Whose Public Space?

Public spaces mirror the complexities of urban societies: as historic social bonds have weakened and cities have become collections of individuals, public open spaces have also changed from being embedded in the social fabric of the city to being a part of more impersonal and fragmented urban environments. Can making public spaces help overcome this fragmentation, where accessible spaces are created through inclusive processes? This book offers some answers to this question through analysing the process of urban design and development in international case studies, in which the changing character, level of accessibility, and the tensions of making public spaces are explored.

The book uses a coherent theoretical outlook to investigate a series of case studies, crossing the cultural divides to examine the similarities and differences of public space in different urban contexts, with a critical analysis of the processes of development, management and use of public space, and their inherent tensions and conflicts. While the case studies investigate the specificities of particular cities, the book outlines some general themes in global urban processes. It shows how public spaces are a key theme in urban design and development everywhere, how they are appreciated and used by the people of these cities, but also being contested by and under pressure from different stakeholders.

Ali Madanipour is Professor of Urban Design at the School of Architecture, Planning and Landscape, Newcastle University, UK.

Whose Public Space?

International case studies in urban design and development

Edited by Ali Madanipour

Routledge
Taylor & Francis Group

LONDON AND NEW YORK

First published 2010
by Routledge
2 Park Square, Milton Park, Abingdon, Oxon OX14 4RN

Simultaneously published in the USA and Canada
by Routledge
270 Madison Ave, New York, NY 10016

Routledge is an imprint of the Taylor & Francis Group, an informa business

© 2010 Ali Madanipour, selection and editorial matter; individual chapters, the contributors

Typeset in Sabon by Wearset Ltd, Boldon, Tyne and Wear
Printed and bound in Great Britain by TJ International Ltd, Padstow, Cornwall

British Library Cataloguing in Publication Data
A catalogue record for this book is available from the British Library

Library of Congress Cataloging-in-Publication Data
Whose public space? : international case studies in urban design and development / edited by Ali Madanipour.
p. cm.
Includes bibliographical references.
1. Public spaces—Social aspects—Case studies. 2. City planning—Case studies. 3. Urban sociology—Case studies. 4. Human territoriality—Case studies. I. Madanipour, Ali.
HT155.W48 2010
711'.55—dc22   2009022165

ISBN10: 0-415-55385-7 (hbk)
ISBN10: 0-415-55386-5 (pbk)
ISBN10: 0-203-86094-2 (ebk)

ISBN13: 978-0-415-55385-8 (hbk)
ISBN13: 978-0-415-55386-5 (pbk)
ISBN13: 978-0-203-86094-6 (ebk)

Contents

Contents

Figures

Tables

Contributors

Müge Akkar Ercan is Assistant Professor at the Department of City and Regional Planning, the Middle East Technical University in Ankara, Turkey.

Shaibu Bala Garba is Assistant Professor at the Department of Civil and Architectural Engineering, the Sultan Qaboos University in Muscat, Oman. He has also taught at King Fahd University in Dhahran, Saudi Arabia, and Ahmadu Bello University in Zaria, Nigeria.

Hong-Che Chen is an architect and a partner with Towerway Architects and Associates in Taichung, Taiwan.

Mauricio Hernández Bonilla is Lecturer and Researcher at the Faculty of Architecture, the University of Veracruz, Mexico. He is a member of the National Researchers System (SNI) of the Mexican National Council of Science and Technology (CONACYT).

Karina Landman is Senior Lecturer in the Department of Town and Regional Planning, the University of Pretoria, South Africa. Before joining the university, she worked as a principal researcher at the Council for Scientific and Industrial Research in South Africa.

Ali Madanipour is Professor of Urban Design and a founding member of Global Urban Research Unit at the School of Architecture, Planning and Landscape, Newcastle University, United Kingdom.

Khalid Nasralden Mandeli is Lecturer in Urban and Regional Planning at the College of Environmental Design, King Abdul-Aziz University in Jeddah, Saudi Arabia. He has worked as an urban design consultant with private companies and government agencies in Saudi Arabia.

Paola Michialino is Lecturer and Degree Programme Director for BA (Hons) in Architectural Studies at the School of Architecture, Planning and Landscape, Newcastle University, United Kingdom. She qualified and practised as an architect in Turin, and developed her research and teaching experience in Italy, Belgium, France, Australia and the United Kingdom.

Peter Rogers is Lecturer in the Sociology of Law and Director of Social Science at Macquarie University in Sydney, Australia. He previously taught at Manchester Metropolitan University and founded the British Sociological Association's Urban Theory and Research (UTR) study group in 2006.

Bahador Zamani is Assistant Professor at the Faculty of Architecture and Urbanism, the Islamic Art University in Tabriz, Iran.

Contributors

Chapter 1

Introduction

Ali Madanipour

Public spaces mirror the complexities of urban societies: as historic social bonds between individuals have become weakened or transformed, and cities have increasingly become agglomerations of atomized individuals, public open spaces have also changed from being embedded in the social fabric of the city to being a part of more impersonal and fragmented urban environments. Can making public spaces help overcome this fragmentation, where accessible spaces are created through inclusive processes? Do the existing and new public spaces of the city serve the public at large, or are they contested and exclusive? Whose public spaces are they? This book offers some answers to these questions through case studies of making public space in different countries.

The book investigates the making of public space in contemporary cities, through analysing the process of urban design and development in international case studies, focusing on the changing nature of public space and the tensions that arise between different perspectives and groups. Two broad frameworks of *place* and *process* are used to study and analyse the urban public spaces in transition. Public spaces, it is argued in this book, should be *accessible places*, developed through *inclusive processes*. With these criteria, therefore, it would be possible to analyse and evaluate the spaces that are being developed in cities around the world.

The book's authors share a common concern about the quality and character of urban public spaces, a concern that has led us to investigate a series of major empirical case studies. Crossing the cultural divides, the book brings these investigations together to examine the similarities and differences of public space in different urban contexts, and engage in a critical analysis of the process of design, development, management and use of public space. While each case study investigates the specificities of particular cities, the book as a whole outlines some general themes in global urban processes. It shows how public spaces are a key theme in urban design and development everywhere, how they are appreciated and used by the people of these cities, but are also contested by and under pressure from different stakeholders.

The book builds on the theoretical foundations developed in earlier publications (Madanipour 1996, 1999, 2003a, 2007), and major research projects funded by the European Commission among others (Madanipour *et al.* 2003; Madanipour 2004). The chapters, with the exception of Chapter 6, are written specifically for this book, reporting on major research projects funded by international organizations, national governments and research councils. All of these research projects, with the exception of Chapter 11, have recently been conducted at the School of Architecture, Planning and Landscape, Newcastle University. This book is the first attempt to bring together the results of these various research endeavours in a single volume. The book is written for scholars and practitioners in built environment and social sciences, including urban design and planning, architecture, urban geography and sociology, with an interest in the relationship between space and society, and the dynamics of change in contemporary cities around the world, as particularly manifested in urban public spaces.

The book's key argument is that, although the social and spatial composition of cities differ considerably across the world, there are a number of general trends that can be observed: that public spaces play a significant role in the life of cities everywhere, and that for cities to work, there is an undeniable need for public space; that the nature of this role, and therefore the nature of public space, in modern cities has radically changed; and that the development and use of these spaces mirror the way a society is organized, shaped by unequal distribution of power and resources, which creates tension and conflict as well as collaboration and compromise. Public spaces, it is argued here, should be produced on the basis of equality for all by being accessible places made and managed through inclusive processes.

Why has urban public space become a subject of interest?

Public space has been an integral part of cities throughout history, so much so that without it, human settlements would be unimaginable. How could people step out of their front doors if there were no public space to mediate between private territories? Like any other part of cities, such as houses, neighbourhoods, political and cultural institutions, it is part of an ever-present vocabulary of urbanism. It has been used in different forms and combinations in many different circumstances, with different degrees of accessibility and control, but they can all be seen as different variations on the same theme. This poses the question: if public spaces, in some form or other, have been a primary part of urban structure everywhere and at all times, why do we see a current wave of interest in public space as a subject of social concern, political action and academic research?

Recent attention to public space is rooted in the structural changes that societies around the world have experienced in the past thirty years whereby the provision of public goods, such as public space, has been under pressure through the ascendancy of the market-based paradigm. The aftermath of the Second World War was characterized by structural intervention by the state in the economy, resulting in large-scale public-sector schemes in urban development, particularly in western countries. Local authorities and their architects and planners were at the leading edge of urban renewal whereby cities were expanded and redeveloped with high-rise public housing schemes, motorways and new towns, implementing the ideas developed earlier by the garden city movement and the modern movement in architecture. As the prosperity of the 1960s was followed by economic decline in the 1970s, the post-war Keynesian accord between the state and the market came under pressure. Industrial decline deprived the public sector of its funds, and urban renewal projects and new town development schemes were abandoned. The solution that was introduced in the 1980s in the United Kingdom and the United States was to dismantle the age of consensus and stimulate economic growth through market revival and competition. Radical de-industrialization, reduction in the size of the state, privatization, individualization, globalization and liberalization of the economy were the new structural directions for the state and society, which spread around the world and lasted for three decades until coming to a halt with a global financial crisis. This paradigm shift had major implications for urban design, planning and development.

With reduction in the size and scope of the state, urban development was transferred to the private sector. The private sector, however, was interested in those aspects of urban development that would ensure a return on its investment. Private companies were answerable to their shareholders, and not to the urban community as a whole. Public goods, such as public space, therefore, were seen as a liability, as they could not be sold and had no direct profit for the private investor. Local authorities and their elected politicians, meanwhile, could not, or would not, invest in those public goods that did not have an immediate political or economic return. They also saw public space as a liability, as something that required higher maintenance costs and was a burden on their dwindling budgets. As a result, both public- and private-sector agencies abandoned public spaces as cities suffered from accelerated decline.

Large-scale schemes, however, could not be developed without some sort of mediating space, some public areas that would link different buildings and spaces. Private developers, therefore, preferred to control these spaces, so that the return on their investment could not be jeopardized by what they saw as potential threats to their operation. New public spaces that were developed after the 1980s, therefore, were controlled and restricted, in contrast to the more accessible and inclusive places of the past. This was a widespread phenomenon, and became known as the privatization of public space. It generated a fear that the city had become private territory in which people could not move easily and the democratic aspirations of liberty and equality would be undermined. This would be a fragmented city, in which some people would be free to go almost anywhere, whereas others would be trapped inside their ghettos or prevented from entering the exclusive spaces of the elite, facilitated through a process of gentrification. The loss of public space symbolized the loss of the idea of the city.

An associated trend was the change in disciplinary and professional division of labour, in which architects and planners both lost interest in public space, leaving it in an indeterminate state. Modernist architecture was interested in refashioning the entire built environment, from the scale of cities down to the level of individual pieces of furniture. Modernism was a relatively coherent, socially concerned movement that sought to solve social problems through physical transformation. With economic decline, which removed the possibility of large-scale urban development schemes, and the collapse of architecture's confidence in its ability to deal with social problems, it withdrew into an aesthetic sphere. The postmodern reaction to modernism was more interested in playfulness of appearance than in grappling with social concerns. It focused on the site, trying to respond to the needs of the client, and paid little attention to what lay outside, the urban context, of which public space was a major part. The architect's clients were private developers, and they were interested in rewards on their investment, which set the parameters for the architect's scope of action. Meanwhile, as a result of rapid economic decline and the heavily criticized consequences of post-Second World War planning schemes, urban planning became focused on social issues, which included large-scale unemployment and the decline of infrastructure. There was no scope for concentrating on public spaces, which would be considered as icing on the cake, a luxury rather than a necessity.

While public and private organizations and their associated professionals had lost interest in the public space, seeing it as irrelevant or expensive, or were encroaching upon it for private gains, the social need for public space in the city had not disappeared. There were increasing concerns about the rise of individualism and the decline of public goods, of which public space was a key manifestation in the urban environment. Individuals were encouraged to follow their own interests, expecting the market to deliver prosperity. But social goods could not be delivered by the market, which had little interest in non-monetary forms of benefit. Social goods could not be delivered by the public sector either, as its financial ability to develop and maintain public spaces was undermined. There was a crisis about public goods in general, and about public space in particular.

As the neoliberal market paradigm spread around the world, other countries adopted, or were encouraged to adopt, the path of economic regeneration through stimulating the market and reducing the state's size and scope. With the collapse of the Soviet bloc, the market paradigm grew in new countries, becoming the undisputed form of economic development. In these countries, therefore, the provision of public goods, which was already, or had become, less effective than in the rich western countries, faced similar issues and problems. Of course, the extent of marketization and the crisis of public space has not been the same everywhere, as is best evident in the differences between European and American cities. However, the global neoliberal trend posed a major challenge to public goods everywhere, as partly evident in the threats facing public space, which has resulted from the restless process of globalization.

The changing nature of public space

The nature and character of public spaces are closely related to the nature and character of cities. As cities have changed, so have their public spaces. In smaller towns and cities of agrarian societies, with their relatively cohesive and homogeneous populations, some public spaces were major focal points, where trade, politics, cultural performance and socialization all took place. As modern cities have grown larger, with heterogeneous populations spread across large areas, public spaces have multiplied and expanded, but have also become more impersonal, losing many of their layers of significance. In the city of strangers, the meaning of public space becomes less personal, more transient, and at best merely functional or symbolic.

There have been major changes in the nature of cities during their long existence throughout millennia (Southall 1998), despite some common features that they share across this time. According to Louis Wirth, cities are identified by size of population, density of settlement, and heterogeneity of inhabitants, and so are perceived as 'relatively permanent, compact settlements of large numbers of heterogeneous individuals' (1964: 68). As these parameters of size, density and heterogeneity, and the relationship among urban inhabitants and with the outside world, have constantly taken new forms, the nature of cities and urban societies has changed considerably. These changes can be seen in the different analyses made of the city. For Aristotle (1992), the ancient city was an association, in which people participated by playing different roles to construct a political community. Max Weber (1966) wrote about medieval cities as a fusion of garrison and market, indicating the defensive and economic functions of cities, as well as their political and legal autonomy. In modern cities, however, the military function of the city has been lost, its political function weakened, its economic function integrated into a larger national and international system, and even its population spread out into the suburbs. This is why one observer decided to write, 'The age of the city seems to be at an end' (Martindale 1966: 62). And yet we know that the age of the city has just begun, as the turn of the twenty-first century has been marked by a shift in the world's balance of population from a predominantly rural to a predominantly urban population.

The nature of public spaces has changed alongside the historic changes in the nature of cities. For most of urban history, the primary public spaces of the city were the core of the urban society, integrating the political, economic, social and cultural activities of a small and relatively

5

coherent urban population. Examples of these primary spaces were the *agora* in Greek cities, the forum in Roman cities, and market squares in medieval cities. The other public open spaces of the city, such as streets, intersections, minor squares, etc., were also essential for everyday sociability and trade. In modern cities, however, the city has grown, with populations so large and heterogeneous that they could not rely on proximity and close encounters to engage in their complex range of activities. Its physical space has also grown to such an extent that co-presence is no longer possible, or even desirable. The role of public space in the close-knit community was fairly clear: facilitating a multiplicity of encounters that were essential for everyday life and helping consolidate the social order. In the modern city, a large number of anonymous individuals are engaged in non-converging networks, while the transport, information and communication technologies have changed the location and shape of these networks. These changes are reflected in the nature of public spaces, which have kept some of their historic functions but now primarily play residual roles.

The change in the nature of urban space can be traced in the relationship between 'space' and 'place' in the literature, whereby space is considered to be more abstract and impersonal, while place is interpreted as having meaning and value. One of the key criticisms of the urban development process in modern cities has been the transition from place to space, through a loss of meaning and personal association. The humanist critics of modernism, as well as others, have raised this criticism in response to the urban redevelopment programmes of the mid-twentieth century (Jacobs 1961). The same criticism was raised in the nineteenth century against the modernization of cities with wide boulevards and soulless public spaces (Sitte 1986). While this criticism partly captures the changing condition of cities, it may also tend to misjudge the complexity of places and identities in cities, hence promoting place as a particular enclosed space with fixed identities, which is not what the spaces of modern cities can or should be (Massey 1994). This is part of a larger debate about the nature of modern cities, and of modernity itself.

The transition from an integrative community to the anonymity and alienation of large modern urban societies has been a key concern in the development of sociology (Engels 1993; Tönnies 1957; Simmel 1950). Behaviour in public spaces has been analysed as the reflection of this transition, from engaging with others to avoiding them, as the overload of encounters and emotional stimuli, and the wide gap between social classes, keep people apart and turn public spaces into residual places of avoidance rather than encounter. Two of the major theorists of the public sphere in the twentieth century, Hannah Arendt and Jürgen Habermas, mourned the passing of these integrative societies and complained about the rise of what was called a mass society. Arendt analysed the ancient polis (1958) and Habermas investigated the early modern bourgeois public sphere (1989), both as examples of situations in which interpersonal communication led to a rich public life. Both of them saw the rigid routines of the industrial city as alienating, and as tending to degrade the qualities of public life.

The result has been a degree of false romanticization of historic public spaces. The Greek *agora* has been portrayed as the material manifestation of this magnificent ancient civilization. This was a civilization, however, in which women, foreigners and slaves had no place in the public sphere. The medieval square has been portrayed as the picturesque heart of the city, in what are often little more than romantic and aesthetic notions of life in the medieval city, and yet at the time it was a place dominated by trade, and it displayed the hierarchies and harshness of life within the city walls. The eighteenth-century coffee houses in London or the salons in Paris are seen as the prototypes for the emergence of a public sphere, in which people were able to discuss matters of common interest and come to an informed opinion about their society, and yet these places were often accessible only to the elite among the emerging bourgeoisie. The early modern city squares and boulevards are portrayed as examples of the rise of a new age of reason and modernity, and yet they resulted from speculative development, monarchical power and suppression of the poor. What we often see is the architecture of the city, or at least a sanitized image of the history, on which we project our own expectations, aesthetic, political and social.

After the decline of industries and the collapse of the rigid routines of the industrial economy, the nature of public space has once again changed, now being integrated into the service economy. The quality of public space becomes an essential support mechanism for the flexible working practices of the service economy, and the consumption-driven basis on which this economy relies. Rather than treating public spaces as functional residues or breathing spaces of the city, which was the attitude of industrial modernism, service-based postmoderns embrace them for their aesthetic value, as well as their provision of spaces of consumption. Public spaces become an essential part of the regeneration of cities through promoting retail development. The association of public space creation and high-value consumption inevitably leads to gentrification, in which one group of people and activities are replaced by another.

The modern large city, which was once a western phenomenon, has now become a global one. The transition from integrative small communities to fragmented large societies, which was associated with the experiences of modernity in nineteenth-century Europe, has now been extended to most parts of the globe through a restless process of colonization, modernization and globalization. In this context, as cities grow everywhere and services form a major part of urban economies around the world, the condition of urban public spaces becomes ever more significant.

Accessible places

Public spaces play many different roles in urban societies and can be defined in a number of ways. The key feature of public space, however, is its accessibility. Without being accessible, a place cannot become public. If public open spaces are conceived as enclosed particular places with fixed identities, their flexibility and inclusiveness will be undermined, and so will their accessibility. They lie outside the boundaries of individual or small group control, providing spaces that mediate between, and give access to, private spaces, as well as performing a multiplicity of functional and symbolic roles in the life of an urban society. In the processes of urban change, the conditions of accessibility are subject to change, hence changing the nature of public spaces. In the controversies about privatization of public space, it is the access to public spaces that has been limited, narrowing the range of social groups who can use these spaces, and making these spaces accessible only to a smaller group of people, often judged by their ability to pay.

The word *public* originates from the Latin and refers to people, indicating a relationship to both society and the state. A public space may therefore be interpreted as open to people as a whole, and/or being controlled by the state on their behalf. Public has been defined as the opposite of private, which is the realm of individuals and their intimate relationships; and so public space is often defined in terms of its distinction from the private realm of the household. Public has also been seen as the opposite of the personal, hence equated with impersonal (Silver 1997: 43), the realm of the non-intimate others. What lies beyond personal, however, can also be interpersonal, where the boundaries between personal and impersonal, private and public, can be blurred.

The distinction between the public and the private is a key theme in liberal political theory, promoting the separation of private and public interests and roles in order to prevent private interests encroaching on and undermining public interests (Wacks 1993; Nolan 1995). The tension has been challenged by the critics of private property, who see this distinction as consolidating the power of the elite at the expense of the poor. It has also been challenged by women, who see it as consolidating the role of men in public affairs and associating the private sphere with women, hence keeping them locked in an inferior position in society (Fraser 1989). The subdivision of the social world into public and private spheres, and the establishment and maintenance of the boundaries between them, has therefore been challenged and criticized from a number of different perspectives.

Yet another challenge to the notion of public sphere and public space comes from social diversity. Public policy has often been justified as directed towards public interest. The idea of public interest has been used to explain and defend the actions of public authorities. Their critics, however, argue that the way this public interest has been defined is too narrow, and often privileges the elite. What is usually considered to be an average citizen, for whom the laws are written and who is the basis of public action, is argued to exclude women, the elderly, children, ethnic minorities and the poor. What is introduced as public interest, they argue, is not really public in an inclusive sense. This poses a challenge to the notion of public: either abandon the idea and replace it with a notion of society subdivided into tribes and interest groups, or try to expand the notion of public so as to include all citizens equally.

In spatial terms, public spaces are by definition public, and as such expected to be accessible to all. However, *public* is not a single entity, as it is composed of different social strata, each with a different set of characteristics, interests and powers. Furthermore, within those strata there are a large number of individual differences. There are strong centrifugal and fragmentary forces that create and separate social strata, which will then be reflected in the constitution of the public. The tension between the public and the private can be seen in the European medieval city, as well as in many cities around the world to this day, where the streets and open spaces of the city are gradually being threatened by the expanding houses and private spaces, to the extent that a minimum amount of space is left for passing through and for conducting trade and other essential functions (Saalman 1968). It is a tension that we can clearly see in our own time, in which private interests tend to claim the urban space, undermining the publicness of its public spaces, in what is termed the privatization of public space.

The nature and character of a public space depend on how it is distinguished from the private sphere. In other words, the way in which its boundaries are constructed determines the type of public space and its quality. If the boundary is rigidly guarded by walls, gates and guards, it is no longer considered a public space. In contrast, the more accessible and permeable a place becomes, the more public it will be. Its degree of publicness will also depend on the types of activities taking place, which can create symbolic boundaries around these activities, or be inviting to as many people as wish to join in. A degree of distinction between intimate and shared spaces, between private and public spaces, is essential for living in society. The controversy is usually about how these two areas are defined, distinguished from one another, and separated by what sort of boundary. Much of urban design has been interested in how this boundary is articulated, how a dividing line can be set up that is protective of the private sphere from the intrusion of others, while protecting the collective sphere from individual interest; in other words, how this boundary can enhance, rather than degrade, the quality of life in cities.

To determine the extent to which a place or activity is public or private, Benn and Gaus (1983) suggested three criteria as dimensions of social organization: access, interest and agency, with access divided further into access to spaces, activities, information and resources. A place is public, therefore, if it is controlled by public authorities, concerns people as a whole, is open or available to them, and is used or shared by all the members of a society. This provides a useful framework for assessing the publicness of a place. The criteria of interest, agency and access, however, approach space instrumentally, seeing it as an asset in exchange, using it as a resource, treating it as a commodity. This interpretation appears to draw on an analysis of social relations as exchange among strangers, rather than a set of emotional and meaningful ties (Madanipour 2003a). There must be additional dimensions at work, which should also be taken into account.

The symbolic dimensions of public spaces are as significant as their functional ones. In the small towns and cities of agrarian societies, public spaces were developed and used as integrative nodes for a variety of instrumental and expressive needs. Performing social rituals in public was as important as engaging in trade or deliberating on how to manage the town. Even before then, as can be observed in the remaining hunter-gatherer societies of today, the common spaces of a group, in which they sing and dance, tell stories and perform rituals, are a significant part of living together as a group. In modern urban societies, however, while humans have remained social beings, it is true that the nature and methods of expressiveness, and therefore the character of urban public spaces, have changed. Much of cultural reading of cities places a performative emphasis on public spaces, seeing them as places for performance and assertion of identity. On the other hand, the functionalist reading of the city appeared to ignore this symbolic dimension and focus entirely on the way cities functioned, hence seeing public spaces as essential for the health of the city, as its lungs. A key argument is that both these camps have failed to see the multidimensionality of public space. Access, therefore, has both instrumental and expressive dimensions. A public space is one that allows a range of necessary activities to take place, but also a place in which 'unnecessary' social activities are performed. An example is the ritual of *passeggiata* in Italian cities, the evening walk in which the inhabitants of the city put on their best clothes and go out of their homes for a slow stroll in public spaces to see and be seen. This is a symbolic and expressive, as well as functional, exercise, a complex urban ritual that cannot be reduced to a single interpretation.

There are major tensions, however, inherent in the symbolic dimension of accessibility. On the one hand, the more accessible a place, the more impersonal it tends to become, particularly in large cities. If a place is reserved for a known group of individuals or a class of society on the basis of their economic or political resources, accessibility decreases and familiarity rises. While individuals may suffer from the anonymity of the large city (Simmel 1950) and prefer to establish a comfort realm of familiarity, they will have to come into contact with a large number of strangers in their everyday life in the city. However, if the city becomes subdivided into zones of comfort for social groups, it has been fragmented and tribalized. Much of the literature in urban design encourages designers and decision makers to subdivide the city into neighbourhoods and identifiable, defendable zones, hence knowingly or unknowingly limiting the accessibility of urban spaces. There is, therefore, a parallel between accessibility and anonymity: spaces that would deter strangers would not be accessible. They may have served local people well, but their accessibility would be controlled and limited.

Provision and free access to public spaces, therefore, are essential for any society. But we should not naively believe in physical determinism, thinking that spatial solutions are sufficient to address societal problems. As public space is a part of the public sphere, we can apply the logic of the public sphere in democratic societies to analysing public space. In these societies, the establishment of a political public sphere did not remove the social divide between rich and poor, but it did provide opportunities for expressing opinion and avenues for trying to influence action. In other words, the public sphere was an integral part of a democratic society. In the same sense, public space is a necessary part of an open society, a space that everyone is able to enter and participate in some collective experience. This may not amount to solving social and economic problems, but it does provide a forum for socialization and a counterweight to exclusionary and centrifugal forces that tend to tear apart the social fabric of polarized societies.

Inclusive processes

Different stages in design, planning, development and management of public spaces have a direct impact on their accessibility and identity. If public spaces are produced and managed by narrow interests, they are bound to become exclusive places. As the range of actors and interests in urban development varies widely, and places have different dimensions and functions, creating public spaces becomes a complex and multidimensional process. To understand places, and to promote the development of accessible public places, therefore, it is essential to study this process and to encourage its broadening, to make it inclusive.

Cities have historically grown and been developed by a large number of people over time. As new technologies have emerged, the size of companies has grown and the areas of expertise have multiplied through a process of specialization, constructing the built environment has become far more complex than hitherto. The process has also become faster than before, in line with the growth in the productive capacity of developers. An army of specialists and a mountain of resources can be employed to create new parts of cities in relatively short periods of time. While this complexity has multiplied the number of agencies involved in the process, it has allocated a specific task to each agency, as cogs in a large machine geared towards a particular mode of operation. As the number of agencies has grown, the organizational hierarchies and the division of labour have focused the process, ruled by technical and instrumental rationality. As technological know-how and the self-confidence of modern city builders have grown, city building has been consolidated in fewer hands, managing and coordinating complex hierarchies and networks of agencies and individuals.

The medieval city, and for that matter the nineteenth-century industrial city, were seen as the result of accidents rather than careful planning. The father of modern rationalist philosophy, René Descartes (1968), preferred cities to be designed by a single designer, who could devise and implement a single well-ordered system. The medieval city, as well as the laws and beliefs of the past, were the result of custom and example, rather than rational thinking. What he advocated was thinking everything anew, according to a rational order. This way of thinking was the basis of the modernist approach to design, aiming to create and impose a new order on the cities of the past, even at the cost of eradicating large parts of these cities. Rather than being conditioned by the past, modernist rationalists wanted a break with the past.

The considerable productive capacities of modern city builders have made this possible. Designers and planners are trained to think strategically and plan for strategic and large-scale transformation of cities. The changing nature of developers has a direct impact on what they build. A century ago, locally based developers could be engaged in single small developments, creating more diverse cities. Now, in contrast, large national or international developers are able to engage in large-scale projects. Developers can mobilize large amounts of capital and large teams of construction professionals, and can use new construction technologies and machinery, enabling them to develop cities at larger scales and faster speeds. A large part of a city, therefore, can be designed by a single organization within a relatively short period of time. As Descartes dreamed, a city can be designed by a single designer and developed by a single organization. The task is complex and will involve a large number of different teams. These are all, nevertheless, under the management of the main developer and the associated design team. However, while this increases efficiency and productivity in city building, it narrows the range of strategic actors and their considerations.

The logic of production, however, is only one among the logics with which cities are built and run (Madanipour 2007). In deciding the best course of action, the ability to make is certainly an important consideration, but not the only one. In deciding how to live our lives or how to manage our cities, we evaluate our options according to a wide range of issues and considerations. To narrow down the range of options to technical and instrumental ones, therefore, would lead to distorted decisions.

A key question in analysing the development process is: who is involved? An associated question is: who do the process and its outcome serve? An inclusive process would involve a larger number of people and agencies and would spread the benefits of the process to larger parts of society, while an exclusive process would limit the number and range of agencies and would reward a smaller number of people. The process of building cities involves complex regulatory frameworks and large financial resources, both of which are often closely entwined with political and financial elites. This tends to give these elites a powerful influence over the process and its outcome.

In market economies, financial resources are generated by the private sector, and it is taken for granted that private investors expect to maximize rewards on their investment. In democracies, the elected representatives are expected to act on behalf of their constituencies. However, the disadvantaged groups, who do not have access to financial resources and are frequently disconnected from the political process, end up having no control or stake in the city building process. The places that are created are not designed to serve them, as these groups are not often part of the decision-making formula. This tends to make city building dominated by powerful agencies and individuals, rather than involving a broad range of citizens. In the development process, development agencies work with resources, rules and ideas in response to the needs of society and demands of the market. However, if the needs and demands of the disadvantaged parts of society are not strongly represented, politically or financially, as is often the case, the process and its outcome may not serve them at all.

Another key question in the development process is the temporal dimension of change. Design as a goal-oriented problem-solving process tends to envisage the built environment as a finished product, working out its structure and details and leaving nothing to chance. Cities, however, are constantly changing, inhabited as they are by intelligent and dynamic people. At no point can there be a final shape for a city. The design and development of cities, therefore, will need to accommodate this change, embracing a dynamic conception of cities rather than a fixed and rigid one.

What is needed, therefore, in investigating, as well as making, the urban space is a multidimensional and multi-agency process involving as many individuals and agencies as possible, and a dynamic process that can accommodate time and change. The result will be a *dynamic multiplicity*, in which city building is envisaged and organized as an inclusive and responsive process. The public spaces that are created by this process will be more inclusive and accessible than the ones that serve narrow interests; will be driven by technical and instrumental concerns; or will be envisaged as fixed, exclusive and rigid places.

An interdependent world

Some readers may wonder why this book has brought together what appear to be disparate experiences from such a wide range of countries. What can African, European, Asian and Latin American cities have in common? Each city and each country has its own history and culture, with different social and economic conditions and prospects. What can we gain from bringing these cases together? On the surface, the differences between our case studies are large and wide, to the extent that the existence of any links or comparisons between their public spaces may seem improbable. Some of these cities are rapidly growing while others are shrinking. They belong to different cultures and economic conditions, each embedded in a completely different reality. What might we find, these readers may ask, in any attempt at placing them alongside one another?

A key answer is the universality of the existence of, and the need for, public space in cities. Everywhere and in any period of history, human settlements consist of a collection of different individuals and households, residing in their own private territories and connected to one another through semi-private, semi-public and public spaces. From the earliest traces of human settlements in Mesopotamia to the metropolises of our own time, this division of space into public and private has been a key feature of urban societies. While the character and use of these public spaces may differ, the universal existence of some form of public space and its social and economic significance for the city cannot be denied.

Another, related, similarity between the cities is in the converging methods of city building, in which the markets and new technologies are prominent. In our time, the spread of capitalism and the extent of global interdependency characterize cities everywhere. Before the arrival of the dramatic economic crisis of 2008, a global consensus seemed to have emerged in which markets were given free rein to come up with solutions to all the economic problems. All of the cities we have studied are part of the global market, albeit occupying different positions in the marketplace, from more central to more marginal. In all cities, the process of city building is subject to the logic of the market, in which land as a finite resource is the subject of competition. What connects these cities and their spaces, therefore, is the mechanism of the market. Even if it operates completely differently in each city, it is subject to the same general principle of risk and reward, and distinction between private and public interests. It also tends to generate, or accelerate, social stratification and division, creating tensions between the rich and poor, and social inequalities that become manifest in the making and use of public spaces.

Also, all cities are subject to the impact of technological change. Transport technologies have allowed them to spread, creating new social and spatial distinctions between the centre and periphery. Construction technologies have been embraced as the solution to city building problems, often applied by architects and planners with little consultation with the city's inhabitants. Cities' position with regard to manufacturing industries also creates overlaps and commonalities: while some are abandoning their industrial past, others are entering a period of industrialization, each with its own distinctive, but ultimately related, impact on the character of public space. Judging by their diverse character and trajectory, we cannot envisage these cities to be on a linear temporal path in which some are further along the line than the others, and the fate of some is going to be a model for the fate of the others. We can, however, see how their linkages, existing and potential, are forged through their current conditions and past histories. More than anything else, they are part of the same global urban process, different components of the same phenomenon and sharing many features of modern urban societies.

Judging by the universal presence and social significance of public space, and the converging economic and technological methods of city building, we can see how the experiences of making public space in different continents of the world can show different aspects of the same phenomenon. While we can emphasize the differences between cities – and there are many – we can also choose to focus on their similarities, which are evident in the making and use of public space, as a manifestation of social organization, and the tensions that arise out of different perspectives engaged in a common concern.

The book is divided into two parts and twelve chapters. After this Introduction, Part I concentrates on the public spaces in city centres, where public spaces have the highest levels of significance and complexity. It investigates the changing nature of city centres and their public spaces, which are the results of structural changes in the urban society, often through fundamental political, economic and cultural transformation. Part II focuses on case studies from peripheral residential areas, particularly low-income neighbourhoods, where public spaces have a significant role in the everyday life of the neighbourhood. The difficulties of conflict and mistrust between different groups, however, have made these places subject to dispute and contest, while the gaps between design and use are evident in the spaces of the city. A combination of central and peripheral areas in a variety of cities around the world reveals the significance of public space in different capacities, and how different forces are at work to shape and control these places in their own image. By using the criteria of accessible places and inclusive processes, and within the spatial framework of centres and peripheries, we analyse the character and quality of public spaces in our case studies. A concluding chapter brings together the results of these investigations and presents some ideas about the way forward.

Part I

The changing nature of public space in city centres

Ali Madanipour

Part I of the book focuses on public spaces in city centres, where demand for and tensions over public spaces' production and control are highest. In post-industrial cities, the changing social and economic bases of the city have eradicated the legacies of the past, sometimes through a struggle for space leading to gentrification. In post-colonial and industrializing cities, the centre has started to lose its hold on the growth of the larger city region. In such cities, other centres of economic and political power have emerged, a change that is reflected in their public spaces.

Parallel to the recent rise in interest in public spaces, the proliferation of alluring, distinctive and exclusive public spaces in many post-industrial cities raises the question of how far these environments are truly 'public'. Chapter 2 discusses the question of the 'publicness' of contemporary public spaces in Britain, where they have been placed at the top of the political agenda since the 1990s. Focusing on the development and use processes of the Haymarket Bus Station in the city centre of Newcastle upon Tyne, renovated in the late 1990s, and regarding the dimensions of 'access', 'actor' and 'interest', it studies its changing 'publicness'. The chapter seeks to show that, contrary to the wide recognition of diminishing 'publicness' of contemporary public spaces in urban design and planning literature, the recent renovation works have in fact had both positive and negative impacts on the 'publicness' of the case study. The chapter concludes that contemporary public spaces may show different shades of 'publicness', in which degrees of 'access', 'actor' and 'interest' can vary widely. It underlines the emerging trends and threats of the blurring distinction between public and private spaces, and image-led regeneration strategies dominating everyday society's needs and civic functions of desirable 'public' spaces, and ultimately violating the 'publicness' of public realms in post-industrial cities.

Chapter 3 investigates another regeneration project in Newcastle upon Tyne. Old Eldon Square sits at the heart of the city centre and can be interpreted in many ways. It is a memorial space, a public park, a locus of local transportation links and a commercial space. As the only green public space in the city centre, and sitting at the heart of the retail development area, in local government strategic plans the use, and potential domination, of the area by groups of young people raised a series of tensions within the redevelopment of the square. This case study, which covers a six-year period (2000–2006), assesses how these tensions rolled out through the regeneration of the area in local planning practices and unpacks the relationship between the concepts underpinning the management and regeneration of the area, the use of the area by a range of groups (particularly the young people), and both perceived and actual tensions between other key stakeholders, including local community interest groups, small- and large-scale business, public and private security agencies, and the city council.

Chapter 4 focuses on change in an Asian city centre. It uses the cases of Ji-Guang Pedestrian Street, Electronics Pedestrian Street and the Green River area in Taichung city centre in Taiwan to discuss the relationship between environmental improvement and city centre regeneration, and also investigate the management and uses of public space after environmental improvement. This chapter explores the efficiency and the impacts of environmental improvement on the city centre by comparing the area before and after the implementation of environmental improvement, and discussing the mutual relationship between relevant factors in city centre regeneration. Could public space improvement be the best way to revive the city centre? The chapter argues that environmental improvement is an essential precondition for the locality and acts as a catalyst for city centre regeneration, even though that regeneration might not be successful. The environmental improvement also influenced the social development and economic regeneration, and many follow-up initiatives that were mostly based on the improved environment. Therefore, the chapter concludes, without an overall consideration of environmental improvement, economic regeneration and social development, the revival of the city centre is hard to achieve.

Cities and societies as historical creations change dynamically in time, with change reflected in their public space. Chapter 5 examines change in the public space of traditional cities in Nigeria, with Zaria as a case study. The chapter examines change in the past two centuries, from a material, social and symbolic perspective, the role that cultural transformation played in shaping change, and the different issues and tensions that characterize social and public life. The chapter concludes that though public space has witnessed changes in its material and social aspects, it is from a symbolic perspective that the greatest change has been witnessed. During the nineteenth century, public space evolved from being the limited communal space of an agrarian society to becoming the central space of a state and a stage for the display of political, economic and symbolic power, and a focus of attraction for migration, contact, trade and exchange of ideas.

Following colonialism in the twentieth century, the importance of Zaria's public space declined as it became a small district in a broader and more fractious metropolitan area, and was gradually divested of its political and economic role in favour of new centres outside. Public space evolved once more to be an exclusionary space for the communal life of residents.

Together, these case studies from three continents show how urban development and regeneration represent both a challenge and an opportunity. They can change the character of an area, threatening the historic and cultural value of some spaces and activities, so that they are reduced to merely an aesthetic and symbolic presence under the new conditions. They put pressure on some existing users and beneficiaries of city centres to make way for new functions and groups, in this way privileging some at the expense of others. When combined with the necessary social measures to avoid injustice, urban development can also act as a catalyst for improving the living and working conditions of urban populations. These challenges and opportunities are particularly evident in city centres, where the symbolic value, the political and economic significance of the place, and the number and complexity of the stakeholders are high; but the same challenges and opportunities can also be found outside the centre, in residential areas of the city.

Chapter 2

Less public than before?
Public space improvement in Newcastle city centre

Müge Akkar Ercan

Introduction

Parallel to the rising interest in the public spaces of post-industrial cities over the past three decades, alluring, distinctive and exclusive public spaces have proliferated in the centres of many British cities (Boyer 1992; Carr *et al.* 1992; Crilley 1993; Francis 1987; Goodwin 1993; Hall and Hubbard 1996; Hubbard 1995; Madanipour 2000; McInroy 2000; Mitchell 1995; Sadler 1993; Tibbalds 1992). Especially since the late 1990s, the Labour governments have put public spaces high on the political agenda, and published a number of policy documents, such as *Towards an Urban Renaissance* (Urban Task Force 1999), *Our Towns and Cities: The Future – Delivering an Urban Renaissance* (DETR 2000), *Green Spaces, Better Places* (Urban Green Spaces Taskforce 2002), *Living Places – Cleaner, Safer, Greener* (ODPM 2002), *Paving the Way: How We Achieve Clean, Safe and Attractive Streets* (CABE and ODPM 2002) and *Living Places: Caring for Quality* (ODPM 2004). The recommendations of the Labour governments, initially centred on the idea of 'well-designed' public spaces (Urban Task Force 1999; DETR 2000), have shifted towards wider approaches and strategies, such as building 'safer', 'accessible' and 'sustainable' public spaces and improving the existing ones in order to create 'liveable' cities (Urban Green Spaces Taskforce 2002); developing more holistic strategies for public space management (ODPM 2004); and encouraging local community involvement in the planning, management and delivery of services of urban public space (Urban Green Spaces Taskforce 2002). Within the government recommendations, public spaces, with their historical and cultural legacies, have also begun to be seen and promoted as one of the key components of urban regeneration projects, together with city marketing and re-imaging programmes (Madanipour 1999; McInroy 2000; Urban Green Spaces Taskforce 2002). Additionally, the Labour governments have encouraged local authorities to improve the quality of public spaces, not only by generating new sources of funding, such as the Heritage Lottery Fund, the Green Spaces and Sustainable Communities Fund and the New Opportunities Fund (Urban Green Spaces Taskforce

2002), but also by launching various schemes such as a Green Flag Awards scheme, the Spaces for Sports and Art Scheme and the new Beacon Council award (DETR 2000; Urban Green Spaces Taskforce 2002). Consequently, beautiful, exclusive and distinctive public spaces, enriched with high-quality construction materials, artworks and design elements underlining the historical and cultural legacies of localities, have been built in British cities.

Despite the resurgence of broad interest in the public spaces of post-industrial cities, recent studies in urban planning and design frequently suggest a diminishing 'publicness' of these public spaces. Pointing out the threat of privatization policies that generated public places undermining the needs of local communities for the sake of private interest, and increased control over access and use of public spaces, which ultimately enhances gentrification, social stratification and fragmentation, all these studies raise the question of the extent to which they are truly 'public' (Punter 1990; Crilley 1993; Madanipour 1995, 1999; Graham *et al.* 1996; Reeve 1996; Loukaitou-Sideris and Banerjee 1998; Oc and Tiesdell 1998; Carmona *et al.* 2003).

This chapter sets out to address this question by examining in depth the Haymarket Bus Station (HBS), a public space redeveloped in the 1990s in Newcastle upon Tyne as a part of the image-led city centre regeneration strategy. The bus station was renewed through a process that was, to a considerable extent, exclusive, and it has experienced a significant change in its 'publicness'. The chapter aims to explore this change. It first defines the 'publicness' of a public space and introduces the framework for measuring its extent. Then it sets the HBS in a wider context, by looking into Newcastle's economic and urban transformation from a heavily industrialized city to a post-industrial city over the past three decades. Third, it investigates the situation before, during and after the HBS scheme with the help of the three dimensions of 'publicness', and develops a discussion on the changing 'public' qualities of public space. Finally, the chapter draws conclusions by questioning the contribution of this type of development to the desirable 'public' qualities of contemporary public spaces and to local economic regeneration.

'Public' dimensions of a public space

The concept of 'public' is rich in meaning and is used in a wide range of contexts. 'Public', as an adjective, signifies 'of or concerning the people as a whole', 'open to all', 'accessible to or shared by all members of the community', 'performed or made openly' and 'well-known' (Gove 1976; Makins 1998). It also connotes 'a political entity which is carried out or made by or on behalf of the community as a whole'; 'authorized by or representing the community' (Gove 1976; Brown 1993). Additionally, 'public' means something 'provided especially by the government, for the use of people in general' (Crowther 1995). As a noun, 'public' refers to 'people in general' (ibid.). However, it is also used to signify 'an organized body of people', such as a community or a nation (Gove 1976). Moreover, 'public' means 'a group of people who share a particular interest or who have something in common', such as the audience at a play or film (Crowther 1995; Makins 1998). Hence, 'public space' can be described as a space concerning the people as a whole, open to all, accessible to or shared by all members of the community, provided by the public authorities for the use of people in general.

Though illuminating, such definitions are not sufficient systematically to describe public space and its 'public' dimensions. Benn and Gaus (1983), who describe the concepts of 'public' and 'private' according to the criteria of 'access', 'agency' and 'interest', offer a valuable empirical tool to define 'public space' and its 'publicness'. First, public space can be defined as possessing four mutually supportive qualities of 'access': (1) physical access; (2) social access; (3) access to activities and discussions, or intercommunications; and (4) access to information (Table 2.1).

The first quality refers to access to the physical environment, as public space is the place in which everybody is entitled to be physically present (Benn and Gaus 1983). Thus, public space is an arena that is physically accessible to all.

The second quality, social access, also called 'symbolic access', involves the presence of cues, in the form of people, design and management elements, suggesting who is, and is not, welcome in the space (Carr *et al*. 1992). 'Environments, individuals and/or groups perceived either as threatening or comforting or inviting may affect entry into a public space' (Tiesdell and Oc 1998: 648). It is therefore important to improve the environmental and social image and ambience of a public space to make it more welcoming and/or less intimidating to a wider range of social groups.

The third and fourth qualities allow us to define the public space in conjunction with the 'time' dimension. The space in which we live, work and experience is not composed of three dimensions only, but rather is a

Table 2.1 The definitions of 'public space' regarding the criteria of access, actor and interest

	Public space
Access	
• Physical access	A space that is physically accessible to all
• Social access	A space that is socially accessible to all
• Access to activities and discussions	A space where the activities and discussions on its development and use processes are accessible to all
• Access to information	A space where the information regarding its development and use processes is accessible to all
Actor	A space that is controlled by public actors, and used by the public
Interest	A space that serves the public interest

four-dimensional entity, an outcome of time, which might be studied under its development and use processes. Hence, the 'public space' is the place where the activities and discussions on its development and use processes are open to all. Markets, concerts, speeches, demonstrations or protests are open to all, if they take place in public environments. Similarly, the 'desirable' development process of the public space must be accessible to everybody, while it includes various stages in each of which the public may not be involved. Yet there are some crucial activities and discussions that must be open to all, such as the decision-making stage of developing a public space, the preparation process of its design scheme. Therefore, the 'public space' is the place where public authorities are responsible for guaranteeing the existence of a public arena in which citizens express their attitudes, assert their claims and use for their purposes. This arena enables the meanings and functions of a public space to change in conformity with citizens' needs and interests, and facilitates ongoing renegotiations of understanding between the public and public authorities. Finally, the fourth quality of 'access' allows us to define the 'public space' as the place where information regarding its development and use processes is available to all members of society.

Second, public space can be defined according to the public–private nature of agencies in control. 'Public actors' means 'agents or agencies that act on behalf of a community, city, commonwealth or state', while 'private actors' refers to 'agents or agencies that act on their own account'. The dictionary definitions of 'the public' are 'the people in general' or 'all members of the society'. Calhoun (1992), Boyer (1993) and Featherstone and Lash (1999) claim, however, that in contemporary society, rather than understanding 'the public' as a 'unitary group', it may be better to conceive it as a series of separate yet overlapping spheres constituting, for example, different socioeconomic, gender and ethnic groups. Boyer (1993: 118), for instance, states that '[a]ny contemporary reference to the "public" is by nature a universalizing construct that assumes a collective whole, while in reality the public is fragmented into marginalized groups, many of whom have no voice, position or representation in the public sphere'. Hence, public space can be defined as a place that is controlled by 'public actors', and used by a public made up of overlapping spheres of groups of private actors.

Finally, public space can be described in terms of the criterion of 'interest' – that is, the status of the people who will be better or worse off in whatever situation is in question. Public interest means the 'common well-being', 'general welfare' or 'benefit that is controlled and received by all members of society', whereas private interest refers to 'the benefit controlled and received by individuals'. Therefore, public space refers to a place that serves public interests.

Analyses of a public space through the dimensions of 'access' and 'actor' respectively would exhibit some overlaps. By identifying the range of user groups, the analysis of a public space through the criterion of 'access' seeks to find out how far the space is socially accessible to the society as a whole, while the part of the study using the dimension of 'actor' involves examination of the various user groups in order to identify the extent to which the public space is used by society. Despite the cross-cutting data of the two dimensions, the three dimensions of 'access', 'actor' and 'interest' can be usefully employed in empirical analyses of public spaces, making it possible to identify degrees of their 'publicness' and 'privateness'.

Also, the suggested definitions outlined here refer to an ideal type of public space. An urban environment, however, is not composed of absolutely public and private spaces. It is, rather, a composition of public and private spaces with different degrees of 'publicness' and 'privateness'. Accepting that the relation between public and private space is a continuum rather than a dichotomy, it is possible to define a public space with varying degrees of 'publicness'. Regarding the dimensions of 'access', 'actor' and 'interest', the extent of the 'publicness' of a public space depends on the degree to which the public space, as well as the activities occurring in it and the discussions on, and information about, its development and use processes, are open to all, are managed and controlled by public actors, are used by the public and serve the public interest.

The 'publicness' of a new public space can be assessed by the examination of its development and use processes through these three criteria, as Madanipour (1995) shows in the analysis of the MetroCentre in Gateshead, a regional-level shopping mall in Britain. In the case of a public space that already exists and is subject to redevelopment or improvement, as in the HBS example, the analysis needs to measure the 'publicness' of the space before, during and after its redevelopment in order to show the changes in the level of its 'publicness'. The data for the research were mainly drawn from documents and archival records (reports, formal studies, articles appearing in the local media and websites), focused interviews with a number of actors involved in the development and use of the case-study area, and direct observations. The research seeks to use data triangulation in order to overcome the common problems of biased, poor or inaccurate articulation. Yet some data used in the research still include limitations, as they do not present direct sources of evidence for the arguments put forward in the chapter. Prior to the presentation of the case study, it will be useful to look at the change in the economic and urban base of Newcastle in the past three decades, and the rising role of public spaces within the recently restructured city economy and cityscape.

Newcastle's transformation to a post-industrial city

The protracted recession of the 1970s and 1980s traumatized a number of previously affluent, heavily industrialized British cities where economic and urban decline had begun to be seen as major threats to their future. Newcastle, one such city, situated in the heart of the north-east of England, was devastated by the decline of the three heavy industries of coal mining, shipbuilding and heavy engineering (Winter *et al.* 1989; Usher and Davoudi

1992; Pacione 1997; Lang 1999; Vall 2001). The recession resulted in the loss of 70,000 jobs in the period 1971–1984 (representing a decline of 43 per cent, while the national average was 6.6 per cent) and a population loss of over 30,000 (representing 9.9 per cent of the city's population) in the 1971–1981 period (Office of Population Censuses and Surveys 1982; Usher and Davoudi 1992). It also hit the city by leaving behind vast tracts of derelict land along the riverside, increasingly deteriorating working-class housing areas suffering from high unemployment and crime rates, and a low standard of education and health service provision (Robinson 1988b; Winter *et al.* 1989; Cameron and Doling 1994; Lang 1999). The city centre underwent a severe decline, accompanied by high rates of unemployment, the deterioration of its urban fabric, the loss of its living and working population, an increase in vacant and underused properties, traffic congestion, limited provision of car parking, a lack of green open spaces, a poor-quality public realm and a lack of investment (EDAW 1996; Healey *et al.* 2002).

Under such traumatic circumstances, since the early 1980s Newcastle has undergone economic restructuring, taking on some of the characteristics of a post-industrial city.[1] One of the major changes is the growth of the service sector, especially in business services. Of the eight most highly industrialized British cities, Newcastle had the highest increase in employment rate in the business sector (93.5 per cent) between 1981 and 1987. The growing service sector has been accompanied by de-industrialization. Among the eight heavily industrialized British cities, the second highest fall in the employment rate in manufacturing industry took place in Newcastle in the period 1981–1987. The manufacturing sector has also undergone a change in character. Instead of heavy industries, it is the chemical, food, timber, furniture and clothing industries that have become dominant in the sector. Branch plants of national and multinational companies, such as Komatsu, a major Japanese company producing earth-moving equipment; Findus, a frozen food company; and Nissan, a Japanese car plant, moved to, and fared reasonably well in, Newcastle and its conurbation adjacent to the banks of the River Tyne in the 1980s and 1990s (Robinson 1988a: 46; Stone 1995). New jobs characterized by a high-quality labour force were created in the 1980s with central government support to increase productivity based on technological improvement (Robinson 1988a: 57). While overall employment fell in Newcastle (−33.7 per cent) between 1991 and 2001, the city's economic profile continued to show the features of a post-industrial city. The manufacturing share of the economy (especially food products and beverages, communication equipment, electrical machinery, plastics, fabricated metal products and furniture), construction, consumer services, education, health and social work, and other services within the total employment in 2001 became much bigger than the equivalent sectors in 1991 (Anon. 2001a). Although the percentages of those employed in finance and business, and public administration services, within the total employment figures in 2001 lessened compared to their share of these sectors in 1991, the recent growth of the consumer services, education, health and social work, and other services, and the change in the profile of the manufacturing sector in Newcastle, are worth noting as characteristics of a post-industrial city.

The city's economic restructuring in the past two decades has gone hand in hand with the creation of a new urban landscape, particularly in the city centre and its immediate periphery. The area-based regeneration schemes driven by public–private initiatives, such as the Grainger Town Project, the Quayside, the Theatre Village and China Town Development Strategy, have created mainly consumption-oriented, highly speculative, commercial and prestigious environments (Figure 2.1). Within this new city-scape, a number of attractive public spaces have appeared, enriched with high-quality construction materials and embellished with artworks and design elements. The Haymarket Bus Station (HBS), one of these public spaces, was seen by the regeneration initiatives as having the potential to improve its good image and attractiveness to inward investment. In many senses, the HBS may be perceived as a textbook example of the privatiza-tion of the public spaces of post-industrial cities, especially those that have become catalysts of urban regeneration projects. But equally, several aspects of the HBS experience stand out as distinctive. As will be argued in the fol-lowing section, in spite of having aspects that diminish its 'publicness' (as compared with its contemporary counterparts), the new HBS also contains features that improve its 'public' qualities.

2.1
Public space improvement in Newcastle city centre: Haymarket Bus Station.

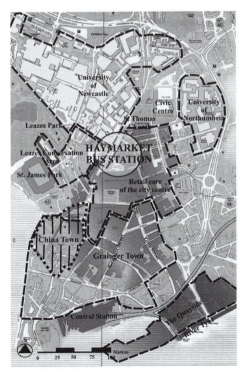

The location and a brief history of the Haymarket

The Haymarket is located in the north-west part of the city centre (Figure 2.2). The bus station, situated on Percy Street, is adjacent to Haymarket Metro Station, the South African War Memorial and St Thomas Church, and the Civic Centre to the north. It is also a neighbour of the University of Newcastle to the north; Leazes Conservation Area (a residential area accommodating listed buildings) is to the north-west; a multi-storey car park on Prudhoe Place and Prudhoe Street surrounded by Eldon Square Shopping Centre (the biggest shopping mall in the city centre) and the bus concourse are to the south; and Northumberland Street, the prime retail street, is to the east.

The history of the Haymarket began in the early nineteenth century when the site started to be used as a parade ground (Mittins 1978). With the rise of Percy Street as a commercial street in the mid-nineteenth century, the site became a marketplace where hay and straw were sold and agricultural servants hired (Collard 1971; Mittins 1978; Grundy *et al.* 1992; Simpson *et al.* 1997). Afterwards, it started to be called 'the Haymarket'. Fairs, travelling circuses, wandering menageries and political gatherings were also held here (Mittins 1978). In the late nineteenth century, a row of houses and a public house called the Farmers' Rest were constructed on the site (ibid.). This was followed by the erection of the South African War Memorial at the north of the Haymarket, the development of Bainbridge Hall and Employment Exchange at the south of the site, and the introduction of a single-deck tram into Percy Street (ibid.).

In the 1930s, the Haymarket's traditional roles were abandoned and it became a departure point for carriers, and a bus station; then the

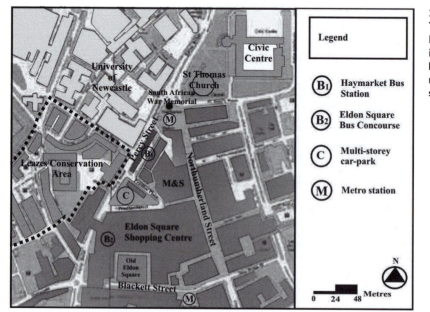

2.2
The Haymarket Bus Station and its surroundings before the redevelopment scheme.

nineteenth-century houses on the site were reconstructed and named 'Haymarket Houses' (Mittins 1978). The 1960s and 1970s witnessed significant changes in the cityscape of the Haymarket and its surroundings. With the 1960 City Centre Plan, the Central Motorway East was constructed, Percy Street was widened and the street frontage was pulled down in order to give way to Eldon Square Shopping Centre and the bus concourse (Simpson *et al.* 1997; Mittins 1978; Newcastle City Council 1963). In the early 1970s, Haymarket Houses were knocked down. A three-storey block was built in the Haymarket and a row of single-storey shops on the south of Prudhoe Place (Harbottle 1990). These changes were followed in 1980 by the construction of Haymarket Metro Station to the north of the bus station and in the mid-1990s by the development of a multi-storey car park (Simpson *et al.* 1997; Winter *et al.* 1989).

Prior to the development scheme
Access and actor
The HBS was an open public space. Despite the lack of statistics on the number of bus passengers using the HBS before its redevelopment, it is still possible to argue that, being a bus station and situated close to the metro station, the multi-storey car park and taxi ranks, it was accessible to pedestrians, metro and bus passengers, and car users. The public space was also used by a wide range of groups working in both the public and the private realms of the site. The Passenger Transport Executive for Tyne and Wear (PTE), bus companies, a private hire taxi company, hackney carriages and street traders were common user groups working in the public space, while small-scale retailers and their employees composed the working population of the private premises. Apart from the bus services provided by private bus companies, the public realm was publicly managed and controlled. The PTE operated the bus station and provided the cleaning and small-scale repair services, while the city council was responsible for the provision of large-scale maintenance services. The local authority also ran the car parks, while the city police were charged with the security of the public space. Being very accessible to and serving a rich variety of groups, and being under the control of public authorities, the HBS was a highly 'public' environment.

Interest
As a communication and transportation node of the city, the Haymarket was the place where people gathered and dispersed. Also, it was a vivid and colourful social environment. People would meet there for various reasons: to have a meal; to take refreshment in a café, restaurant or the pub; to shop; or to go on to somewhere else. Small retail units and the Farmers' Rest, with its austere decor but inexpensive food and drink services, attracted a large number of people to the site. Because this was a location for takeaway restaurants, the bus and metro stations and taxi ranks, people ended up in the Haymarket after closing time in the pubs and clubs to have their

midnight meals and then to take the bus, metro or taxi home. In this sense, the Haymarket was of considerable public service.

Yet it could also be said to have undermined the public benefit. HBS users, and thus the HBS's qualities as a desirable public realm, suffered from traffic congestion, from conflict between pedestrian and vehicular traffic, and from the fact that the public space was chaotic, disorganized and physically run-down with poor street and traffic signs. The bus station lacked public convenience facilities (such as toilets or baby changing rooms) and integration with those primary activities (especially Northumberland Street and Eldon Square Shopping Centre) surrounding it. In general, it did not function efficiently or safely for bus passengers, bus companies or the operator of the bus station. The old and modest-looking shops in the Haymarket, the dirty and ugly appearance of the rear of the buildings facing Northumberland Street, and the rather chaotic, crowded and physically deteriorated public space did not create an appealing environment either (see Figure 2.4 later in the chapter). All these factors diminished the public space's economic role, as it could neither make much contribution to increasing the land values of its environs, nor attract investors, developers or potential occupiers to the site.

The development process

From the beginning of the 1980s, the City started to look for an investor to redevelop the Haymarket. The site was put forward for redevelopment three times in these years, yet none of these attempts succeeded (Newcastle City Council 1994a). In the early 1990s, Marks & Spencer (M&S), a big high-street retailer, which owned the land on which the M&S store and service yard were located, decided to extend the store into the Haymarket with the aim of turning it into its biggest store in Britain outside London. It bought the three-storey building on the Haymarket and became one of the main property owners of the site (ibid.). After deciding to venture a £30 million investment on the redevelopment of the HBS, it approached two other major property owners of the site: Scottish & Newcastle Breweries (S&N), which owned the Farmers' Rest and the former Ginger Beer Works; and the local authority, which owned the temporary shops on Prudhoe Place and Percy Street, as well as the highways on the site, including the bus station (Newcastle City Council 1994b; Young 1994). M&S negotiated with S&N Breweries and the City by offering a new pub and restaurant and a new bus station on the site at a very low cost to both parties (Newcastle City Council 1994a).

The development process, which was highly exclusive, was carried out by a small group of public and private actors. The City and the PTE constituted the public side of the scheme, while the private side consisted of M&S, S&N Breweries, the main bus companies operating in the HBS (Northumbria Motor Services and Stagecoach), the organization of hackney carriages in Newcastle (the Northern Owner Drivers Association, NODA) and the M&S planning and design consultants and contractor (Newcastle City

Council 1995; Broomfield 2000). The domination by M&S of the development process led to the shaping of the HBS design according to the interests and needs of large-scale business, and jeopardized the desirable development process of public space. Despite the initial agreement between M&S and the City, the size of the operational area of the bus station became smaller and smaller, while the M&S extension gradually expanded towards the bus station. The main entrance of the M&S extension with the new food hall was deliberately located on the Haymarket to face directly onto the pedestrian walkway and the passenger waiting area, and thereby to attract customers to the store (Newcastle City Council 1994a). Also, by avoiding the improvement in the accessibility of the public passageway between the Haymarket and Northumberland Street, M&S encouraged the public to use its store as much as possible and therefore to purchase from the store (Newcastle City Council 1996a). The public actors, especially the City, played collaborative, facilitating, coordinating and regulatory roles in many design issues, such as the layout of the bus station, and thus enhanced the 'publicness' of the development process. Nevertheless, the design issues relating to the aesthetic and symbolic qualities of the public and private space, such as the size, height and architectural style of the retail development, the hard and soft landscaping of the public space, the style of the canopy, the lettering of the railing of the bus station, the size of the M&S logo, and the clock on the tower on the new retail development, became primarily the concern of the local authority (Denton Hall 1994; Broomfield 2000; Newcastle City Council 1996b, c, d; Perry 1996; Young 1997). In this sense, the City's involvement, driven by the desire to improve the image of the Haymarket and thereby attract investment to the site, arguably resulted in the use of the public space as a visual and functional component of the Haymarket's regeneration.

Public involvement in the development process, however, was kept limited. Prior to the procedural public consultation, the primary and daily users of the Haymarket, such as the bus passengers, shoppers, shopkeepers and bus and taxi drivers, were absent from the process. Neither were any surveys or interviews undertaken by the local authority in order to understand the problems of the Haymarket users. During the consultation period, the City received a number of objections to the development scheme. The opposing public views were concerned about:

- the exclusion of the local and small-scale enterprises in favour of a big upmarket retailer (Rutter 1994);
- the architectural style of the retail development, which did not reflect its function and disregarded the historical and cultural legacy of the Haymarket (Cousins 1994; Hartwell 1994);
- the potential increase in the traffic problems on Prudhoe Street and Percy Street due to the new size of the bus station (T. Jackson 1994; McDonald 1994; Newcastle City Council 1994a; Serfaty 1994);

- ventilation problems that could arise because of the new layout of the bus station (Lowes 1994).

Despite their relevance, the City mostly ignored these public objections. The public consultation was predominantly a one-way process of expressing the public's views, rather than a discussion forum where public and the public actors exchanged opinions. Therefore, it is arguable that community needs in no way shaped the design of the proposed public space.

During the development process, three opposition groups emerged against the HBS scheme:

- the tenants of the shops at the Haymarket, protesting against their displacement from the site;
- the regular users of the Farmers' Rest, objecting to the shift from a modest, local and traditional type of pub to an upmarket, exclusive, theme-based and more commercial pub and restaurant that disregarded the Haymarket's characteristics (Wood and Openshaw 1994);
- the Northumberland and Newcastle Society (a local charity), seeing the demolition of the Farmers' Rest and the Ginger Beer Works as a loss to the Haymarket's historical and symbolic values (Newcastle City Council 1994a).

These three groups, rather than raising their concerns during the public consultation, opted to voice their protests in other ways. The tenants of the shops and the customers of the pub showed their reactions by reporting to the press (Wood and Openshaw 1994: 6; Henderson 1994: 3; Anon. 1994: 9). The Northumberland and Newcastle Society applied to the Secretary of State to examine the historical value of the Farmers' Rest and the Ginger Beer Works (Newcastle City Council 1994a). Despite these reactions, there was no evidence that the City genuinely made an effort either to create an inclusive public arena or to include these groups' needs and opinions in the design of the public space. The restricted public access to the discussions related to the development of the public space therefore frustrated the desirable public realm's qualities.

Following planning permission granted by the City in 1994, the old bus station and other premises on the site were demolished. A two-storey building was constructed as an extension to the M&S store with a service yard and customer collection facilities, together with three kiosks, a public house and restaurant (called the Old Orleans), as well as a new bus station with a glazed canopy, and improved hard landscaping associated with the taxi rank and the multi-storey car park (Newcastle City Council 1994c) (Figure 2.3). The new bus station was opened to the public in 1997.

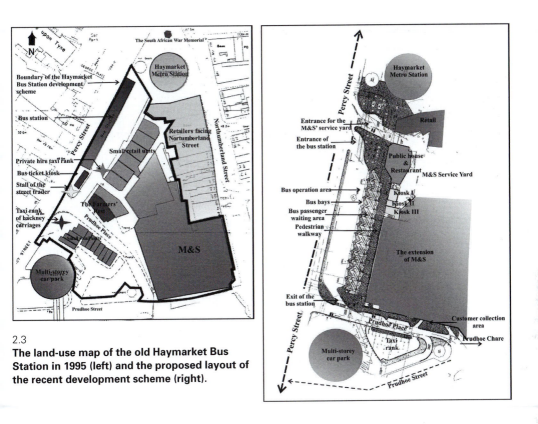

2.3

The land-use map of the old Haymarket Bus Station in 1995 (left) and the proposed layout of the recent development scheme (right).

The use process

Access and actor

The recent redevelopment scheme brought about a good-looking and a relatively accessible safer and healthier public space. The HBS, used by over 7.5 million people according to the NEXUS statistics for 2001 (NEXUS n.d.), is still one of the busiest public spaces in the city centre. The new design has improved the Haymarket's physical and social accessibility to some extent by eliminating various undesirable factors, such as noise, smoke and untidy and disorganized taxi ranks, and by introducing a better-organized queuing system and a glazed canopy protecting users from bad weather conditions (Figures 2.4 and 2.5). It has brought 'order' and 'discipline' into the space, and has provided comfort and convenience for the users. It is now more predictable what types of activities (such as queuing and waiting for buses, taking taxis, walking) will occur, where they will occur and who will be involved in them.

The new management has also enhanced to a degree the physical and social accessibility by increasing the standard of maintenance services and the level of control imposed on the public space. The City has improved not only the cleaning services of the site, but also its aesthetic quality by introducing multilayered pots placed on the pavement, pots of flowers

2.4
The old Haymarket Bus Station in the 1960s (above left) and in 1995, just before its redevelopment (below left), and the new bus station (right).

hung on the street lights, and railings for the bus station (see Figure 2.7 later in the chapter). Access control over the public space has become much stricter than before through the installation of surveillance cameras at the site and an increase in the level of street lighting. The classical music played in the bus station relaxes people, discourages violence and keeps teenagers away from the public space. The city police and NEXUS (previously called the PTE), by monitoring and patrolling the site, impose a direct significant control on the public space in order to eliminate so-called undesirable groups such as beggars, homeless people and noisy teenagers, and, accordingly, undesirable activities such as sleeping on benches, drinking alcoholic beverages or simply hanging around. As well as area-based management and design strategies, the local authority has taken a city-wide coordinated approach to tackling graffiti in public spaces through a dedicated Graffiti Forum, which monitors graffiti incidents, cleans up graffiti and actively monitors public spaces against graffiti writers in order to catch and prosecute them, but also to educate them (ODPM 2002). The City also enacted new by-laws, which have empowered specially trained traffic wardens to deal with litter, dog fouling and the distribution of free literature in public spaces by issuing a £50 penalty notice (ODPM 2002). Although both the Haymarket-specific and city-wide management and design policies of public authorities can be regarded as a part of public policy to create and maintain a cleaner, safer and more ordered public space, arguably they have also turned the bus station into a more or less desirable public space, which, in reality, has never been so clean, disciplined and stratified. By infringing on the public's right of full access to public space, such policies no longer allowed for much 'chance' and 'spontaneity', promoted social filtering and inevitably led to social exclusion and stratification. They therefore naturally reduced the social accessibility of the public space, and frustrated its 'publicness'.

The recent scheme also brought about a drastic change in the user profile of the Haymarket. By displacing small retailers and their budget shoppers, and welcoming large international businesses and their affluent consumers, it considerably reduced the variety of Haymarket's user groups, and resulted in gentrification (Table 2.2). Despite the protests of the shop tenants at the Haymarket against their displacement, the only small-scale retailer that kept its location on the site was Greggs. A few retailers, such as Pizza King, Get Stuffed and Newcastle United souvenir shop, were able to set up business in another part of the city centre, while the rest probably went out of business after their displacement. As well as the budget shoppers of the small shops, the regular users of the Farmers' Rest make up another user group now deprived of the Haymarket. The development of the Old Orleans brought about the shift from a modest, local and traditional type of pub to an upmarket, exclusive, theme-based and more commercial pub and restaurant, which disregarded the Haymarket's characteristics and has no attraction for the former users of the

2.5
The new design brought 'order' and 'discipline' into the Haymarket.

Farmers' Rest (Wood and Openshaw 1994). Hence, the new upmarket retailers, by attracting affluent groups to the Haymarket, and the new management, by pushing 'undesirable groups' out of the site, have promoted gentrification, and thus impoverished the social accessibility and 'publicness' of the space.

Table 2.2 The user profile of the Haymarket Bus Station before and after its redevelopment

Before the redevelopment	After the redevelopment
Large-scale retailers: • S&N Breweries	Large-scale retailers: • M&S • S&N Breweries

Small-scale retailers:
• Get stuffed   • Gus Carter
• Newcastle Kebab   • The souvenir shop
• Pizza King   of Newcastle United
• Greggs   • Park Lane
• Park Café   • Bobby Ann
• Mayfair   • Pasha
• Stages Truck   • Casa Del Florio
  Dance-wear   • Eldon Antiques
• Timpsons   • Top Style hairdresser
• M&N News
• Cascade
  Amusement Arcade
	Small-scale retailers:
	• Greggs
	• Finlays

PTE (the operator of the bus station)	NEXUS (the operator of the bus station)
Street traders Taxis: • Hackney carriages • Private hire taxi company	*Street traders* Taxis: • Hackney carriages
Bus companies: • Northumbria Motor Services • Stagecoach	Bus companies: • Arriva • Stagecoach • Go Ahead
The public: • Bus passengers • Pedestrians • Shoppers mainly using small-scale retailers in the site • Modest customers of the Farmers' Rest • 'Undesirable' groups	The public: • Bus passengers • Pedestrians • Shoppers mainly using large-scale retailers in the site • Affluent customers of Old Orleans

Gentrification was also reinforced by the 'principle of exclusivity', embedded in the new design through elegant and highly expensive construction materials and high-quality artworks (Figure 2.6). According to Hajer (1993) and Loukaitou-Sideris (1993), the 'principle of exclusivity' intends to impress and attract, and at the same time promote the 'feeling of affluence'. Hence, the new design, tending to attract affluent groups, has further promoted gentrification, and thus impoverished the social accessibility and 'publicness' of the space.

2.6

The enhanced aesthetic and visual quality of the public space, and its aesthetic and symbolic roles – overemphasized by the new design.

The public space is still managed and controlled publicly. Nevertheless, there have been some interventions of private actors into the management and operation of the public space. For example, the bus companies and some high street retailers (especially M&S, Bainbridge, Eldon Square Shopping Centre plc and Fenwick's) pay for traffic wardens to ease the traffic congestion on the site; public transportation services are mainly provided by private bus companies; and M&S's and the Old Orleans' security guards and cameras intervene in the operation of the bus station when their security is jeopardized. These are the key elements that partly privatize the management of the public space, and frustrate to an extent its 'publicness' (Table 2.3).

Public interest

The recent development scheme brought about a public space that served the public benefit considerably. The public gained a brand-new bus station at very low cost to the City. The new bus station, in a way, has become a source of pride for citizens of Newcastle. With the new design and management improving the visual and aesthetic qualities of the public space and creating a strong visual identity, the new public space has arguably started to function as a catalyst for image-led regeneration of the city centre. For example, the management policies aimed at creating a more attractive, cleaner, more ordered and more disciplined public environment have strengthened the visual quality of the public space. Similarly, the new design has enhanced and promoted the aesthetic qualities of the site through the use of expensive construction materials, such as York stone for the hard landscaping, and the introduction of artworks embellishing the Haymarket, such as the clock tower, glass-panel artwork on the canopy of the bus station, the ornamental and elegant railings of the balconies of Old Orleans, and the well-considered details of the bus station railings, such as lettering (Figures 2.6 and 2.7). The new design has also generated a strong 'visual identity' for the Haymarket. The use of high-quality construction materials, particularly ornamental and elegant ones, and expensive and distinctive artworks and design elements has embellished the Haymarket and created a 'chic' architecture (Figure 2.6 and 2.7). Further, the strong visual identity has been developed by introducing 'variety and diversity' into the design of the bus station through various manufactured and imported images, which are not in harmony with each other but create a landscape of visual variety, called a 'scenographic variety' by Crilley (1993). By reflecting the architecture and construction materials of a Victorian building on Percy Street, the new design has attached the bus station and its environs to a 'grandiose' historical image. It has also brought an imported image into the Haymarket through the new pub and restaurant, whose design reflects 'New Orleans' themes (Figure 2.7).

Those design and management elements, improving and enhancing the attractiveness of the public space, have turned it into a means of increasing the land values around the Haymarket, and thereby a tool for

Table 2.3 Changes in the 'publicness' of the Haymarket Bus Station (HBS)

	Before the improvement	After the improvement

Access	• Physically open to all
	• Accessible for public transport and private car users, and pedestrians
		• Still physically open to all and accessible for the same groups
		• More public because of its improved physical and social accessibility through the new design and management, which have made the public space safer, more attractive and ordered
		• Less public, owing to its diminished social accessibility:
		  • promotes social filtering, social stratification and exclusion
		  • promotes gentrification

Actor	Agencies in control: • Public authorities (except the private bus companies providing bus services) User groups: • Used by a wide range of user groups (see Table 2.2)	Agencies in control: • Still dominantly managed and controlled by public agencies • Less public because of the partial privatization of its operation and management User groups: • Still used by a large number of people • Less public, owing to the diminishing variety and diversity of user groups of the Haymarket (see Table 2.2)

Interest	• Served the public interest because of being:
	  • a vivid and colourful social environment
	  • an inclusive public space
	• Undermined the public interest due to:
	  • traffic congestion;
	  • conflict between pedestrian and vehicular traffic;
	  • chaotic, unorganized and physically deteriorated public space;
	  • poor traffic signs;
	  • lack of free-of-charge public convenience;
	  • lack of integration of the bus station with primary activities surrounding it;
	  • inefficiently and insecurely functioning bus station;
	  • insufficiency in performing the economic and aesthetic qualities of the HBS.
		• Still serving the public interest because it:
		  • became more attractive, cleaner, safer and healthier than it used to be;
		  • has functioned as a source of pride for the city;
		  • has contributed to the city centre regeneration and city imaging campaigns;
		  • is a brand-new bus station at no cost to the public.
		• Still undermines the public interest due to its:
		  • overemphasized economic roles by being used as a means of consumption and an economic-value generator;
		  • overemphasized symbolic qualities;
		  • diminished social accessibility;
		  • unresolved problems:
		    • traffic congestion
		    • conflict of pedestrian and vehicular traffic
		    • inefficiently functioning bus station
		    • lack of free-of-charge public convenience
		    • lack of integration of the bus station with primary activities surrounding it;
		  • poor ventilation as a new problem.
		• Serves more private interest (see Table 2.4)

2.7

The Victorian building whose façade was copied for the façade of the Marks & Spencer store extension (above), and the embellished façade of the Old Orleans pub and restaurant brought a 'New Orleans' theme (below), all aiming to create a grandiose image for the Haymarket.

attracting investors, developers and potential occupiers to the site, helping bring the underused buildings back into use, creating new jobs and resources for the economy of the city and contributing to the regeneration of the city centre. A number of projects have been under way since the late 1990s. The east of the Haymarket – that is, the site stretching from Morden Street to St Thomas' Street – is being developed as offices, shops, a hotel, leisure facilities or a multi-storey car park (Anon. 2001b), while schemes to convert the Eldon Square Bus Concourse into a new shopping area as an extension of the Eldon Square Shopping Centre (Anon. 2003), to develop a new cultural quarter to the north-west of the Haymarket (Young 2003a) and to redevelop the Haymarket Metro Station as a new five-storey building comprising a new bus station concourse, travel agency, shops, offices and a restaurant and bar to the north of the bus station (Young 2004) have been recommended for approval.

Yet the new design of the bus station has turned the space into a means of consumption. Public spaces, as the major places where commercial activities and exchange have taken place, have naturally been used as means of consumption for centuries (Gehl 1996). What is remarkable about the new design of the bus station, however, is the creation of a public environment that is more consumption oriented than it used to be. While the design of the old Haymarket set some distance between the bus station and the retailing activities through the traffic road, the new layout, by removing this distance and setting a very close proximity between the passenger waiting area, the pedestrian passageway and the shops, has created a public space that encourages those who come, wait or leave the public space to purchase goods from the shops (Figures 2.3–2.5). By using the public realm as both an economic-value generator and a means of increasing consumption, the new design is undermining the public interest, and thereby the desirable 'public' realm qualities.

Equally, the improvement of the environmental image and ambience of the HBS has made it more welcoming and less intimidating to a wider range of social groups, and thus improved its 'public' qualities. Yet it has uttered threats against the symbolic values of the public space. Public spaces, with their images and symbols, are meant to serve as social binders (Loukaitou-Sideris 1988; Lynch 1992; Moughtin 1999). In the case of the HBS, however, the new design, embedded in imported and manufactured images that have never belonged to the modest history of the Haymarket, has generated confusion over the public space's symbolic meanings, and therefore raised doubts about how far the new public space will be appropriated by the public, and how well it will perform as a social binder. Hence, the design interventions in the symbolic values and meanings of the public space have diminished the social accessibility of the Haymarket, and the public interest, thereby violating the desirable public realm's qualities.

Additionally, in a number of different ways the new design has undermined the public space's physical accessibility, as well as the public

interest. Twenty-one interviews conducted in 2000 with the working population of the HBS (the Old Orleans public house, M&S, Eldon Square Shopping Centre plc), with the groups who operate in the public space (NEXUS,
Arriva bus company, taxi and bus drivers, street traders) and with the daily
users (pedestrians, shoppers, bus or metro passengers) show that conflicts
between pedestrians and vehicular traffic and traffic congestion are still the
site's predominant problems (Figure 2.8). Direct observations and interviews at the Haymarket also reveal that the bus station remains inefficient
and continues to suffer from the lack of free-of-charge public convenience
facilities. Equally, the new design is unable to strongly integrate the bus station with its surroundings. The closest connection between the bus station,
Northumberland Street and the shopping mall is via Eldon Square staircase,
which is used only during the hours between the opening and closing times
of Eldon Square Shopping Centre (that is, between 9.00 a.m. and 5.30 p.m.
on Monday, Tuesday, Wednesday and Friday, between 9.00 a.m. and 8.00
p.m. on Thursday, between 9.00 a.m. and 6.00 p.m. on Saturday, and
between 11.00 a.m. and 5.00 p.m. on Sunday). It therefore does not enable
twenty-four-hour public access. Neither is it adequately accessible for disabled or elderly people (Figure 2.8). In addition to the old problems, the
new glazed canopy has led to poor ventilation, which appears to be an
increasing problem for bus passengers. Several design and management features that impinge adversely on the desirable public space's qualities are to
some extent the outcome of public exclusion from the public realm development process, as doubts had already been expressed through public objections, protests and reactions.

Private interest

Although the new HBS design has undermined the public interest in various
ways, it has significantly favoured the private interest (Table 2.4). The main
private actors benefiting from the old HBS were S&N Breweries, the small
retailers (the tenants of the retail units at the Haymarket and Prudhoe Place,
and street traders), a private hire taxi company, hackney carriages and bus
companies (especially Stagecoach and Northumbria Motor Services – or,
with the new name of the company, Arriva). Apart from the small retailers
and the private-hire taxi company, these private actors became the primary
beneficiaries of the new HBS, as they were able to keep their position in this
important part of the city centre and also gained a highly disciplined and
ordered environment that made their operation much easier than before. Of
the private actors, the HBS new design predominantly favoured M&S and
S&N Breweries, which have not only increased their trading areas but also
gained a good position next to a very busy bus station and thereby increased
their commercial profits, as claimed by the manager of the Old Orleans:

> Obviously as a business we're trying to benefit from the fact that
> the bus station is outside the door. Because people waiting for a

bus are coming and having a drink, while they're waiting, or they get off the bus, and may decide to have something to eat in the restaurant before they go out or before they go shopping. So we do benefit from that. But we noticed that when the bus station is closed, it actually had an impact on our business.

M&S especially has obtained a significant privilege, since its store, functioning as a major passageway between the Haymarket, Northumberland Street and the shopping mall, has increased customer capacity by 35 per cent. Pinpointing the advantages of the new store, the M&S financial assistant manager explains the company targets as follows:

We know that the route between Northumberland Street and bus station is used as a short cut by a lot of people. We know that only 70 per cent of the people who come through these doors

Table 2.4 Changes in the private interests of the Haymarket Bus Station (HBS) before and after the improvement

	Before the improvement	*After the improvement*

Private interest	Those benefited by being adjacent to, or close, to the public space, or using it:
	 • S&N Breweries
	 • small retailers
	 • private-hire taxi company
	 • hackney carriages
	 • bus companies
	 • street traders
		• Those benefiting by gaining a disciplined and ordered environment to operate smoothly:
		   • M&S, S&N Breweries, hackney carriages, bus companies and street traders;
		 • Those who operated in the site before the improvement of the public spaces and who were able to keep their position in the sites (hackney carriages, bus companies and street traders)
		 • Upmarket retailers and business groups benefiting by the improved image and design attracting affluence:
		   • M&S, S&N Breweries, retailers of Eldon Square Shopping Centre
		 • Those benefiting by moving into and starting a business in these sites:
		   • Finlays
		 • Those benefiting by gaining privileged positions and facilities for trading:
		   • M&S and S&N Breweries
		 • Landowners, developers and investors benefiting by the increasing property values
		 • Business interests in the finance and construction industry, and estate agencies benefiting by the good image of the area, which has boosted development activities in and around the HBS

2.8
Conflict of pedestrian and vehicular traffic (above right and left); traffic congestion in the Haymarket (below left and middle) is continuous.

actually spend money. So the big challenge of M&S is how to make the invitation to shop better, to persuade them to stop and buy when they pass through. That's the real commercial challenge for us.

Moreover, M&S has acquired three kiosks, and gained better service yard and customer-collect zone facilities for trading. The public space also benefited new private-actor groups. Having a good position in the Haymarket, Finlays, a tenant of the M&S kiosks, is doing very good business. The HBS, with its new and exclusive images and design attracting affluent groups, favoured the interests of upmarket retailers and business groups. Landowners, developers and investors in the private spaces around the Haymarket are other private actors who have benefited from the remarkable increase in property values due to the improved image of the site. Furthermore, in a wider context the new positive image of the Haymarket boosted the development activities in the private space of this part of the city centre, and thus benefited the business interests in the finance industry (building societies, banks, personal loan investments, etc.), the construction industry (building contractors, agents that hire plants and supply construction materials, etc.) and estate agencies involved in the regeneration of the site. Therefore, in comparison with the number and variety of private-actor groups that the HBS served before its redevelopment, the new public space can be seen increasingly to favour private interest.

Becoming less or more 'public' than before?

The investigation of the three stages of the Haymarket development in terms of the dimensions of 'access', 'actor' and 'interest' showed that the redevelopment of the HBS has had both diminishing and improving impacts on the desirable 'public' space qualities. The 'publicness' of the public space has been undermined by partial privatization of the development, management and operation of the HBS. Although the Haymarket is still serving a large number of people, the investigation revealed that, with the diminishing variety of users and the strict control measures, it is predominantly serving a more 'homogeneous' public than it used to do, and is increasingly characterized by a strong tendency towards enhancing gentrification, social exclusion and stratification. With its impoverished social and physical functions, and strongly emphasized economic, aesthetic and symbolic values, the new HBS has also undermined the public interest, while favouring the private interest much more than it used to do.

The undermined 'public' qualities of the HBS remarked above show similarities with at least four main trends, which have also been noted elsewhere as hallmarks of post-industrial cities' public spaces:

- the increasing involvement of the private sector in the provision, management and control of public spaces;

- increasing restrictions on the social accessibility of public spaces through surveillance and other strict control measures in order to improve their security and 'good' or 'sanitized' images;
- the tendency of public spaces to promote gentrification, social exclusion and stratification;
- a new urban form that significantly favours private interest rather than community needs.

Four areas of similarities between the HBS and post-industrial cities' public spaces reflect the ever smaller, more internationalized and more homogeneous world in which we live. Nevertheless, there are also some dissimilarities between the HBS case and other contemporary public spaces, reflecting the different experience of Newcastle. After the improvement of the HBS, the 'publicness' of the public space was secured in terms of the provision, operation and control of the public space, since the agencies in control are still public authorities. Similarly, the redevelopment project, using and promoting the public space as a catalyst of urban regeneration and a means of consumption, has also turned the Haymarket into a remarkably good-looking, well-maintained, safer, more organized and controlled space. Hence, despite the new design and management promoting gentrification, social exclusion and stratification, the physical and social accessibility of the Haymarket have been relatively improved by the recent scheme. With its attractive and distinctive look, the HBS is an example of favouring the public interest by providing a relatively inclusive and accessible environment, helping attract inward investment, creating new job opportunities, bringing economic vitality back to the declining parts of the city centre and boosting civic pride. The investigation also shows that the use of the public space as a means for the improvement of a city's image and attractiveness can offer an opportunity for cities not only to improve the quality of their public space, but also to enhance the aesthetic quality of the city centre.

Conclusion

Two major conclusions can be drawn from all the investigations and discussions on the 'publicness' of the HBS. First, contrary to the wide recognition of a diminishing 'publicness' of post-industrial cities' public spaces in the urban design and planning literature, the redevelopment of the HBS has had both improving and diminishing impacts on its 'public' qualities. The general point that can be drawn from the case study and extended to its counterparts is that contemporary public spaces may show different shades of 'publicness', in which the degree of 'access', 'actor' and 'interest' can vary widely. Nevertheless, the trend for post-industrial cities and their public spaces, and the threat to their 'publicness', is the blurring of the distinction between public and private spaces. The challenge for planners, designers, architects, developers and other place-making agents is to deal with the rising ambiguity between the two realms in the new cityscape of post-industrial cities.

Second, as in the Newcastle case, for many post-industrial cities in Britain, especially those that have suffered from decaying urban economy and environments, there is an increasing tendency to use enhancement of the quality of public spaces, and the promotion of their economic, aesthetic and symbolic roles, as a crucial policy instrument in economic and urban revitalization. At the same time, this generates threats against the 'public-ness' of these public spaces. The challenge for local authorities, planners, architects and other regeneration initiatives therefore is to take into con-sideration the needs of everyday society, and the wider civic functions of public spaces in cities, and not to allow the economic or image-related effects to dominate. The creation of genuine 'public' spaces, which can ensure the sustainability of any regeneration initiatives and the generation of vital and viable cities (especially city centres), can only be achieved if the image-led regeneration strategies balance the needs and interests of every-day society, as well as the genuine civic functions of public spaces.

Acknowledgements

The initial research for this chapter was made possible by grants from the Higher Education Council (HEC) of Turkey, and the University of Newcastle. The author acknowledges their support. The author also owes her greatest thanks to those interviewed in the fieldwork programme, including bus and taxi drivers; pedestrians, passengers and street traders, as well as Jim Cousins MP; Dolly Potter, the Planning Officer of NEXUS; and the representatives of the Highway and Transportation (HAT) department; the design team and the ex-Planning Chief of the NCC; Nathaniel Lichfield & Partners; the Old Orleans Public House; Eldon Square Shopping Centre; M&S and Arriva.

Note

1 McClelland (1988: v) identifies three major indications that define a 'post-industrial city': (1) the part of the economy that specializes in service and technology-based activities; (2) the part of the economy that experiences de-industrialization represented by a shift from labour-intensive production to capital-intensive production in which the labour force is highly qualified (that is, it has a high level of education and specialization); and (3) the part of the economy that is mostly dependent on footloose industries and multinational companies and institutions.

Chapter 3

Youth participation and revanchist regimes

Redeveloping Old Eldon Square, Newcastle upon Tyne

Peter Rogers

The context

In a rapidly changing landscape of research, it has become clear that gentrification and revanchism are subjects of study gaining momentum. These
themes are increasingly seen to be underpinning both the experience and the
management of the city in many critical reviews of globalizing, and increasingly urban, society. This research offers an opportunity to reframe discussion of gentrification and revanchism by connecting the broader theoretical
themes that inform research to a grounded empirical case study of a post-
industrial city on the cusp of the world stage. In this case study, that city is
Newcastle upon Tyne in the United Kingdom. The empirical part of this
chapter pulls together previous research into the broader understanding of
Newcastle upon Tyne to focus on the social and spatial exclusion of young
people from the city centre.

   The exclusion of young people from public space has increasingly
been highlighted as an effect of redevelopment following the strategic legacy
of urban renaissance (Rogers 2006). Often this occurs through a series of
implicit and *explicit* exclusions. It is argued in this chapter that *implicit*
exclusions occur at the level of governance in two main ways: first, young
people are often given a minor or passive role in public consultation –
particularly consultations affecting public 'amenity' spaces or open plazas;
and second, they are often reduced to playing a minor active role in specific
projects that target the development of appropriate 'play spaces'. The
explicit exclusions are more often tactical practices targeting 'inappropriate'
young people with the intent to 'disperse' problematic gatherings and 'move
on' groups of youth from commercial areas, encouraging them to use spaces
provided explicitly for youth 'playfulness' out of the broader public milieu.
This might often be operated under the guise of managing nuisance and
potential anti-sociability. In this case study, the tensions arising from such
management of conduct through design, consultation and tactical spatial

management are unpacked. The primary focus of this chapter is therefore the concept of a key public space in Newcastle upon Tyne city centre. By narrowing the focus to a particular site, the difference can be demonstrated between the approach of government agencies to regeneration – using limited strategic and typologically driven concepts of public space – and the everyday reality of using that location for the citizens who work, play and even pray in Old Eldon Square (Figure 3.1).

Old Eldon Square sits at the centre of the commercial core of Newcastle upon Tyne and offers the only central green public space in the heart of a bustling commercial district. As such, it is a perfect example of intersecting tensions among key groups. The remainder of the chapter will attempt to tease out the tensions and contradictions in the rhetoric of inclusion and consultation from the reality of increasingly exclusionary practices governing conduct, particularly where the extraction of maximum exchange-value from the public space that is Old Eldon Square appears to take precedence over the 'publicness' of the location. This seeks to highlight the contrast between the rhetoric of inclusion, the 'explicit' provision of space for young people and the reality of 'implicit' exclusion that underpins the roll-out of city-central urban renaissance in Newcastle upon Tyne. This type of 'renaissance' appears increasingly retail and commercially oriented, with significant ramifications for the 'publicness' of city-central public space.

3.1
Old Eldon Square in Newcastle upon Tyne city centre.

Theory and methods of the study

This case study draws on *The Production of Space* by Henri Lefebvre (1991), developing the now much-discussed conceptual triad of spatial production towards an analytically researchable process, as well as some elements of Foucauldian notions of governmentality and the management of the 'conduct of conduct'. The relationship between these approaches is tied to the three major elements of 'spatial production' and the processes of government as they appear in 'regimes of practice'. It is argued that through this theoretical lens can be viewed the means by which the concept of a given site is embedded into specific regimes of practice for the management of that location through apparatus and techniques for mobilizing power (*dispotifs*) (Foucault 2003, 2007) in order to exert control over the sovereign territory of state, region or, in this case, the city. The theoretical framework harnesses representations of space (conceived spaces), representational spaces (lived everyday spaces) and spatial practice (perception of and reaction to these interweaving elements) to construct an analysis of the regime of practices through which change is occurring. It also seeks to show how the requirements placed upon sovereign government (as conceptualized in a more Foucauldian narrative) to enhance the economic offer of the city on behalf of the citizens are implicitly and explicitly displacing the concept of 'public trust' in which the ideal of public space has been traditionally managed at the local level. Much of this is emerging from the reaction to urban decline alongside the entrepreneurial turn in government, and related issues discussed widely in urban geography and sociology (Kearns and Philo 1993; Eisinger 2000; Evans 2001).

The argument here is that the concept of space held in trust by local authorities and agencies tasked with the redevelopment and marketing of urban spaces is increasingly dominated by commercial and entrepreneurial concepts (Rogers and Coaffee 2006), inherently reducing the 'publicness' of these locations (Akkar 2005a). The intricacies of hegemonic negotiations occurring through both democratic channels and governance form a discursive 'regime of practices' that legitimates the entrepreneurial governance of the city. This implies and enforces a 'conduct of conduct' (Dean 1999) that excludes those not amenable or conducive to the reapplied notions of appropriate behaviour in these spaces. The result is a less public form of urban open space, and citizens on the fringe of political negotiations become marginalized in favour of stakeholders from private commercial interests – who have more access and better-defined needs and wants for the future of the city. These can be seen as key contributors to the regime of practice associated with the development and management of safe, clean spaces for the fluent exchange of capital and the orderly flow of commerce in the everyday life of the city centre. Through the creation of a coherent concept for each of the spaces that comprise the city centre, a managerial composite of appropriate activity in each location is created. The appropriateness of activities thus influences the formation of a typology of spatial resources,

resources to be held in trust by the government and managed on behalf of the populace. This includes the streets as spaces of transition from one location to another; plazas and open areas used as showcases, event or multi-purpose 'amenity' spaces; memorial spaces; and private areas under private management, as well as parks and playgrounds, or 'play spaces'. A notion of appropriateness is tied to each type of location, forming a key thread of the appropriate management of conduct within those locations in liaison with partner agencies. Thus, governance brings together the city councils and local authorities with public–private partners (from investors to private security), emergency services (the police, fire and related services), key lobbyists and public interest groups (e.g. residents' associations), as well as the general public themselves.

However, through the interweaving of people's perceptions and actions in using these spaces, there are changes to the moral consensus underpinning each site and location. This consensus operates in a different – more fluid and dynamic – fashion as compared with the regime of practices emerging from the interplay of governors and stakeholders. Within given locations or sites, the membership of users changes over time; ergo, at different times of day, different groups interact and the consensual codes of appropriate conduct flex and change in response to the balance created by that interplay. This complicated, and at times dense, body of theoretical work has led to numerous interpretations of the layering between the concepts of space brought forth by the regime of practice emerging from governance of specific locations, the lived everyday spaces created through the use of given locations, and the complex minutiae resulting from the interplay of competing forces and interests upon all the actors and agents involved at differing levels of spatial production. This research seeks to draw out the interplay of these elements and apply the theory of spatial production empirically to research on the given site or location, in this case Old Eldon Square. In order for it to do so, the terms have to be defined in a researchable context.

If one assumes that the conceived or conceptual space is the 'rational space' of design and planning (Allen and Pryke 1994), then the discourse that is constructed around a given location in strategic planning documentation offers us a critical unit of analysis for developing a deeper understanding of these locations. However, if, as has been suggested, these discourses on space are also inclusive of discursive regimes, then it is also necessary to incorporate the institutional and social memory of the space and its appropriate uses to offer a complete analysis of the concept of space being represented (Shields 1992; Elden 2001). First, in order to engage with these managerial threads the research has to understand and develop the regimes of practice underpinning conceptual space by reviewing the documents of design, the architectural scheme and the activities for which the space is organized through this process, and by looking at who are the key stakeholders in the redesign and redevelopment of the given location. This involves interviews and archival analysis as well as the longitudinal study of the site as it is redeveloped over a period of time.

Second, the lived space under investigation requires an approach that enables the subtle nuances of diverse everyday use-values of a given location to become more evident. If there is more than one concept of use in the historical memory of the location, then it is necessary to engage with the local populace to tease out the memory of past uses and see whether they are elided by or conflated with those of present dominant uses. It is equally likely that a researcher may assume that these are contributing factors to the perception of that space. The way in which people use the space and have used it previously thus informs the patterns of activity and behaviour sanctioned in that location; the cycle both reinforces the consensus of appropriate conduct and illuminates the transgressions upon the broader awareness of the appropriate potential use of the site. It is also through this discursive reinvention of locations that rules or a moral consensus of appropriateness are constructed, so the researcher must understand the key demographic groups associated with a location and their frequency or consistency of use by engaging in observation and interviews with those who constitute the dominant user groups in the past and the present.

This raises tensions with the final and most complex element of the triad, spatial practices. There are several approaches to this particular aspect of the production of space as an ongoing process. It is intended in this research that spatial practice represents the difficult and messy parts of the process, which are difficult to unpack in depth. It also binds and informs elements of abstract and social spaces as flexible, permeable and constantly changing subsystems within spatial production. These subsystems act as a lens of interpretation through which every action occurring is *perceived*, but also at that moment of perception *reacted to*, informing the ongoing decision-making process of the individual and any collectives engaged in activity with the specific site. By developing these as rhythms of interacting processes occurring in both space and time, we begin to see the dynamic nature of spatial production in more depth (Lefebvre 1991, 2004). This may also result in the identification of specific subsets of users through identifiable identity markers such as single-parent shoppers, veterans and elderly people, or subculturally identifiable youth groups (e.g. goths, chavs, etc.).

What makes this research different is the ability of this theoretical framework to offer unprecedented depth to the analysis of connections forged between ethnographic cultural research methods, policy review and theoretical frameworks of spatial production. This offers opportunities to develop more culturally grounded interpretations of how users view and engage with public spaces within a regime of practices. The analysis of these interactions demonstrates the ongoing shift in government where the over-privileged input of entrepreneurial stakeholders is subsuming the role of citizens in the conceptual orientation of public spaces. Furthermore, the resultant management tactics as a coherent regime of practices *in situ* can be clarified, making distinct the potential of these regimes of practice both to create social divisions and to undermine the fluent social environment at the heart of the broader idealized concept of 'publicness'. In order to assess street-level experiences of all citizens (including the general public and private business) alongside strategic concepts in policy (strategic documents from a range of agencies) and management of perception around a particular location (through media content analysis of local and national news on subjects of concern, such as anti-social behaviour, or the problem of youth), a case-study strategy was developed. This broad framework offers in-depth profile management of minority groups in the city centre; a qualitative policy review of strategic documentation; and interviews with a range of operatives at local and regional levels in the civil service, public and private security services, the emergency services, both large and small businesses, and a wide range of special interest groups. Taken together, these allow the researcher to construct an 'anthropological stage of reality' from which to draw an analysis of the connections between concepts of public space, experiences of public space, and the intersection of *perceptions of* and *reactions to* activities that occur in Old Eldon Square by all those who have a stake in either the *development* or the *use* of the location. This theoretically informed but empirically grounded approach offers a unique reflection of the production of urban public spaces as an ongoing and perpetually shifting process, but one not out of the reach of a more inclusive regime of practice. This potential is not currently realized in the current framework of translating policy into practice, as seen in studies of gentrification and revanchism (Smith 1996; MacLeod 2002; Slater 2004).

Typologies and public space

In understanding the importance of the concept or representations of a given space to the wider process, there are a number of factors that must be taken into account. First, the role of strategic documentation, the representations of space underpinning the concept itself, is made manifest through the operations, briefs and tactics of managing the design and consultation process for any urban development. This design assumes a range of factors, such as particular uses to which the space is to be put, and its role in the network of spatial assets held in trust for the local populace by the city council, but is also concerned with ambience, presentation or style and with less aesthetic and more practical issues such as the delivery of the construction, and maintenance of the site after completion. A key change from the managerial approach to governing the city towards the entrepreneurial governance of the city-region can be seen in the treatment of public spaces in the community, where they are being repackaged in strategic documentation as resources. This change towards a strategic assessment of space as a series of assets, to be mobilized for a range of uses (both public and commercial), implicitly redefines the publicness of each given location through categorization as an asset for a specific 'conceived' purpose. In the national government agenda for urban development as set out in the policy document known as the 'Urban White Paper' (DETR 1999), it is clearly stated that public space must be

> somewhere to relax and enjoy the urban experience, a venue for a range of different activities, from outdoor eating to street entertainment; from sport and play to a venue for civic or political functions; and most importantly of all as a place for walking and sitting out.
>
> (DETR 1999, quoted in Amin *et al.* 2000)

But what then happens if a specific location fulfils more than one of these aims? How is it to be managed and – an even more complex problem – to be redeveloped in a way that ensures it remains public in all of its capacities? As no public space is hermetically bounded or sealed from other spaces, be they streets or buildings, then to treat each as defined by a singular use would appear to be problematic. This is the tension in management that is teased out through the following reappraisal of typologies of public space in Newcastle upon Tyne.

Four dominant concepts of Old Eldon Square

In order to enable an understanding of the specific site at the heart of this case study, this section outlines the four concepts of Old Eldon Square and links these to the lived space itself. Links are made between particular interest groups and each of the concepts through their live experience and social memory of these locations, as evidenced in observation and interviews over a period of five years (2000–2005). The city centre of Newcastle upon Tyne has a number of open public spaces; however, the majority of these are hard-surfaced locations, considered broadly as plazas or squares. Old Eldon Square is one of the only significant open green spaces within the boundaries of the city centre – though the centre is skirted on the periphery by several larger parks and public gardens.

As a green open public space, at the time skirted by walkways, this area has a long history as a gathering place for local youth. Young people often gather at evenings and weekends to sit and socialize on the grassy area, out of the main pedestrian flow through the commercial core of the city. Local history suggests that this has been the case since the 1960s, when several covered public arcade areas within the city were redeveloped or privatized within the broader redevelopment of the city occurring as a part of the unitary development plan at that time (Pendlebury 2001). As a result of this removal of the core locations with which young people identified, these groups began to congregate in the liminal area of Old Eldon Square and have continued to do so till this day.

Old Eldon Square can also be seen as a commercial space for big and small businesses. The square is surrounded on three sides by the Eldon

Square shopping centre. This is owned by a large public–private partnership between the city council, Shell Pensions Trust and Capital Shopping Centres (CSC), with the local council owning the controlling share in the venue. However, the day-to-day operation of this shopping centre, which dominates the commercial core of the city, resides with CSC. The centre has private security and a private closed-circuit television (CCTV) network, the control room for which is located in the shopping centre itself and is isolated from the public CCTV in the surrounding area. In addition, the centre is also patrolled by private security guards to enforce the regulations for conduct affecting the public thoroughfares through the commercial area (e.g. no skating, rollerblades, stereos, etc.). The fourth side of the square is the final remaining architectural element of the original buildings, most of which were destroyed during the development of the shopping centre in the 1970s. In this Georgian terrace there is an ensemble of small local businesses ranging from specialist stores (from jewellers to youth cultural clothing, musical instruments and wedding dresses) to cafés and private services (e.g. accountants) (Figure 3.2).

These two dominant elements of the space are also underpinned by more functional use of Old Eldon Square as a transitory space. The main road that runs along the south end of the square (Blackett Street) is a main east–west thoroughfare through the city centre for buses and taxis – with no general motorized access. Since the opening of the shopping centre in 1975, the local bus station has been located underneath the shopping centre and could be reached through a number of throughways running off Eldon Square into the shopping centre itself. Also adjoining the road and along

3.2
The final remaining side of the original square.

the pavements are a number of bus stops for major routes into the city. This also encourages the use of Old Eldon Square as a gathering location, convenient for those coming into the city from outlying towns, villages and suburbs. Old Eldon Square has often been used as a conduit from north to south through the shopping centre. The original design of the square made an uneasy space of transition for pedestrians, and the space had become somewhat marginalized from the city centre; the nearby Grey's Monument formed the primary pedestrian locus through the urban core.

Finally, the fourth concept of the location is as a sacred space. In the centre of the grassy area on Old Eldon Square is a stone paved area accessible by a paved access point from the southern pavement. At the centre of this paved area stands the dominant feature of the site, a memorial to soldiers who fought in the world wars. This is a site of great importance to the local ex-servicemen's association, and an important feature of the city centre. Proposals have been made to move the statue from the area but have been met each time with a public outcry, and have resulted in the memorial space becoming a key feature of the city, and the site of Holocaust and Remembrance Day ceremonies.

The typology of city centre public spaces

As an agenda for urban renewal, the urban renaissance was always an ambitious project and has been widely discussed and researched (Evans 2001; MacLeod 2002; Imrie and Raco 2003; Lees 2003; Moulaert *et al.* 2004). In arresting and in fact reversing the decline of the central city over the twentieth century, a tightly defined package of processes was generated to create a new concept of the public city. It can be argued that by rationalizing public spaces as community 'assets', governance groups unintentionally initiated a different approach to public space, an approach encouraged by the strategic rhetoric of 'renaissance' and combined with commercially driven practices of partnership, which to some extent subsumed traditional public consultations. This 'asset management' boiled down to a typology of activities prescriptively grounded in broadly defined categories of explicit use – and implicitly assuming a typology of users (i.e. memorial space for older citizens, playgrounds for younger). The emphasis thus shifted from national guidance to the interpretation of how to enact this at a local level. The emphasis on stakeholder partnerships and the documentation of local strategies, combined with corporate entrepreneurialism – itself encouraged by emerging pseudo-civic actors such as city centre management – encouraged local authorities to create locally specific typologies of 'use'. The typologies ascribe certain activities to certain areas, thus maximizing the communities' public assets – to improve their communal quality of life within the boundaries of the normative understanding of acceptable behaviour and activity in public space. Furthermore, this appears to increase the 'added value' of public space by maximizing its earning potential as a resource. In addition, the emphasis on aesthetic improvements rather than social rewards and a focus on ensuring the perception of cleanliness, safety and accessibility led to accusations of 'gentrification'. This also gives an implicit focus on categorizing and controlling vulnerable groups that are often highly visible yet remain on the fringes of 'appropriateness'. Several projects in similar locations undergoing redevelopment have noted that renaissance in this form – and both the entrepreneurial partners and practices it encourages – risks creating a programme of revanchism (Reeve 1996; MacLeod 2002). However, the prescriptive effect of renaissance a priori can be critiqued for its lack of an understanding of the use and re-appropriation of space as inevitable and unmanageable. This proposition conflicts with the inherent orderliness of the concept of the city as proposed by the renaissance.

Specifically, the treatment of city centre public space has a tendency not to provide spaces for groups who are inherently different from the dominant perceptions of appropriateness that permeate the entrepreneurial concept of public space. The treatment of public spaces as commercial resources engenders a concept of conduct that encourages the orderly flow of capital through appropriate forms of consumer-oriented behaviour. This concept, having been created by the hegemonic processes of consultation and the strong influence of commercial stakeholders, reinforces the resultant imbalance of interests, and hence leads to concerns about the over-dominance of commercial needs and priorities in the production of specific public spaces. In particular, research has shown that young people, who are not *criminal* but are *noticeable*, may be perceived as disorderly and potentially dangerous (Rogers and Coaffee 2005). These groups often make use of public space as an arena for an autonomous exploration of the boundaries of acceptable behaviour during adolescence (Kelly 2003; Valentine 2004). This makes these youth groups particularly vulnerable in this context, as the perceptions they generate and the playful activities they engage in are frequently in direct conflict with the concepts of orderly commerce promoted by renaissance. The 'disorderly' spaces of youth also often tend to be focused in the marginal or 'liminal' spaces targeted by renaissance for regeneration (Cloke and Jones 2005), such as Old Eldon Square, which was targeted for a major regeneration project in 2001, culminating in extensive regeneration work between 2002 and 2009.

In the Newcastle City Council 'Parks and Green Spaces' strategic plan (Newcastle City Council 2004), a typology was created of all public parks and open spaces in the city centre. This demonstrates effectively the broad understanding of use-values attributed to each location by the council, outlining the location, the resources and the particular focus of use seen to be appropriate for each venue. While the strategy focused on green spaces only and not civic spaces or private land (including gardens, countryside and private sports grounds), there are a number of locations – such as Old Eldon Square – that do not fit neatly into this assessment framework, and as such require a more focused typological definition. This particular strategy draws on Planning Policy Guidance 17 (PPG17) (DCLG 2002) to this end (Table 3.1).

Table 3.1 Typology of green spaces in PPG17

	PPG typology	*Primary purpose*
Green spaces	Parks and gardens	Accessible, high-quality opportunities for informal recreation and community events
	Natural and semi-natural green spaces, including urban woodland	Wildlife conservation, biodiversity and environmental education and awareness
	Green corridors	Walking, cycling or horse riding, whether for leisure purposes or for travel, and opportunities for wildlife migration
	Outdoor sports facilities	Participation in outdoor sports such as pitch sports, tennis, bowls; athletics or countryside and water sports
	Amenity green space	Opportunities for informal activities close to home or work or enhancement of the appearance of residential or other areas
	Provision for children and young people	Areas designed primarily for play and social interaction involving children and young people, such as equipped play areas, ball courts, skateboard areas and teenage shelters
	Allotments, community gardens and urban farms	Opportunities for those people who wish to grow their own produce as part of the long-term promotion of sustainability, health and social inclusion
	Cemeteries, disused churchyards and other burial grounds	Quiet contemplation and burial of the dead, often linked to the promotion of wildlife conservation and biodiversity

Source: Newcastle City Council (2004: 22)

Old Eldon Square was listed as an 'amenity' space in this typological framework (Newcastle City Council 2004: 23), but is also listed in the City Centre Action Plan (Newcastle City Council 2002) as a part of the 'Eldon Retail Core' area. This aspect of the plan noted that Eldon Retail Core was the heart of the city and emphasized, in the managerial priorities for this area, the need to improve public spaces and access to (and egress from) those spaces, and to improve the parking facilities for the city centre. It highlighted the importance of integrating Eldon Square Shopping Centre into the rest of the commercial city, including the minor shopping centre in the 'Grainger Town' cultural quarter known as the Newgate Centre and the newly built high-profile 'Gate' leisure complex, which has since become a form of commercial gateway between the southern city centre and the dominant northern retail core. It is clear in this conceptual orientation of the locale that the commercial concept is the dominant one. The amenity focus of the Old Eldon Square green space as requiring the provision of 'opportunities for informal activities' is elided within the corporate planning for the 'reduction of traffic' and plans for the upgrade and relocation of the bus station underneath the shopping centre. This incorporates the eventual integration of Old Eldon Square into the Eldon Square Shopping Centre as an outdoor and publicly owned pedestrian conduit between the north and south of the shopping centre.

The commercially oriented conceptual focus becomes much clearer through the subsequent redevelopment of the area between 2002 and 2008. Extensive work was undertaken with the southern shopping centre redevelopment and is still under way at the time of writing.[1] The plans for the redevelopment were put out for private tender; the winning proposals were then opened for public consultation at a private viewing or view by appointment; and public notifications of the consultations for residents and businesses in the area were held at a private venue near to Newcastle, often during weekday working hours. Subsequent public viewings of the plans could be seen in the area itself, following approval of the scheme and the undertaking of redevelopment. These plans sought to add crosswalks through the grass area to enable pedestrians to move through the area north to south and east to west without having to circulate around the grass. They also sought to move the bus station from underneath to the rear of the shopping centre, enhancing the bus station already on offer outside the northern 'Haymarket' area of the city centre. The relocation of the bus station would then allow for further commercial space to be added to the shopping centre and a more fluid access from the bus station into the city centre through Old Eldon Square itself. Links would thus be forged into the new redevelopment of the 'Southern Gateway' linking up with the neighbouring Gate complex to the south-west.

Tensions with lived and perceived spaces

The process of developing and implementing these plans was not uncontested, nor were the final plans universally welcomed. Newcastle upon Tyne has a long history of planning conflicts between the local population and the city council, and the activities associated with this redevelopment brought both widespread praise and public outcry from particular interest groups (see, for example, Akkar 2005b). It was noted earlier that the area has a long history as a gathering site for a wide range of youth groups in the region. The dominant group of users in the area at the time of the planning and redevelopment were these youth groups. There is a broad split between two large demographics of inner-city youth. The first is often from low-income working-class families with strong links to the appropriation of 'high culture' fashion and accessories in creative forms (labelled 'chavs' in the local media and popular culture). The second consists more often of youths from suburban and out-of-city areas, often from middle-class or slightly wealthier families and following a musical subculture linked to rock and heavy metal music (often labelled 'goths'). These labels are highly simplistic, but for the purposes of this chapter will not be investigated further. The focus here is much more on the interaction of these groups with the planning process, the broader perception and propaganda associated with the need to move these users from the area to more appropriate play spaces assigned to teenagers and adolescents in the schema of public spatial resources, and the problems that their presence was perceived to cause to the orderly flow of commerce targeted in the 'Eldon retail core' as the means of enhancing the city centre.

Concurrent with the public consultation on the three-scheme redevelopment plans was another consultation practice undertaken on behalf of the city council by the Brunswick Young People Project (BYPP), located in the Brunswick Chapel near to Old Eldon Square. The consultation was focused not on garnering youth opinions on the redevelopment but on the potential for providing alternative locations and sites for them to gather away from the area, and understanding what types of developments were practical and manageable, and would stimulate use by the youth groups (Thompson 2001). It is a strong implied theme in the consultation protocols that any changes should be focused on uses that would direct the youths away from the Old Eldon Square area into new spaces that would fit the typological understanding of 'areas designed primarily for play and social interaction involving children and young people, such as equipped play areas, ball courts, skateboard areas and teenage shelters' (Newcastle City Council 2004).

The consultation highlighted that while there was no cogent agreement among young people on what was required, a strong theme existed in the consultation and in community work proposing the need for some form of 'skate park' in, or near to, the city centre. This was a recurring theme in local policy as several 'amenity' areas or plazas throughout the city centre, including the memorial itself, were becoming covered by anti-skating by-laws throughout this period. This was also the subject of other tactics of dispersal, such as the spreading of gravel near the Haymarket Metro, a popular site for BMX riders, rollerbladers and skaters, the closure of some known popular skating areas including the open spaces outside the city council offices, and the introduction of fines alongside the by-laws.

This developed into a comprehensive scheme for the development of a skate park in the city centre. During this process the skaters themselves were able to interact with the designer and were able to assist in developing the park that they felt they wanted (Rogers 2006). Significantly, though, the site chosen for the park was on the northern periphery of the city centre, nestling between a busy road passing Newcastle University and a motorway overpass into the city centre; this is as far away from the Eldon Retail Core as it is possible to get while still being within the limits of the city centre.[2]

The local media often reported on youth-related issues linked to skateboarding and youth subcultural gangs in the city centre. In particular, the 'blight' of 'gang brawling' (Young 2003b) was noted in the media, alongside other concerns over surveillance and youth safety (Rogers 2006). The removal of the original trees whose dense foliage prevented the surveillance cameras around the area from effectively overseeing the centre of Old Eldon Square also caused local controversy. The trees were replaced with a species of saplings with sparse foliage, less imposing on the broader vista (Rogers 2005). Equally, the local media coverage suggested that surveillance cameras were installed to 'keep an eye on the goths', but also attempted more exploratory pieces of the 'angels with pierced faces'. Any coverage of the local skateboarders was linked to problems of safety and the need for spatial provision to remove these youths from public arts and memorial areas, where they were committing criminal damage against architecture and endangering other users of these spaces (Young 2002a, b).

There were also organized protests by the youth groups, supported by many other groups, including the ex-servicemen's association (which was anecdotally implied by the city council to be in favour of removing youths from the area). This was by no means a unanimous or blanket opinion among the elderly, to whom the area was so symbolically significant (Rogers 2005). These protests were further supported by work from the Heritage Foundation (awarding £24,800), which worked with young people in the area to produce a DVD entitled '50 Years in the Making', charting the youth-cultural history of the location. Further public consultations were mooted but the plans for the area were eventually implemented substantially unaltered from the three-scheme redevelopment plans.

The resultant changes to Old Eldon Square

Since the beginning of the redevelopment, areas of Old Eldon Square have been closed off for substantial periods as the building works have been rolled out. While there is little substantive evidence of attempts to eliminate the young people from the area, the explicit redesign strategy and redevelopment, coupled with the two streams of consultation practice, and more implicit schemes that seem subjectively focused on encouragement to relocate, seems to indicate a clear attempt to displace and disperse young people as a core element of the broader conceptual space represented by the corporate plans, design and development of the location. This is best evidenced by the plaque embedded in the stone walkway on the eastern side of the square in 2008, which states, 'Welcome to the Old Eldon Square, the city's principal war memorial. Everyone is invited to enjoy this area, but please do so with respect for its meaning and consideration for others.'

The redevelopment of Old Eldon Square itself has seen the introduction of shops at the ground floor level of the square on the western side, facing the Georgian terrace (Figure 3.3). Owing to rent increases and rebuilding works, many of the smaller shops in the Georgian terrace have been forced to relocate away from the area, and the northern side of the square has a new glass frontage leading into the basement shops linked to the new bus station (Figure 3.4). The effect of these developments on the use of the square by young people is varied. Anecdotal evidence has suggested that many of the young people have in fact moved from the Old Eldon Square area to the nearby Grey's Monument as the main place for gathering, partly because of the speciality shops linked to the youth subcultures in the Georgian terrace (which have a long history and loyal consumer base) and partly because historical identification with the site means that there is still an effective and noticeable youth presence in the area.

Significantly, much of the territorial issue associated with the conflict between youth subcultures has been alleviated by the removal of the first-storey walkway around the top of the square, which has now been brought into the shopping centre itself within the new frontage on the north side. The full impact of the redevelopment will be difficult to ascertain until the completion of the Southern Gateway redevelopment in 2010.

It is difficult clearly to allocate accountability to specific agents and agencies for the development of a regime of practice that creates divisions between different types of citizens. The consultation processes used throughout the process of redevelopment clearly show that the residents, businesses, contractors and young people, as well as specific interest groups such as the ex-servicemen's association of veterans, were all consulted in subtly different ways. The rhetoric of consultation under the regime of democratic process installed in local government allows for this to be a targeted approach in order to better understand the needs of each

3.3
The new frontages on the north and west sides of the square.

3.4
The entrance to the new underground mall area between the bus station and Old Eldon Square.

demographic, and in many ways this has been successful. The development of specific skate park provision has shown this to be the case, not only with the involvement of young people in the democratic process but also with the successful involvement of the skaters themselves in the design, development and eventual setting of rules and code of conduct for use of the area. It also allowed the governance groups better to understand the needs and concerns of these young citizens, particularly with regard to safety and to the cultural differences between youth subcultural groups. The use of specialist skate contractors to help develop these proposals went a long way towards demonstrating a serious desire to help and provide for these groups. However, the means and nature of the information gleaned by independent contractors on the city centre's skate provision was at once *enabling* in terms of understanding what provision was needed but also *exclusionary* in the identification of skate 'hotspots' and the subsequent legislative 'banning' through anti-skate by-laws regarding skating activity in almost all of the areas identified in the independent report (Rogers 2006).

Implicit tactics of relocation were used throughout the consultation and redevelopment of the locale. These included legislative action (by-laws), environmental amendments (spatial closures, gravel spreading, textured pavements), overt observation by security agencies (police photographing the area and regular police presence), covert observation (use of CCTV and expansion cameras throughout the urban core), provision of alternative venues (in the form of day-clubs playing music targeting the goth groups), and so forth. Taken as a whole, this operates as a harmony of practices creating an implicit and explicit regime of provisional exclusion underpinning the democratic practices of local government – a regime aligned with the expansion of economic imperatives for the orderly flow of commerce.

Conclusion

The examples given in this research offer some critical insights into the means by which the lifestyle, activities and 'lived experience' of the youth groups in this area played a role in the conceptual alignment of the space under redevelopment for the city centre as a whole. The main goal of the redevelopment was to find ways to bring the liminal space of Old Eldon Square back into the commercial offering of the Eldon Retail Core. In the process, however, the users who had claimed a form of ownership of the area appeared to be stigmatized as detrimental to the extraction of maximum added value from the site. The uncomfortable equilibrium these groups had attained with the surrounding commercial area (both big and small businesses), the memorial space itself and the need for a transitional pedestrian conduit to increase footfall in the southern areas of the city centre intersected in a dynamic interplay of competing interests, values and uses. The end result of this was that the youth groups were deemed surplus to requirements and a regime of practice emerged by which they were to be moved out of the area through all the tools and techniques of governance available, including design, participation, consultation, criminalization, demonization through the media, and so on. While on the one hand the young people played an active role in the decision-making process, through consultation on their needs and the subsequent provision of a skate park, it should be noted that the skaters made up a minority, albeit a significant one, among the youth in this area. Skating as such was by no means a monolithic activity – not an oriented activity of the young people writ large, simply a highly visible 'solvable problem'. The diversity of interests inherent in the adolescent groups in this area required the application of broader perceptions of appropriate conduct to non-consuming activities such as 'hanging out'. While not conducive to the orderly flow of commerce, and often boisterous or on the fringes of public acceptability, the youth groups are not illegal under any form of liberal democratic social contract. Where concerns over the implicit criminalization of this fringe behaviour are apparent in the emergence of a literature assessing anti-sociability, nuisance behaviour (Squires and Stephen 2005) and the legitimacy ascribed to enforcing the location of these marginal groups in the spaces provided for them. This literature began with understanding gentrification through assessments of the homeless, surveillance of prostitutes and observations of criminality, but has now expanded this remit to incorporate elements of revanchist policies towards nuisance behaviour often attributed to the unsupervised young. When grounded in the spatial understanding of tourism and the myth-making associated with given locations (see, for example, Shaw *et al.* 2004) the importance of the Old Eldon Square war memorial to the myth of 'place offer' in the construction of a cultural economy in Newcastle upon Tyne (particularly as a leading competitor in the contest to become Capital of Culture for 2008, where Newcastle was a finalist but eventually lost out to Liverpool), the potentially disruptive elements of youth culture in the city centre could be seen, and were anecdotally referred to by many (see Rogers 2005) as a problem to be solved.

While there is a great deal of research dealing with issues of youth exclusion from space and the commercial regeneration of the city and the city centre at the expense of marginal demographics – much of which has been noted throughout this chapter – there is much less work that brings this together with a critical theoretical framework of the changes implied by such shifts on the broader democratic project. If this project has highlighted nothing else, it has shown that a more nuanced understanding of the rhythmic interplay between *time* and *space* and *process* is required to advance our understanding of these phenomena. These shifts should not be noted as interesting footnotes to the planning and redevelopment of cities and spaces; they are emblematic of broader changes to the hierarchy of sovereign power and its use in everyday life. These changes are becoming ever more 'impactful' alterations to the framework of rights and responsibilities that underpins the liberal social contract of advanced capitalist society, with wide-reaching implications for the future.

Notes

1 See www.eldon-square.co.uk/.
2 See www.newcastle.gov.uk/skate.nsf/.

Chapter 4

Can public space improvement revive the city centre?

The case of Taichung, Taiwan

Hong-Che Chen

Introduction

The issue of the importance of city centres and the strategies for city centre regeneration have been the subject of considerable attention (DoE 1992; Scotland Development Department 1999; Ravenscroft 2000). The decline of city centres not only affects commercial development but also has wider implications such as the provision of employment opportunities, the quality of the physical environment, and the attractiveness of city centres to the region (Thorpe 1983). The various reasons for the decline of city centres include the changing commercial environment, the disappearance of employment and population, the transferring of competitiveness, and problems within the city centres themselves (Bromley *et al.* 2003). It is hard to clarify which of the reasons for the decline of city centres is the crucial one, as these reasons are spread out across economic, social and environmental factors. Moreover, there are many diverse strategies for reviving city centres, though they produce a variety of outcomes and varying degrees of effectiveness. Environmental improvement is considered to be a catalyst, one of the essential drivers in city centre regeneration (Bromley *et al.* 2003; Hall 2000). However, successful urban regeneration cannot be examined merely in terms of physical improvement; it is necessary to measure how beneficial the regeneration strategy is in improving the social and economic conditions in the declining city (Hubbard 1995). Thus, it would be significant to know how the improvements of public spaces are related to city centre regeneration.

This chapter sets out to explore this question by way of three case studies on the implementation of public space improvement. Besides providing an understanding of the impact of such improvements on the commercial environment and social development, this chapter also investigates the tension and conflict in the transformation of the public spaces from different perspectives. Evaluating the efficiency of environmental improvement and examining its impact is a way to understand whether environmental improvement benefits city centres and to recognize the elements that influence it. The three case studies in Taichung include public open spaces, pedestrian streets and waterway spaces, in order to explore the impact of environmental improvement and to discover whether public space improvement can revive the city centre.

The context of Taichung city centre

All three cases are located in Taichung city centre in Taiwan, which is a developing country in South-East Asia with an expanding economy based on hi-tech and computer manufacturing industries. Taichung City, located in the west-central area of Taiwan, is the third biggest city in Taiwan. The mayor of Taichung City has attempted to raise the profile of the city by proposing the vision of turning Taichung into an international metropolitan centre in order to increase work opportunities, raise the quality of life and promote tourism. The promotion of hi-tech manufacturing, cultural industries and local services has been adopted as the main strategy for the development of Taichung City (Taichung City Government 2004). Several major construction projects are due for implementation in the Seventh Redevelopment Zone, a newly developing area for culture, administration offices and commerce. The decisions on design authorization were made by way of an international competition, which was expected to introduce various perspectives for improving the quality of the urban environment.

Projects such as the introduction of a branch of the Guggenheim Museum sought to propel Taichung City onto the international stage. The Taichung city government expected that the 'Guggenheim effects' could be replicated in Taichung City to bring economic prosperity to the city, creating more working opportunities and uplifting the city's international reputation. The preparation of this project started in 2002. Negotiations between local government, the Guggenheim Museum and Parliament were long-drawn-out, and it was hard to reach an agreement between the government and the Guggenheim Museum, especially as the matter of funds for the project was not resolved. This project eventually fizzled out in December 2004. Yet although the introduction of a Guggenheim Museum to Taichung City was aborted, the Taichung city government is still striving enthusiastically to organize large construction projects in new districts to stimulate the urban economy. However, competition from the new developing districts has gradually eroded the dominance of the city centre itself, reflecting the higher priority given to these areas by the Taichung city government. To address the decline of the city centre, a number of environmental improvements and commercial promotions have been implemented by the local authority.

The early development of the city centre benefited from convenient transportation and local industries such as clothing and weaving. The convenience of city centre transportation is based on the presence of the railway station and bus terminal, which not only serve as hubs for public transport but also bring about commercial development. At an early stage in its history, many products were gathered together for trading in the city centre, which became famous for its street markets and developed into the most prosperous area in Taichung City, with Ji-Guang Street as the most renowned street. Three department stores opened in the city centre in the 1970s and then two more during the 1980s. The arrival of these department stores attracted more investment, and the development of shopping streets expanded all over the city centre, reaching a peak of prosperity in the early 1990s. However, the widespread use of motor cars intensified suburbanization and decentralization, leading to the relocation of commercial development to the newest and most popular developing district in Taichung, the Seventh Redevelopment Zone. This area attracted the attention of investors and the government, threatening the dominant position of the city centre.

Nowadays, Taichung city centre has lost much of its economic strength and is heading towards a situation of decline. Regeneration has become an essential task if the city centre is to recover its previous prosperity by creating new opportunities. Among the possible strategies for city centre regeneration, the Taichung city government has focused on environmental improvement as being the most feasible and practical to implement, with the highest visibility and greatest potential impact on the physical and economic conditions of the centre. It is considered to be the catalyst and motivation for city centre regeneration. Therefore, three physical improvements to the city centre have been implemented. Two of them, improvements to Ji-Guang Street and Electronics Street, are concerned with the implementation of pedestrianization, while the Green River area scheme involves improving the riverside space.

The locations and photographs of these three cases can be seen in Figure 4.1. All of them are located in the hub of the city centre and are adjacent to the railway station and the bus terminal. Most of the land is used for commercial purposes. Ji-Guang Street is a 10-metre-wide street with various shops on both sides and has become a shopping street for students and youth groups. Electronics Street is famous for selling electrical and computer products but is just 6 metres wide. Green River is an important asset for Taichung residents, particularly for the communities of the city centre. Initially, Green River was an essential source of life and leisure, but over time it changed from a natural river to an urban drainage system. This change brought about much debate on the use of this waterway space. The three schemes play important roles in the development of the city centre, and it is worth knowing whether or not they could be key elements in driving city centre regeneration.

Theory and methodology

Urban regeneration usually refers to the physical, economic and social renewal of areas that have been to subject to decline (Parkinson 1989). Urban regeneration is a complex and dynamic procedure of urban change. It reflects the various transitions in policy and the economic, social and environmental context, and itself represents an outcome of the interplay between these many influential factors. The case-study method was adopted as being suitable for understanding the different dimensions of city centre regeneration. In a case study, 'the background, development, current conditions, and environment interactions of one or more individuals, groups, communities, businesses, or institutions are observed, recorded, and analysed for stages or patterns in relation to internal and external influences' (Mauch and Birch 1998: 117). The case-study method is an empirical inquiry in depth and breadth to recognize the holistic aspect of cases. It is a comprehensive strategy relying on multiple sources of evidence to carry out the investigation and analysis of the research. It is therefore suitable for exploring the situations and problems of city centre regeneration, encompassing the multiple dimensions of environmental, economic and social factors.

4.1
The location and image of the three cases (Ji-Guang Street, Electronics Street and the Green River area).

Ji-Guang Street   **Electronics Street**   **Green River area**

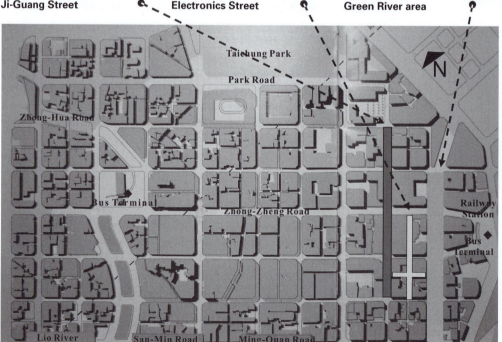

The selection of cases through which to explore the impact of public space improvement on city centre regeneration had to pay attention to the time when the environmental improvement was implemented. The three main projects were carried out in 2000 (the pedestrianization of Electronics Street and the Green River improvement scheme) and 2001 (the pedestrianization of Ji-Guang Street). They were introduced after the start of decline and were completed at a time that would allow an evaluation of their impacts. Information was collected through collecting the existing surveys and documents; through direct observation; and through interviews, including preliminary interviews, with visitors and traders, and key informant interviews with consultants, managers and executives. The initial preliminary interviews, conducted in 2005, aimed at understanding the perspectives of shoppers and traders in order to establish the key questions for the main interviews. For the shoppers, the questions focused on shopping satisfaction and preferences in the city centre. The traders were asked in detail about the turnover and the expectations for improvement in retail development. The selection of key informants for their roles in the managing and executing of city centre regeneration was considered of great value in providing perspectives on the changes to the city centre. The key informant interviews were conducted between 2005 and 2006. They were designed to offer more understanding about the problems and situations of the target cases, highlighting perspectives not presented in the documents and data. The managers, the heads of management committees, are closely involved with the commercial development of the city centre, with understanding the demands of traders and shoppers, and with the problems involved in implementing city centre regeneration.

The transformation of public space
The most directly visible change in environmental improvement is to make the public spaces fresh and new. According to the surveys, most visitors are satisfied with the environmental improvement, including street furniture, plantings and pavement. These improvements transform the image of public spaces into a neater and tidier one. Visitors and locals alike can obviously feel the improvement tangibly and visibly. That is partly why the Taichung city government considers environmental improvement to be a catalyst for city centre regeneration, as widely recognized and visible changes are expected to pave the way for other changes in the area.

A key theme in these schemes has been the relationship between environmental improvement and commercial development, which is particularly supported through pedestrianization, providing safer spaces for a variety of activities. After the implementation of pedestrianization, the shopkeepers who wanted to advertise the changes and attract customers initiated promotional activities in these pedestrian streets, making a closer link between the shops and the public spaces. In the case of Ji-Guang Street, besides special festivals and holiday events that involve large-scale celebrations and parties, there are always casual activities at weekends, such as performances by singers and entertainers. These casual activities are aimed both at attracting customers and at letting the visitors enjoy the various performances during shopping time. The most essential activity in Ji-Guang Street is called 'Chinese New Year Purchase', the traditional custom in which every family buys some special materials to celebrate the Chinese New Year. This celebrated activity is expected to create a new commercial feature for Ji-Guang Street, with businesses hoping that Chinese New Year shoppers will think of Ji-Guang Street. In the case of Electronics Street, the prevalence of electrical and computer products allows the retailers to successfully stage many promotional activities, even though the street is not wide enough to host massive activities. Nevertheless, many small, private promotions take place in Electronics Street.

In addition, the most important transformation after the environmental improvement in the Green River area, besides the improvements alongside the waterway, is in the covering of part of the waterway as an open space, called Green River Square, to make it easier for crowds to disperse from the bus terminals and also to make space for new activities (Figure 4.2). This change responds to the demands for space for outside public use, as the city centre in general lacks enough open spaces. However, unlike those in Ji-Guang Street and Electronics Street, the activities of Green River Square are not related to commercial promotions. Its activities are usually related to public welfare and are held during special festivals. There is a weak relationship between this open space and the shops alongside Green River. Although these activities can attract people and business opportunities, the benefits for the retailers are limited.

4.2
The covering of part of the waterway as an open space.

The themes of commercial streets and the scale of public space are some of the key factors affecting the use of public spaces in the city centre, closely related to the image of the city centre and its spaces. The purpose of commercial activities in Electronics Street is to reinforce the electric theme for the street and to remind the visitors to visit Electronics Street when they wish to buy electrical and computer products. However, Ji-Guang Street presents a very different image, the key feature of the street being the diversity of the products that can be bought there. Although the businesses target students and youth groups, the theme of Ji-Guang Street is not as clearly defined as that of Electronics Street. Moreover, Ji-Guang Street businesses hope to create a new image to increase competitiveness, such as the annual promotional activity 'Chinese New Year Purchase'.

However, this kind of short-term commercial activity is not enough to change the image of Ji-Guang Street. Although it can persuade more customers to visit Ji-Guang Street, and the street itself also has a good reputation for its festivals, the retailers of Ji-Guang Street do not benefit from it during normal days. Most of them do business in products relevant to youth and fashion, which have little association with traditional and festival themes. Therefore, Ji-Guang Street is still in the transitional stage between the traditional and the modern identity of a shopping street. Furthermore, the size of a public space dictates what activities it can accommodate, and narrow streets limit the opportunity for certain commercial activities. In the case of Electronics Street, a 6-metre-wide lane may be suitable for shopping but it is not wide enough to host certain commercial activities.

A linear space, such as a pedestrianized street, possesses the functions of linking and leading. At the same time, it offers the opportunity to develop the utility of a square should it be of sufficient size. In the case of Ji-Guang Street, the space for consumers is not only a 10-metre-wide pedestrianized street, but also includes 4-metre-wide arcades on both sides. The shoppers can normally walk through Ji-Guang Street along the arcades in front of retailers, even though sometimes the street is closed in order to host commercial activities. Therefore, when the scale of linear open space reaches a certain size, the street can be used for a variety of activities.

The impacts on economic regeneration

The impacts of public space improvement on the commercial environment can be reflected in the property value and business turnover. First, according to the statistics of the Taichung Land Administration Bureau, land value in the city centre always appears to display negative growth; in particular, it reached its lowest value in 2001. As economic conditions improved overall, land values in the city as a whole started to show positive growth in 2005. However, land values in the city centre are still declining. Although the overall economic environment may not be the factor that has the most influence on the decline of the city centre, the occurrence of the decline is by no means due to the economic recession.

Moreover, as we can see from Figure 4.3, which compares the variation of land values for Taichung City as a whole with those for the city centre, there was a sharp reduction in property value in the city centre between 1999 and 2002. However, after the implementation of environmental improvements from 2000 to 2001 the land value decline slowed down but it was still negative. The gap between Taichung City as a whole and the city centre began to widen in 2004 and the trend continues to the present day. The average value of land in the city as a whole is increasing, yet the value of land in the city centre remains the same. This means that the relative decline of the city centre began at that time. According to these statistics, the short-term benefit may be reflected in property values in the city centre, but it is not enough for the centre to catch up with the average value for Taichung City. The speed of growth of the other areas is more rapid than that of the city centre. The long-term competition will constantly face the city centre.

Moreover, during this research, interviews were held with the tenants of the retail units in these three cases to obtain the relevant information about business earnings and shop rentals. Although it is hard to obtain exact statistics that show the variation of turnover and shop rents, as retailers always consider these to be business secrets, we can get some clues about the general situation from the tenants of the retail units. They felt that business turnover had not greatly increased and that rental values were lower than previously. The average earnings and lower rental values, the indicators of successful commercial development, reveal that the improvement projects in the city centre did not increase commercial prosperity. Meanwhile, some new tenants believe that this is a good moment to move into the commercial environment of the city centre because the rental values are lower than before and they think that the potential of the commercial environment in the city centre is such that it is worth making an investment. Although the commercial development of the city centre has an unclear future, the lower rental value is an attractive reason for investing there. This signals the possibility of a change in the character and economic status of the city centre.

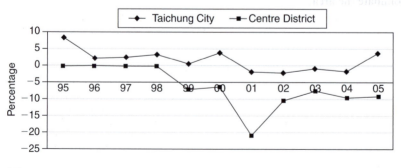

4.3
The modulation of announced current land value between Taichung City and Centre District (amplitude modulation (%) = (value of this year – value of last year)/value of last year x 100%.

Furthermore, the data on the vacancy rates in retailers' rent could be an essential indicator to demonstrate the extent of prosperity in the shopping environment. Table 4.1 shows the statistics of the vacancy rate in these three cases before and after environmental improvement. It can be seen that the vacancy rate of retailers in Electronics Street showed a decrease (–10 per cent) and that of Green River area remained the same from 2000 to 2005. However, there is an increase (of 1.6 per cent) in the vacancy rate of retailers in Ji-Guang Street. This means that the environmental improvement did not persuade more investors or retailers to move into Ji-Guang Street. By contrast, Electronics Street maintained its strong position in the computer business. The pedestrianization seems to have benefited Electronics Street, whereas in Green River area the number of vacancies among retailers remained stable. That is to say, the environmental improvement did not increase the number of retailers in Green River area, and the area maintained its high vacancy rate (40.5 per cent). This reveals that the commercial environment of Green River area is facing a serious decline. The improvement did not seem to benefit the commercial environment of the city centre overall; it only attracted more retailers to Electronics Street.

Thus far, we can see that the land value still shows negative growth, but the decline tends to be slight and the vacancy rate of renting is stable. It seems that the commercial environment did not gain direct benefits from the public space improvements, but the area was stabilized, which is a positive development when one considers the strong competition from the new suburban commercial areas. The impacts of the three case-study areas on each other are also noticeable. They are all located in the city centre and are close to each other, and there could therefore be some interaction and correlation between them. The ripple effect occurs when the dominant retailers could have an influence on the adjacent and surrounding commercial environment. In Taichung city centre, the vivid theme of Electronics Street is attractive to the young people and student groups who now dominate the area.

The surrounding shops feel the strength of the theme, and some businesses have attempted to change the nature of the goods they sell to link

Table 4.1 Vacancy rates for the three cases

	Ji-Guang Street		Electronics Street		Green River area	
	2001	*2005*	*2000*	*2005*	*2000*	*2005*
Vacancy (amount/ rate)	14 (11%)	16 (12.6%)	6 (15%)	2 (5%)	34 (40.5%)	34 (40.5%)
Change	+2 (+1.6%)		–4 (–10%)		0 (0%)	

with Electronics Street, particularly the retail units that are located in the nodes of the pedestrianized street. This research also found that the traffic artery is the factor that cuts and stops the ripple effect, in contrast with the pedestrianized street, which is the catalyst for causing the ripple effect. The ripple effect has changed the distribution of retailers in the city centre, in particular after the implementation of environmental improvements. Retail investors see the success of Electronics Street and understand the benefits of the link between the pedestrian spaces. Therefore, they gradually move into this area and the surrounding areas where the theme of computers is growing; it is also gradually changing the image of the shopping spaces from a traditional to a younger and more modern one.

Safety in public spaces

The sense of safety is an essential indicator to show the efficiency of city centre regeneration. The fear of crime could reduce the occurrence of social and community activities and also damage the image of city centres (Hass-Klau *et al.* 1999). To avoid this fear and to provide safe public spaces will benefit the development of city centres. Security is established in freedom from fear and dread. Pedestrians' fears mainly originate from vehicles and darkness. Although some natural disasters are adequately managed, other human threats in urban spaces, like road safety and fear of crime, are seemingly on the increase (Carmona *et al.* 2003). Thomas and Bromley (2000) argued that the decentralization of city centres causes safety issues to emerge, particularly as regards night-time activities. Hass-Klau *et al.* (1999) also noted that fear of crime, which can discourage individuals from using certain streets at night, would be a serious problem if it were extended to the daytime.

Pedestrianization can provide the opportunity to eliminate the fear caused by vehicles and the darkness. A pedestrianized street can be well lit and is car-free, so naturally these fears are reduced. Although currently the pedestrian streets are not for the exclusive use of pedestrians because the traffic is restricted only on a part-time basis, and pedestrians therefore still have some concerns about vehicles, the security is better than before. The improved streetlamps installed during pedestrianization and the fact that the majority of shop lights stay on until ten o'clock make the street at night similar to what it is in daytime. These factors allow activities to be extended into the evening without shoppers needing to fear the darkness. Therefore, pedestrianization has reduced the fear of vehicles and darkness.

According to a survey carried out by Taichung City Police Bureau in 2006, covering the period 2001–2005, the annual statistics for criminal activities for the city centre and for Taichung City demonstrate that the percentage of city centre crime compared to that for Taichung City as a whole decreased from 2.82 per cent to 1.95 per cent. The survey reveals that the number of criminal cases in the city centre is tending to decrease and public security to improve. Although it is hard to be certain that the improvement of public security in the city centre is wholly a result of the environmental improvement, it certainly had a positive impact on the sense of safety on the street. At the very least, it did not cause the public safety of the city centre to deteriorate. Hass-Klau *et al.* (1999) argue that crime in the street space of city centres is always an inevitable cause of reducing the social activities that occur outdoors. The fear of crime may make the public prefer to stay at home and avoid meeting others. It reduces participation opportunities in social activities as well as more commercial activities, which could gradually weaken the vitality of a city centre. Thus, a decrease of crime in public spaces could encourage the occurrence of social and commercial activities to vitalize the city centre. However, other statistics show that the rate of theft is gradually increasing, in line with the growth of the commercial activities, and CCTV units are being installed in Electronics Street.

The benefits of environmental improvement have been mentioned in the previous sections, but there have been some conflicts or negative effects between the public spaces and social development following the environmental improvement. The environmental improvement of the Green River area attracts many foreign workers, particularly in Green River Square. Every weekend, the various foreign workers from the towns surrounding Taichung City congregate in the city centre around the railway station and the bus terminals. The Green River area is the closest open space to convenient transport. The foreign workers take advantage of the weekend to meet together and socialize. However, the concentration of various groups of foreign workers is associated with occasional fights, which have negative implications for the Green River area as a whole. Therefore, environmental improvement needs to be carried out in conjunction with improvements in the economic and social conditions, providing support facilities for international workers. Otherwise, a superior open space can soon acquire a poor reputation in the minds of the citizens.

The management of public spaces

After pedestrianization, it was essential to develop the necessary management infrastructure for managing, controlling and maintaining these spaces. First of all, pedestrianization changes traffic circulation: the originally busy streets now prohibit the passage of vehicles through the city centre, and thereby the amount of space available for the use of vehicles is reduced. This appears to cause the city centre traffic to be more congested. More importantly, the arrangement of unloading services needs to be resolved after pedestrianization. The traffic-restricted times and unloading bays are the essential elements to be considered. Lorries usually utilize the times when traffic is not restricted in order to deliver merchandise, but not all of them can do that. They sometimes take advantage of the unloading bays to dispatch the goods during the limited time. The sites of unloading bays are set up near the entrances to pedestrian streets, which are always full of crowds and vehicles (Figure 4.4). This produces a negative impact on the accessibility of shopping streets and also causes conflicts between pedestrians, lorries, and vehicles at the entrances to pedestrian streets. The shortage of unloading spaces and the traffic-limited times are inconvenient for the retailers to stock up and to dispatch their merchandise. Pedestrianization needs to confront the challenge presented by unloading issues.

Motorcycles represent the major type of transportation that accesses the city centre. Pedestrianization aims at controlling the parking and the passing of motorcycles. Before pedestrianization, motorcyclists could always park haphazardly at the side of the street or in front of shops. However, the restriction of vehicle entry into the pedestrian streets is inconvenient for motorcyclists. This change brought about a loss of advantage in the mobility of motorcycles. Motorcyclists have also complained that the government does not provide sufficient parking spaces for motorcycles. The outcome is that the motorcyclists always park haphazardly as close to their destination as they can, which then clutters up the public spaces (Figure 4.5). They even break the regulations by entering the pedestrian areas, as it is more convenient for them to do so. However, this kind of behaviour has a negative impact on the sense of safety for pedestrians. What the visitors originally believe to be safe and comfortable pedestrian spaces turn out not to be traffic-free areas. Furthermore, in the Green River area there is no pedestrianization, but the problem of the parking of motorcycles is still an issue for pedestrians and the Taichung city government. Although there are parking spaces for motorcycles alongside Green River, there are still insufficient of them, and this leads to congestion and misuse of pavements. Parking for motorcycles is a critical problem for the Green River area because it could damage the landscape of the waterway area and interrupt the movement of pedestrians.

The issue of whether the implementation of environmental improvement can provide more comfortable, high-quality and usable spaces

4.4
The unloading situation in the narrow Electronics Street can cause congestion and conflict.

4.5
Motorcycles parked in Ji-Guang Street.

for the public causes some tensions and potential conflicts. These public spaces are located in the commercial districts, close to shops and commercial activities. The question is, who will benefit from the environmental improvement – the retailers, visitors, shoppers or investors? It is also of interest to ask how these public spaces can provide 'usable spaces' for the retailers and the visitors in the commercial environment. These three case studies revealed two types of conflicts between the public spaces and the retailers.

The first conflict involves some restaurants that extend their service range by arranging tables and chairs on the pedestrian street to attract more customers. This is the advantage of the open spaces for the restaurants, but it is also seen as an obstacle for pedestrians, preventing them from walking freely in the public spaces. These restaurants hope to create an outdoor atmosphere for the consumption of food and drinks like that of the cafés of European countries, so that visitors can enjoy the outside sunshine and the streetscape. This kind of usage began immediately after pedestrianization, helping to form a closer relationship between the visitors, public spaces and restaurants. From the viewpoint of restaurants, the usable space is an advantageous opportunity to extend their business area. However, as public spaces function as a resource for the general public, they are also used for other purposes, and so should not be monopolized by the restaurants and their customers. Although the decision makers could not have expected this outcome, they see that it creates a different streetscape in the city centre and also could attract more visitors. The government faces a dilemma as to whether or not to ignore the general function of public spaces and allow the occupation by the restaurants, which could make the city centre environment more vibrant.

The second issue is that pedestrians and motorcyclists are in conflict for the use of public spaces. The meaning of usable spaces from the viewpoint of motorcyclists is spaces where it is convenient for them to park their motorcycles. They do not consider whether this haphazard parking will cause inconvenience to pedestrians and adversely affect the landscape of public spaces. From the point of view of retailers, the priority is that shoppers are able to visit their shops, irrespective of whether motorcyclists park in proper positions. These disputed uses always cause conflict between the government, visitors and the shops. There are different perspectives on the 'usable spaces', which produces tension between the various groups; this also reveals that management of public spaces is essential to control their use, particularly after environmental improvement.

Tension and conflict between different groups

The different groups have various perspectives on the use of public spaces in the city centre, sometimes resulting in tension and conflict between them, which has an impact on the city centre regeneration. However, tension is not always conflictive or necessarily bad while it provides an opportunity for awareness of the relationship between different groups concerning the public spaces (Franck and Stevens 2007). Various voices, forces and actions will give shape to public spaces, even though the conflicting perspectives may seem confusing and troublesome during the process. The tension will provide a way to more clearly understand the strengths and weaknesses of the transformation.

First, there are the various views on the two issues in the usage of the Green River area: is the covering of the waterway a good way to utilize the space and is the Green River to be a space for commercial or for leisure use? At an early stage, in order to allow the urban development of Tai-chung, Green River was transformed from a natural river to urban drainage. The features and functions of the surrounding waterway space changed as well. At that time, there was an increased demand for traffic capacity and public spaces in the city centre. The purpose of the coverings is to resolve the congestion of the area surrounding the railway station and to provide more public spaces for the city centre. Therefore, as the natural river had already changed to become an urban drain, it was decided that it should be covered, to resolve the problems of traffic circulation and to increase the amount of public space. In addition, the covering in the front of First Square is an open space through which the crowd from the bus terminals can disperse. It does mean that the coverings need to have the capacity to cope with increasing crowds and traffic and to supplement the lack of public spaces.

However, nowadays public opinion has become aware of the importance of rivers, and people are determined to avoid repeating the error that was made when the upper reaches of Green River were covered. The city's residents have already forgotten the whereabouts of the origin and upper reaches of Green River, because roads and parkways have replaced the waterways. They increasingly consider that rivers should retain their original features, even if they have become no more than urban drains. Although many waterway spaces have already been covered up for non-water functions, it is at least to be expected that no more covering of urban waterways will happen. Moreover, the suggestion from the local residents and the head of Green River Neighbourhood suggested driving the plan for a 'light corridor' with European-style café culture and art activities to create a leisure atmosphere for the Green River area. Also, implementing pedestrianization on both sides of Green River Street supplements the waterside space by expanding the range of open space, so creating a leisure space that is available both during the daytime and in the evening.

The Green River area has many opportunities to develop social welfare, art, leisure and commercial activities. It is hard to say whether the Green River spaces should be for commercial or leisure use, but a combination of the two could benefit the Green River area. Therefore, regenerating the area does not necessarily need to focus only on the promotion of commercial activities. The introduction of activities related to social welfare could be one means of attracting people to visit the Green River area, which could improve the area's quality and reputation, as well as helping the retailers.

The three cases are three parallel linear open spaces. The weakness of these open spaces is the lack of enough connections between them to construct a network and to improve permeability. Only if all of them were connected to form an open space network could the whole city centre benefit fully, whereas at present the interruption by traffic arteries weakens any existing links between the pedestrian streets. The linking of open spaces would allow them to share resources and expand the effects to the whole city centre. Moreover, after the environmental improvements, the images of these three cases have changed to some extent, but the overall picture of the city centre is hardly affected. Once the potential of the Green River area is realized, it could play a more central role in the regeneration of the city centre. However, this research found that, given the number of different organizations and contexts, cooperation is not easily achieved. The tendency towards competition is more obvious than the willingness to cooperate, even though the benefits of cooperation are understood. Retailers' pride in their individual street names, 'Ji-Guang Street' and 'Electronics Street' respectively, means that they refuse to look for a common identity for the area. They are not confident that cooperation could improve in the future. The retailers of the city centre see themselves as belonging to their own particular street, not to the city centre.

The product of tension and conflict, however, gives us more of an understanding of the relationship between different roles; we also need to build a bridge through which to coordinate and reconcile. The establishment of a management committee plays this role in these three cases. The development of town centre management in the United Kingdom could be considered a strategy of urban regeneration (Page and Hardyman 1996). Town centre management is a strategy for urban regeneration to resolve the conflict between town planning, collaborative funding and economic functions (Thorpe 1983). Town centre management could play an essential role in coordination between the local authority, private investors, and users of a city centre.

The Taichung city government understands the importance of city centre management; in all three cases, it assisted in setting up the committees for managing and maintaining the public spaces. The essential tasks of the management committees are to manage and maintain the overall environment. Assisting with traffic management, beautifying the urban landscape and maintaining the relevant facilities should also be the responsibility of the management committee. It also needs to coordinate and negotiate between different views to achieve consensus. For example, the implementation of promotional activities in Electronics Street might meet with less opposition than it would in Ji-Guang Street. The retailers always do their best to collaborate in every activity, as they understand that the common aim is to make the commercial environment of Electronics Street more prosperous. However, as there is a greater variety of retailers in Ji-Guang Street, it is harder to achieve a consensus regarding promotional activities, as different retailers have different opinions concerning the types of activities. Even though they have the results of the meetings, not all of them are willing to cooperate. Therefore, we can see that successful management of the commercial environment depends on the corresponding management committee.

The reaching of a consensus in the community will be a way to increase the efficiency of the management committee and also reconcile the tension resulting from the differing views of the retailers. Moreover, the government also plays a role in integrating and coordinating between the bureaux and the management committees. Even the individual bureaux need to have mutual coordination, as do the management committees. Many locals express their views to the government by way of the management committee. Also, plenty of planning and implementation is needed to achieve cooperation with the various bureaux. Coordination is essential to reduce the conflicts between them and complete the planning efficiently. In addition, the management committees of the commercial environment in the city centre should be integrated in order to reinforce the competitiveness and improve the image of the city centre.

Can public space improvement revive the city centre?

The value of public space improvement is not only the visible and tangible refinement of the physical environment, but also the effect on commercial regeneration and social development. Environmental improvement is always expected to maintain the competitiveness of the city centre and to improve the economic conditions. Public investment in environmental improvements is doubtless invaluable when it attracts sensible expectations of private investment (Bromley *et al.* 2003). When the public authorities invest in environmental improvement, it can not only improve the quality of the project at hand, but also create an opportunity to attract more private investment on more related domains. However, it has been argued (Hall 2000) that environmental improvements did not bring about an instant and short-term improvement in the economic development of the city centre, nor did they increase its competitiveness. This research found that the land value and retail turnover of the city centre have not obviously increased after the environmental improvement; also, there is no apparent change in the vacancy rate of shop units. The environmental improvements did not directly and instantly benefit commercial regeneration, even though it slowed down the tendency towards decline when the city centre faced the threat of a new developing area.

If city centres are to keep their dominance in twenty-first-century cities, they must maintain these two roles: the enforcement of symbolic elements and the location of public gatherings (Rypkema 2003). The characteristics of city centres are still environmental decline, insufficient accessibility, the conflict between vehicles and pedestrians, and weak management and maintenance of public spaces (Scotland Development Department 1999). To revive the city centre, besides reinforcing the original meaningful and valuable elements of the city centre and the merit of convenient transport, the image of decline needs to change. The transformation of city centres' image is crucial in estimating the efficiency of public space improvements and a key point in attracting visitors and investment. Undoubtedly, in terms of physical environment, environmental improvement gains the approval of visitors and shoppers. Most of them can appreciate the image of regeneration and the image of a more attractive commercial environment.

Conclusion

Could environmental improvement be the best strategy for city centre regeneration? This research found that the environmental improvement did not give the city centre any direct, instant benefit, but it did slow down the process of decline and turned it into a tendency towards improvement. Moreover, improvement of the public space also influenced social development and economic regeneration, and many plans and implementations that were mostly based on the environment brought improvements.

It was important to carry out some planning and implementation for the environmental improvement and economic regeneration of the city centre. Taichung city government is now keen to reverse the decline of the city centre, aiming to use comprehensive strategies, including environmental improvement and community involvement, to support the commercial environment as well as to develop a sustainable environment in the city centre. The management committee plays an essential role as the promoter of community involvement in commercial and neighbourhood development. Not only is it responsible for promoting the shopping spaces, but it is also a linkage for neighbourhood relationships. However, for the city centre regeneration to be successful there needs to be a comprehensive strategy. It is not enough to have only environmental improvement, even though it could be an essential precondition. It is necessary to put relevant measures in place to coincide with the environmental improvement.

Chapter 5

Change in the public spaces of traditional cities

Zaria, Nigeria

Shaibu Bala Garba

Cities and societies, as historical creations, are participants in a dynamic process of change and transformation that is reflected in public space as the context for community life. This chapter presents the findings of research into change in the public space of traditional Hausa cities with Zaria as a case study (Garba 2007). The chapter examines how cultural transformation in Zaria has shaped change in its public space over the period from the Fulani Jihad in 1804 to 2004. It also examines the issues and tensions that characterize the social life and public space of the city. The traditional Hausa cities are a group of seven city-states (*Hausa Bakwai*) founded around the ninth century in present-day northern Nigeria (Figure 5.1) (Hogben 1967). The Hausas are a cultural group of mixed origin and race united by a common language found in the savannah region of West Africa. Islam was introduced to the Hausa cities between the fifteenth and the sixteenth centuries and gradually became the established religion. The early nineteenth century saw a wave of Islamic movements in the Sudan region that resulted in the establishment of a Sokoto Caliphate as a loose federation of city-states that included the Hausa cities in present northern Nigeria. The Sokoto Caliphate lasted until the beginning of the twentieth century, when it was integrated into a British colonial holding. Under the colonial government, the northern and southern parts of Nigeria were united to create a single country, which was granted its independence from British rule in 1960. During the colonial period, the focus of growth in the Hausa cities shifted to areas outside their walls, resulting in their evolution as traditional cores of larger metropolitan areas. Zaria City's history is closely tied to that of the Hausa cities as a group. The Fulani Jihad led to its integration into the Sokoto Caliphate. It came under colonial rule in 1903 when its ruler invited the British army to assist in fending off attack by hostile forces. Population and spatial growth since the colonial period has seen Zaria transformed into a large metropolitan area, with the traditional city as one of its districts.

The nature of the change that the Hausa cities have experienced since the jihad was a major motivator in their choice for the research. Additional motivations included urban problems associated with their current growth and development, and the general perception that they have been inadequately studied in order to facilitate informed intervention. Zaria was specifically chosen because it classically manifests the problems faced by the cities, but has also retained substantial elements of its traditional character, making it a good candidate for study to support intervention. The focus on public space was dictated by its importance as the arena for socialization and social production and its role in the image content of cities.

Approach to public space

A review of the academic literature reveals that space as a concept is subject to competing understandings (Van de Ven 1980: 46; Jammer 1969: 17; Massey 1985: 9; Madanipour 1996: 29). Mitchell (1996: 127–8), commenting on public space, notes its ambiguities, including 'as a place, an idea, an ideal, and a contested concept'. Further examination suggests that the competing understandings are a product of the multidimensional nature of space. With regard to public space, five applicable dimensions can be identified: material, social, symbolic, cultural and historical. The material dimen-

5.1
Map of Nigeria showing the Hausa city-states.

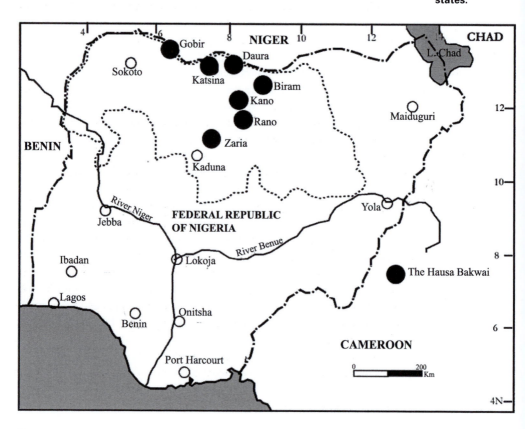

sion of public space deals with its physical aspects. As material space, public space is recognized as having properties that define its form, including its functional typology (Mitchell 1995: 115–16; Carr *et al.* 1992; Tibbalds 1992; Krier 1979), its morphological organization at the two- and three-dimensional level, its enclosure pattern and its structural organization in a public space web (Carmona *et al.* 2003: 111; Scruton 1987: 16). It is also constituted at different spatial scales ranging from individual public places to the public space of a whole city (Ruddick 1996: 140). The social dimension of public space deals with people and their activities in creating, using and managing public space. It is viewed from this perspective as the material setting for non-familial social life (Walzer 1986: 470; Mitchell 1996: 128). It embodies freedom of access for the public and provides the setting for social activities, social interactions and the production and reproduction of society in a social and cultural setting. The symbolic dimension of public space focuses on the meanings, connections, behaviours and attitudes that people develop through participation in the social life of communities in public places (Carr *et al.* 1992: 187; Goheen 1998: 479; Tuan 1980: 6). The cultural dimension of space focuses on group properties and the systems of power relations in society and how these shape the built environment and everyday social life (Castells 1977: 126; Knox and Pinch 2000: 59). Public spaces are acknowledged to be situated within broader cultural settings, with cultural orders and their embedded structures expressed in political, social, economic and symbolic terms, and providing a means of seeking explanations about patterns observed in space (Benn and Gaus 1983: 5; Carr *et al.* 1992: 3). The historical dimension of public space focuses on the fact that space and societies are in a process of dynamic historical change (Madanipour 1996; 38–9; Pred 1984a; Gregory 1989). As historic entities, both societies and cities accumulate forms from the past that influence present and future forms and practices.

Based on the academic literature, the research adopted a five-dimensional approach to public space, viewing it as material space with a social and symbolic dimension situated in a cultural setting, and with both public space and the cultural setting in a process of dynamic transformation with and over time. The research viewed the integration of the five dimensions as being necessary to enable a more comprehensive examination and understanding of public space. To integrate the dimensions into a consistent model, the research adopted structuration and time-geography based on the work of Giddens (1981) and as further developed by Pred (1984a, b). The model (shown in Figure 5.2) essentially relates the broader structuration process of society expressed in political, social, economic and symbolic structures with the public–private structuring of social life and urban space. The structuration process results in a cultural definition of the public and private that is reflected in the organization of urban space. Public space at the macro urban scale consists of the aggregation of material spaces supporting the public life of society. At the micro level, public space becomes material places where people engage in activities to socialize and be socially produced, acquiring meaning and connections to both place and society in the process. As socialization occurs from the macro cultural level to micro place practices, society and public spaces are transformed dynamically in time.

Based on the model, a framework of issues and questions was derived that was used to establish the parameters of the research and address its objectives. Public space is defined in the context of the research as 'spaces accessible to and used by the public as the focus of community social life'. In the tradition of the literature, public space is taken to include both open and enclosed spaces, such as religious facilities and markets, which play a significant role in the social life of communities. Change in the public space of Zaria was examined from the perspective of the material, social and symbolic dimensions of public space in the period from 1804 to 2004. The period was divided into three – jihad, colonial and post-colonial – in line with events in the city's history. Examination of change proceeded from the examination of cultural transformation in each of the three periods, to identifying patterns of change in public space, and examination of how historical and cultural transformation has shaped change and the evolution of public space to its contemporary form. Data for the research were collected using both documentary and fieldwork methods. The approach to analysis was qualitative, aided by the use of various morphological tools and techniques. Data on cultural setting were analysed to understand historical forces and cultural changes happening in the different periods. Data on public space were analysed to understand change in public space from a material, social and symbolic perspective by period. Comparison was carried out across periods to isolate changes and, by linking changes with cultural transformation, to explain the identified changes. The simultaneous examination of public space and cultural context in time also led to the identification of issues and tensions that characterize social life.

Public space in the pre-jihad period

In the pre-jihad period, the Hausa cities shared a common city form consisting of an urban space that is walled and protected by moats, with the walls penetrated by gates (Figure 5.3) that led to the twin centres of market and palace, located towards the centre of the city (Urquhart 1977: 10). The typical structure evolved without any distinct form of land-use zoning or sharp distinctions between function of built-up areas (Moughtin 1985: 43).

In the case of Zaria, the wall was penetrated by nine gates, with roads from the gates converging at the market, which is still in the same location, and the Juma ward of the city, where the old palace and Friday mosque were located. The morphological organization consisted of a dense inner-city area, with development concentrated around the market and palace, and buildings defining road spaces as open paths, and outer-city areas where the land is open space or small clusters of family houses located

5.2
A model of public space.

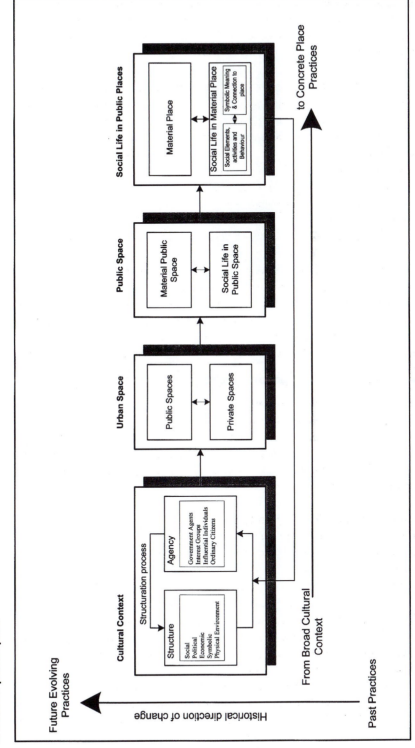

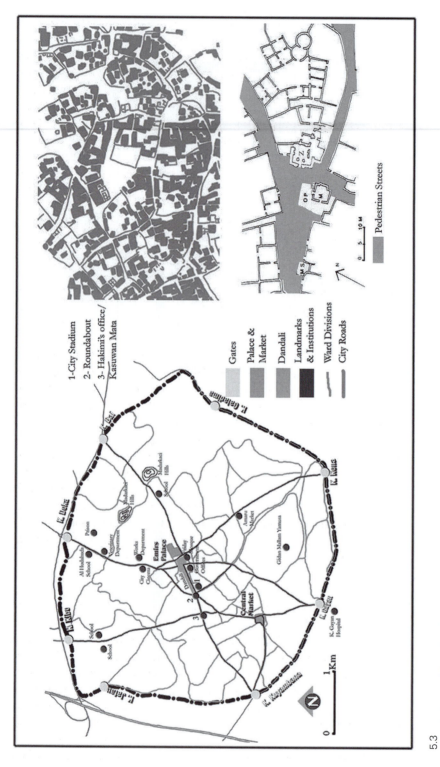

5.3
Morphology of Zaria's urban space.

1-City Stadium
2- Roundabout
3- Hakimi's office/
Kasuwan Mata

Gates
Palace &
Market
Dandali
Landmarks
& Institutions
Ward Divisions
City Roads

Pedestrian Streets

in open land. In the inner city, open public spaces were defined by one-storey walled compounds of rectangular buildings or round huts. The city was united and given form through its organic movement system that criss-crosses the built fabric connecting places, people and activities. The principal public places included gates, road spaces, spaces for craft production, residential community spaces, markets, open areas and religious spaces in the form of mosques and spaces for the traditional Bori religion. Gates served as points of control and were differentiated in importance depending on the city that they served. The road spaces existed as a network of streets that penetrated and connected the fabric and served as a means of transport for animals and people. Spaces for craft production were nested within roadways, markets or residential quarters. Residential community spaces existed as spaces formed by the grouping of residential houses. Open spaces were found around the periphery of the city wall. The market functioned as a centre for commerce and production. The city had a Friday mosque located in Juma ward, where the palace then existed. Islam was then a religion of the ruling class, with lower-class residents practising the Bori religion, sometimes combining it with Islam.

The society in pre-jihad Zaria consisted of a resident Hausa population with a social life that was focused on farming, limited craft activity and some trading. Activities in public places were limited to movement, functional income-earning activities, limited rituals and celebrations mainly of a religious nature, and native forms of entertainment and socialization. Security was a major issue in view of the warring nature of the period. The city's public space was significant and of symbolic importance mainly to its residents; it was a community space that rooted the people in place and provided them with a stage on which to undertake the mundane activities of social life. The market was the most significant space because of the primacy of economic activity and its role as a centre for visitors to the city. Gates were also significant as connectors to the external world. Though the Islamic religion might have played some role in the definition of the fundamental values of the society, this role appears to have been limited, particularly as regards public institutions and governance.

Time and change in public space

Zaria's public space evolved and became transformed from its roots in the pre-jihad period following fundamental changes in the cultural setting of the city during the jihad, colonial and post-colonial periods. The jihad in 1804 initiated the first wave of change and transformation. The jihad was conceived as change designed to produce the marriage of political and symbolic religious power in a more just and egalitarian society built on an Islamic foundation. The jihad resulted in the institution of a new set of political actors, the gradual evolution of a monarchical system of governance with four established ruling houses, elaborate political structures with many offices handed out as patronage, and competition for political office.

The administrative system of the period did not embody any ideal of large-scale public intervention in development. The religious ideals of the jihad vanished shortly after, as materialism took over from reformism (Mahdi 1974: 184). Political power evolved, being synonymous with accumulation, and the two became mutually reinforcing in establishing social position. Accumulation was strongly linked to slave and large farm holdings. Emirs evolved as the most powerful persons in the society, combining a trinity of political, economic and symbolic religious and cultural powers. As a member of the Sokoto Caliphate, Zaria had elaborate security arrangements, leading to improved safety and increased migration, contacts and trade across the caliphate and beyond. Overall, the jihad initiated a process of transformation that saw Zaria elevated in importance as the capital of an emirate and a member of the caliphate, and led to the transformation of its pre-jihad cultural order into one that is more diverse in the constitution of its social elements and broader in its contact, and one that embodied a stronger tie to the Islamic value system even when knowledge and practice of the religion were at a very basic level for most people.

Changes happening in the society as a result of the jihad were also reflected in the material, social and symbolic patterns of Zaria's public space. The most significant change from a material perspective was the establishment of a public space, the Dandali, which has evolved as the premier public space of the city (Figure 5.4). This followed the construction of a new palace fronting an open space by the first post-jihad ruler of the city (Urquhart 1977: 14), and the subsequent addition of a Friday mosque and shariah court around the vicinity of the space, all contributing to giving physical expression to the jihad aspiration of combining political and symbolic power. Architecture evolved as a strong symbol of status in the period and served to reinforce the competition for office and influence. The increased patronage of builders by the ruling class in competition with each other led to the rise of a new style of mud architecture, *Soro* style, with rooms of rectangular shape constructed with engaged columns, flat roof and wall decoration. A class of expert builders also emerged to service building needs. The Friday mosque, whose construction stretched the possible limits of mud construction, became the ultimate arbiter of taste and aesthetics of the new architecture. Architectural developments affected the visual character and morphology of Zaria City and contributed to establishing the concept of the traditional form of a Hausa city. Zaria City during this period witnessed an overall expansion in the density of development within its walls, though the organic nature of the organization of the fabric inherited from the pre-jihad period remained.

Social changes occasioned by the jihad were manifested in public space in the form of the diversity and spatial organization of the city's population, and in activities in public places. Improved safety and increased migration led to Zaria having a public space that was most diverse. The centrality of the city as the capital of an emirate, its geographical location and its importance in the caliphate all led to the inflow of migrants from places as far away

as Senegal and Gambia. Diversity was also enhanced by the presence of a large number of slaves from different places. Diversity was reflected in the ethnicity and place of origin of the population, and was manifested spatially in the organization of people into neighbourhoods. Public space evolved in the period as a principally male domain with limited female participation restricted along age and social class lines. Farming and craft production remained the dominant functional activities. There was an expansion in the scale of craft production activities due to expanded trade and contact, and also to satisfy the needs of an emergent ruling class. The prevailing value system of the period led to certain activities such as traditional Bori religious practices, gambling and prostitution gradually receding from visibility but not completely disappearing. The seasons played an important role in structuring daily life. The rainy season was the time for farming and limited craft activity, while the dry season was the time for craft production, entertainment, travel and warfare. The dry season was also the period for events and festivities.

The three most important public spaces of the period were the Dandali, market and residential quarter spaces. The Dandali became the most important space of the city, serving as the place for official events and celebrations, and the display of the power and authority of the emir as a head of state and a client ruler of the Sokoto Caliphate. The importance of the Dandali was complemented by the entourage of the emir, the greatest signification of power and the most important symbol of the period. This evolved, consisting of uniquely dressed escorts, a eulogist, musical sounds and decorated mounts that accompanied the emir in public. The practice appeared to have its roots in war preparations during the pre-jihad period, but became more elaborate in the jihad period and laid the foundation for festivities and celebrations that have now become part of yearly festivities in the city. The market acted as a regional hub of economic activity and served to extend the economic influence of the city beyond its wall. The residential community spaces remained significant as the place for community socialization and interaction.

Colonialism initiated the second wave of transformation in the cultural life of Zaria. This started as political change that saw the supervisory role of Sokoto over the caliphate replaced by British administrators. The British administrators were of upper-middle-class background with Victorian/Edwardian ideals, and saw their mission as being to civilize and transform the lives of the colonized (Urquhart 1977: 25; Orr 1965: 215). The colonial administration adopted a system of indirect rule whereby people were administered through their local institutions and associated customary practices. They introduced the concept of modern administration, establishing native authorities with emirs as their head, and municipal planning and development administration, including the concept of efficient management. British planning led to the discontinuation of repairs to Zaria's city wall, created a segregated system of settlement by directing new migrants to areas outside the traditional city, and ultimately led to the emergence of a Zaria metropolitan area, with the traditional city as a component district. Other changes introduced by the colonial administration included the abolition of slavery, the introduction of western education and the introduction of a new export-based economy operational in districts outside the traditional city. British decision making ultimately led to Zaria being a part of a broader northern Nigerian political grouping initially, and ultimately of Nigeria as a country.

The active regime of development intervention during the colonial period impacted material public space in three ways. First, the Dandali witnessed the addition of more administrative facilities that included a new shariah court and dispensary, and vehicular access, all strengthening the place as the political centre of the city. Second, there was an increase in the construction of public facilities, including a prison, a school, works and veterinary departments, which added new public places and provided for activities such as recreational sports. Finally, there was an expanded programme of road development, which altered the hierarchical organization of road spaces, introduced new centres of activities and generally restructured connectivity in the fabric. The early part of the colonial period witnessed a golden age of architecture in the city as prosperity and the creation of a new middle class increased the patronage of traditional builders, resulting in the expansion of decorated *Soro* houses, and the expansion of decoration from entrance ways to the full façades of buildings. Towards the later part of the period, new materials and construction technologies led to a gradual transformation of architecture, starting with the use of tin roofs and gutters, and later the use of cement plasters with etched decoration, and the construction of concrete block structures. Decorations also incorporated new symbolic items such as cars, aeroplanes and licence plate numbers. The introduction of new materials resulted in the structures becoming more permanent, and the built fabric losing its inherent ability to disintegrate and be recycled. Permanency made latent environmental problems, particularly of drainage and refuse collection, more visible in public space.

The decline in migration to Zaria City following the redirection of migrants to areas outside the city walls, coupled with action to stop slavery, which depopulated the city, contributed to a decline in the diversity of the city's social character. This decline was further enhanced by an expansion in the practice of wife seclusion and a decline in female participation in public space as a result of improvements in income and Islamic education, and the ending of slavery. As has already been mentioned, changes in activities saw the gradual disappearance of gambling, prostitution and Bori religious practices within the boundaries of the city, and the introduction of recreational sports. Cultural festivities linked to the two Eid prayers became formalized as events in the city's cultural calendar. Daily life evolved, being centred on the market and residential-quarter spaces. Activities were gradually extended into the night as services improved and people began to engage in full-time non-farm employment. The expansion of Zaria beyond the space of the traditional city led to a dichotomy in the image of the metropolitan area, with Zaria City associated with tradition and culture, and areas outside the city associated with modernity and change. This dichotomy marked the beginning of a process of the gradual decline of the importance of Zaria as the principal centre of the city and its region, and the emerging importance and significance of areas outside the city. Along the same lines, a social identity of 'indigene' evolved, constructed spatially around being associated with residency in the city and membership of its society. The later part of the post-colonial period also witnessed changes in values, with western education as the most significant beneficiary. New western-educated bureaucrats became both symbols and carriers of change in society, being closely associated with new artefacts and symbols of prestige and status such as service quarters and cars. The educated bureaucrats emerged as the most significant challenge to the power of the emirs and traditional institutions as they assumed the political leadership of an emergent nation.

The granting of independence by Britain to Nigeria in 1960 marked the beginning of the third wave of transformation for Zaria City. Independence led to a reorganization of the national polity, including the institution of a new political class and structures of administration. The diverse nature of the people making up the country led to the rise of competition for power and control of resources among the various ethnic and social groups of the country, and to instability. The 1970 oil crisis led to a period of national affluence that was reflected in improved public finances, substantial investment in service provision, diversification of the employment base and improvements in health care and life expectancy. This was followed by a period of fiscal problems in the 1980s, which led to unemployment, widespread poverty and a decline in public service delivery. Changes happening in the country were reflected at the local level in Zaria, mostly in the broader metropolitan area, with the traditional city remaining isolated. Political reorganization saw an independent local government council established for the city and the consequent loss of political power by the emir. Employment remained largely in craft production, but this was gradually rendered irrelevant by industrial goods. The period witnessed improved connectivity to the outside world following the introduction of satellite broadcasting, which partly led to demands for more puritan Islamic religious practice.

The overall expansion in facilities provision, especially schools and vehicular roads, during the post-colonial period resulted in an increase in the supply of public places and activity centres in Zaria City. Certain city gates were also transformed into unique places following the construction of new portals. The new portals contributed to the institutionalizing of the separation of the city and its spaces from areas outside. The adoption of new materials and construction technology continued, leading to a gradual change in the character of the fabric and the adoption of villa and bungalow as new house forms in development. The city also witnessed a tremendous increase in development density and a consequent decline in the amount of open space. New house forms contributed to the rise of a new development pattern that was usually straighter in arrangement and emphasized efficiency in land use. Zaria City witnessed a reorganization of social activities in the period, with traditional entertainment and craft production gradually declining and being replaced by commercial trading and recreational sports. A new focus on electronic entertainment available through the cinema and satellite broadcasting also emerged. Daily routine in the city continue to be focused on daytime economic activities and recreational sports, and evening and night-time social interaction in residential neighbourhoods. The seasons diminished in importance, even though many people continue to engage in farming during the rainy season. From a symbolic perspective, the importance of Zaria City and its public space declined during the post-colonial period. The city lost its association with political power and its geographical centrality in the city and region. Residents of Zaria City continue to be homogeneously perceived as 'indigenes' compared to those outside the city walls. The city's public space has evolved into the community space of city residents again, with its attraction and significance to 'other outsiders' limited to occasional visits to witness festivities and appreciate the relics and aesthetics of past social and spatial forms and practices. Values in the city continue to be rooted in the Islamic religion, which is increasingly informing action. The society also appears to be going through a period of discourse aimed at re-examining, reshaping and modernizing its values, with new values being more amenable to the acceptance of technological change.

Zaria City's public space

Zaria City's public space, as at the time of detailed fieldwork in 2004, was contained in an urban space that is still defined and set apart from the broader metropolitan area by its dilapidated wall. Within this urban space are found nine types of public spaces that constitute the city's public space: the Dandali, road spaces, residential community spaces, gates, and open natural spaces, markets, religious spaces, institutional spaces, and entertainment and recreation spaces. Four spaces – the Dandali, Road Spaces, Residential Quarter Spaces and Markets – stand out as the most important in the life of residents and usually have the other spaces nested within them. The Dandali is still the most important public space of the city. It is organized as an informal open space in front of the emir's palace, with the Friday mosque, the shariah court, the local government secretariat and city's police station (Figure 5.4) in its vicinity. The space is used for events and festivities of a cultural or religious nature. These include the weekly Muslim Friday prayers, festivities associated with the Muslim Eid prayers, ceremonies for visiting dignitaries, and conferment of traditional titles and political receptions. Roads host a variety of activities that include functional income earning, social interaction, entertainment and recreation activities. The nature of road spaces makes going through the city an exposure to a collage of people, activities and sounds. Residential community spaces serve as an interface between the public domain and the semi-private domain of house entrances. The spaces would normally have a mosque, shop or kiosk and a canopy of trees located within them, and serve as the main social gathering area for the residential neighbourhood. The city market serves as the main location for commerce in addition to social interaction, production and entertainment. Its importance in the city has been diminished now because of the presence of many smaller markets. The city's fabric is still organic in character, with houses, mostly irregular in shape, still making up the bulk of it and roads serving as the connecting tissue. In older areas of the city, house entrances (*Zaure*) provide the link between the private spaces of the house with public residential quarter spaces, while in the newer areas gated villas or bungalows front the streets. Built form, which serves to enclose open public space, is predominantly a single storey high, but there are some two-storey and three-storey buildings. The enclosing surface displays variety and contrast in treatment as a reflection of the evolving nature of construction technology and of differences in status. The contrast is evident between traditional and modern construction, concrete and mud construction, richly designed houses and incomplete or poorly constructed and poorly maintained houses (Figure 5.5).

Activities in Zaria's contemporary public space can be classified into everyday life activities, and cultural events and festivities. Daily life in public places is dominated by city residents. Access and participation vary with regard to gender, age and social class. Social life is dominated by males, with female access and participation varying with age, class, activity and location. Daily life is centred principally on economic activities, complemented by social, recreation and religious activities (Figure 5.6). In addition to people working, most spaces will have people sitting idly and conversing. There will be hawkers, itinerant service providers and entertainers marketing their wares and services, in the process creating a unique social ecology. This will sometimes be complemented by calls for prayer or the rhythmic chanting and recitation of the Qur'an by groups of Islamic students.

The major events and festivities in Zaria City's public space are of a religious or cultural nature. The major religious events are the weekly Friday prayers, and the two Eid prayers of *Adha* and *Al Kabir*. On Friday, activities generally come to a halt at midday as people, dressed in their best clothes, troop out for the Muslim congregational prayer. After the prayer, the Dandali becomes transformed into a place for socialization, entertainment and commerce – activities that from all indications appear as important as the prayer (Figure 5.7). Eid activities generally start with a prayer in the prayer ground outside the city wall, followed by three days of festivities. The festivities include a parade through the city by the emir accompanied by his entourage, followed by traditional greeting by title holders at the Dandali, where they race on horseback for about 200 metres, stop in front of the emir and offer greetings of allegiance and loyalty (Figure 5.8).

5.6
**Daily life
activities in
public spaces.**

Each official is adorned in unique colours, adding to the ceremonial look of the occasion. Cultural festivities occur during the installation of a new chieftain or to honour visiting dignitaries. The festivities are very similar to the Eid festivities. Cultural events and festivities attract people from far and wide, and remain the most significant attraction of the city for outsiders.

5.7
**Friday prayer in
Zaria.**

5.8
Eid festivities in Zaria.

From a symbolic perspective, Zaria City's public space is now space for the social life of the city's residents, who attach the most value to it. The city's residents tend to assign value and significance to public places depending on their association with the identity, history and roots of the society. Places like the Dandali, the Friday mosque and the central market, which represent the tripolar centres of political, symbolic and religious power in the glorious days of Zaria as a political power, are the most active centres of social and community life, and the locations where meaning and connection are established at the broader level of the city's society. Places like the residential-quarter spaces operate at a lower level of significance as the social nexus of neighbourhoods, where people interact and the social reproduction of the society occurs.

Issues and tensions in public space and social life

The examination of Zaria's public space highlights five important issues that have become important or are a source of tension in social life: the role of religion in social life; access and participation in public space with respect to the female gender; the issue of social identity, inclusion and exclusion; the management of public space; and the issue of heritage retention and prospects of the loss of traditional character.

Religion has played an important role in Zaria City's develop-ment but is now evolving as a source of tension both within the traditional city and in the broader metropolitan area. The Islamic religion has evolved as a strong force shaping the social and cultural setting of Zaria and its public space. Its influence is manifested in activities, symbolisms and in the material fabric of public space. The role that religion has played has changed over time. Hogben, commenting in this respect, notes that Islam 'started as a religion, but it later became a state, and finally a culture' (1967: 10). As a culture, Islam has played a fundamental role in establishing the operative norms, values and morality that govern the daily life of people and their interactions with others. It also has a strong influence on the structuring of social roles and responsibilities. Since the 1980s, religion has increasingly become a source of tension and fraction in social life. Improvement in religious education has led to challenges to dominant traditional sects such as the Qadriyyah and Tijjaniyah movements, and their decline. In their place, new sects and groups have emerged, with exposure to diverse and competing ideologies. These competing ideologies have led to alignment among groups, sometimes placing them in conflict either with each other or with the general society. In addition, there are also tensions between the predominantly Islamic residents of the traditional city and the large Christian population living in the broader metropolitan area. The national competition for power and influence sometimes takes on a religious dimension, which is manifested locally in civil disturbances. Taboos that essentially remain based on Islamic proscriptions also sometimes force people into relative choices to avoid harsh social sanctions (Renne 1997; Abdullahi 1986). There is a growing perception among the population of a decline in morals and discipline (*tarbiya*) in society, which is linked to the rise of an indigenous Hausa film industry and the perception of its being out of tune with religious prescription.

The concept of public space necessarily embodies the ideal of universal access and participation. The Hausa cities have been the object of gender-based scrutiny in this respect, in view of the Islamic nature of the society and the association of Islamic city models with gendered public and private domains. Examination of Zaria's public space shows a model that is different from the Islamic city model. Public space in the Hausa cities is gendered, in that males are the dominant participants in public activities. This gendered nature does not, however, preclude female participation. Female access and participation have varied over time, with three factors as the main determinants: age, social status and marital status. Young children and teenagers usually have access to all public spaces without any restrictions. Old women also have unfettered access to public space. Slaves (before the abolition of slavery) and low-income women, whether married or unmarried, have always had free access to public space, with slave women engaging in commerce and other functional activities. Married high-status women have experienced the greatest restriction on access and participation. Most of the remaining population would usually be able to move in public space but without actively participating in activities. The issue of identity, social inclusion and exclusion is one that has become important both for residents of Zaria City and for those of the larger metropolitan area because of the national competition for power and resources and their

103

allocation based on place of origin. Since the colonial period, there has been a freeze on migration to the traditional city and the identity of its residents, in contrast with the fluid nature evident in previous periods. Residents of the traditional city view themselves as 'indigenes' of Zaria and those outside the city as temporary residents or visitors. Within the traditional city, there is a further fractioning of the population along title-holding, wealth and other lines. This has led to tension, as less powerful groups increasingly feel that more powerful groups are using association with the city to struggle for, acquire and accumulate resources to the detriment of the less powerful groups. This tension is pushing some residents to repudiate the concept of identity associated with the city, viewing it as a tool more of oppression than of progress. At the broader metropolitan level, there is also a tendency for those outside the traditional city to feel aggrieved because they are not given equal opportunities as permanent residents of the metropolitan areas.

Management and servicing of public spaces has evolved as an issue because of the generally poor state of services and facilities delivery. The regime of management in the city has evolved with minimal active public participation in the management and maintenance of public places. Though public development intervention has expanded over time, this has not been adequate, or matched by the provision of structures for the servicing and management of public places and facilities. Most public spaces are therefore serviced and maintained by interested users. The result is that public places are poorly serviced and maintained, and this is manifested in visible problems in the environment. The rapid change that is happening in Zaria's built environment is also leading to concerns about the impact of this change and the prospect of the loss of the city's traditional character. This character, stemming from the spatial definition of the city, the structure and organization of its built fabric, the unique spatial layout of residential quarters, and the unity of material and technology of construction, has come under pressure as a result of population growth and the adoption of new materials, methods of construction and development form, and is leading to questions about how to retain and preserve heritage. The issue assumed significant importance following attempts to destroy and replace the Friday mosque constructed in the jihad period with a new concrete construction. Protest led to the encasement of the old mosque in a concrete shell, and to a national initiative to create a museum of Nigerian traditional architecture, in which the Zaria Friday mosque was reconstructed. The incident raised a fundamental question regarding how to address change in ways that at least preserve elements of the city's heritage and tradition – an open question that is still in search of an acceptable answer.

The issues and tensions highlighted are directly manifested in Zaria's public space and in broader public discussions about the Hausa cities. The issues are manifested as patterns in material and social public space, in social actions and discourse, and in behavioural attitudes. The issues of access, identity, inclusion and exclusion are all manifested in the social character of public places, where normative values and rules dictate limits of participation. The social exclusion of others is visibly evident from dress and other customary practices and is reinforced by the close-knit nature of the society. Tension from differentiation and exclusion within the city's population is manifested in public attitudes and behaviours that are increasingly becoming more aggressive and anti-authority and leading to discontent and disaffection. Abdullahi (1986: 40–1) notes in this respect that the society is undergoing a fundamental shift as people are moving away from a society built on the self in relationship to the unknown in a religious setting, to one in which the self is viewed in relationship to a material environment. Changing attitudes are sometimes associated with a decline in religious values, and this has produced conflict with the indigenous film industry because of its perceived role in such a decline. Tension is also exacerbated by poor public-sector development, visible in the form of various urban problems. These include lack of employment opportunities, poor drainage and sanitation, a chronic refuse problem, the presence of large stagnant pools of water and an overall poor amenity situation. The problems have made politics the prime subject of discussions in public places, with negligence in services and opportunities provision the main topics. Tension resulting from the issue is so high that there is a growing antagonism against public agencies and their workers, and disaffection is linked to some of the riots and public disturbances that have occurred in the city. Some sources in the city have linked observation of declining decorum and discipline in the city and the rise in drug use and consumption to the poor service situation and lack of opportunities. Religious tension is manifested in public space in the form of confrontations and conflicts, which have become frequent in the city. Several such disturbances have occurred within Zaria City as a result of conflict between Islamic groups. Civil disturbances have also occurred between Muslims and Christians living in the metropolitan area. The broad implication of the issues identified has made them subjects of discourse among residents of the metropolitan area. They are also active topics of broader discourse on the Hausa cities in forums that include the media and academic circles.

Conclusion

The examination of Zaria City's public space reveals a pattern of gradual change and transformation that is in tandem with significant historical events and changes in the cultural setting of the society. Changes are manifested in the material, social and symbolic patterns of public space in the form of addition to, modification of or complete abandonment of practices, and occur in response to events, actions or policies introduced in different historical periods. From a material perspective, Zaria's public space has witnessed a reorganization that has seen some space types added and some modified or eliminated, and a reorganization of its morphological pattern resulting in an increase in density and changes in structural organization, enclosure elements, surface treatment and general visual character. From a social perspective, public space has witnessed changes in the patterns of access and social character, and in the types, and spatial and temporal organization, of activities. It is, however, from a symbolic perspective that the public space of Zaria has witnessed its greatest change. Zaria's public space evolved from being the communal space of an agrarian society in the pre-jihad period to becoming that of the capital of a large emirate and a powerful member of the Sokoto Caliphate. This elevated the centrality of the public space, imbuing it with significance as a stage for the display of political, economic and symbolic power, and a focus of attraction for migration, contact, trade and exchange of ideas. The colonial period saw a gradual decline in the importance of Zaria and its public space, as it was divested of its political and economic role and at the same time became a small district in a broader metropolitan area. Public space in Zaria has evolved once more into the space for the communal life of residents, with its attraction to 'others' outside restricted to visits to watch cultural events and to appreciate the aesthetics of traditional environment and practices. This traditional heritage and aesthetics is, however, currently threatened, as indicated by the review of issues and tensions. The issues and tensions identified point to challenges that must be addressed as part of any effort aimed at improving the management of change and development of Zaria City and its public space.

Part II

Public space and everyday life in urban neighbourhoods

Ali Madanipour

Part II brings together case studies from urban neighbourhoods outside the centre, particularly from low- and middle-income residential areas. Here public spaces are intertwined with everyday life in the neighbourhood and display the various gaps that exist between different perspectives and groups, to the extent that these gaps may even lead to the setting up of physical barriers. When the making of public space happens through official channels, by public- or private-sector designers, the result displays a gap in understanding between the abstract ideas of the designer and the diverse patterns of life of the people. The solution often lies in the participation of the people in the process of creating the public space.

The main public spaces in European cities are the focus of much attention, whereas marginal public spaces, which are the focus of Chapter 6, are places of neglect and decline. The concentration of disadvantaged and vulnerable groups in limited spaces creates a sense of entrapment. The social fragments that are placed next to each other in deprived neighbourhoods, either by market forces or by public planning, start to crack in the public places of these neighbourhoods. On the one hand, intensive use of space by some groups excludes and intimidates others. On the other hand, the limited amount of public space is under threat of encroachment by other demands on a finite resource. In these places of fragmentation and competition, communication is often difficult, if not impossible, as different social groups speak different languages, have different attitudes and have different frameworks. A public space that allows this diversity to become aware of itself through free expression can be a significant asset for such a diverse population. Improving public places can improve the actual conditions of life in these neighbourhoods, while injecting a sense of hope and a better image in the eyes of residents and the outside world. Although it is a key part of good governance, there is no doubt that this should be put in perspective, as one among a number of issues that need addressing.

The focus of Chapter 7 is on the transformation of public space in South Africa through gated neighbourhoods and its implication and meaning in the country and more broadly for urban design. Research findings on the development of gated neighbourhoods have indicated that they are a significant mechanism of urban transformation in post-apartheid South Africa, changing both neighbourhoods and cities in many ways. The chapter briefly explains what is understood by 'space' and its relation to 'place', as well as how this relates to the understanding and modification of public space in cities. It then discusses the nature of public space in South Africa through a short discussion of apartheid spaces (spaces of yesterday) and the vision for public space in the post-apartheid city (spaces of tomorrow). The following section shows how, despite these aims, and as a result of pressures such as insecurity and crime, public spaces are significantly transformed through the proliferation of gated neighbourhoods. The penultimate section explores the implications of these changes as related to urban function (use of space), form ('definition' of space) and meaning (interpretation and/or experience of space), both in terms of South Africa and for urban design in general.

Chapter 8 is a case study of public spaces in modern residential areas in Jeddah, Saudi Arabia, engaging with the shortcomings of planning and design of these neighbourhoods. Contemporary public policies and spatial planning practices for regulating urban growth and urban space have led to fragmentation in the layout of modern residential areas. This fragmentation, together with a highly mobile and heterogeneous population, has deprived inhabitants of possibilities for socialization and caused a breakdown in one of the mechanisms of crime prevention (i.e. natural surveillance combined with self-policing). Such practices have increased residents' perceptions of vulnerability to criminal and sub-criminal activities, as well as actual levels of anti-social behaviour. In addition, residents are exposed to higher levels of risk from traffic, noise, air pollution and other urban hazards. Therefore, awareness of risk, fear of victimization, and nervousness about the outdoor environment are heightened and common in the rhythms of the quotidian residential environments. Consequently, individuals (or at least certain sectors of society) have withdrawn from public life, and life in general has become more insular, inward-looking and home based. This withdrawal has resulted in widespread withdrawal from life in public, alienation and social polarization. The main purpose of the chapter is to examine the contemporary practice of public space provision, dissecting the different aspects concerning the planning, design and management undertaken by the stakeholders involved in public space provision with the aim of developing a multidimensional approach that could inform urban design principles and practice for future provision of this amenity.

Chapter 9 is a case study of the design and development of public open spaces in a new town in Esfahan, Iran. The study shows that the new town's residential areas are mainly organized under the modernist functionalist approach in the form of building blocks where streets have segregated residential areas, dividing the town in such a way that separation of semi-public and public space is not of any importance and has lost its value. In addition, the chapter demonstrates that the unresponsiveness of outdoor residential public spaces is a weakness deriving from the existing process of design, implementation and maintenance of these spaces. Apart from the specific differences in the studied cases, their general common gaps and shortcomings can be summarized as follows: the economic gap and deficiency of necessary infrastructure; producers' imagination versus consumers' expectation; the cultural gap between designers and users; design quality and cultural identity; social, educational and administrative gaps; and questions about the role of professionals in terms of providing a high-quality living environment. Despite their gaps and shortcomings, the residential public spaces examined are still of great importance for local residents and are noticeably being used and patronized by different user groups. This enduring importance confirms the significance of outdoor public spaces in residential areas for people's everyday life.

Chapters 10 and 11 address the possibility of people's involvement in the design and development of public spaces, to overcome the divide between the designer and the user. Chapter 10 studies the development of public space in low-income neighbourhoods in Mexico. From the second half of the twentieth century up to the present, a great part of the urban environment in Latin American cities has grown through the development of informal settlements. These are settlements created by the low-income population, who mostly appropriate the peripheral territory of consolidated urban cores spontaneously and illegally. In the past two decades, governments and urbanists have recognized these settlements as a way to satisfy pressing housing needs, which in turn has led to the improvement and upgrading of housing, urban services and community facilities. In this context, the improvement and development of public spaces play an important role in the urban integration and consolidation of such settlements. Although the development of these low-income neighbourhoods has received much attention by urban researchers, very little attention has been paid to processes related to the consolidation of their public spaces. Drawing on qualitative research based on in-depth interviews and participant observation, this chapter illustrates how the production of public spaces takes place. It looks at how the main stakeholders interact in the development process (planning, design, construction and management) of public places; it also covers the social and spatial transformations of the urban public environment within settlements' consolidation process. Finally, it explores the use of, the possible conflicts over usage, and the values and meanings attributed to public spaces in this context.

Chapter 11 investigates case studies from north-west France. This chapter approaches the co-production of public space in participative laboratories as a new urban design strategy leading to redefinition of urban development and social identity. Making explicit the various uses', users' and stakeholders' conflicts of meaning allows debate and redefinition of both the design process and the decision making, and becomes an educative process that gives social meaning a primary role in the development of public space. The study analyses five projects realized in France, in the Nord-Pas-de-Calais region, with the support of the French government and regional authorities, in a pilot project driven by the research team 'Habitat and Development'. The chapter discusses the experimental method developed for facilitating participative laboratories, involving experts, elected representatives and lay citizens in multicultural and interdisciplinary participation throughout the design process, in the context of the *Politique de la Ville*, the national policy for urban and social development established in France from the 1980s. The participation of the whole panel of stakeholders gives social meaning and legitimacy to the process, institutes a forum that extends the boundaries of the design process to include an educative process for all concerned, and changes the relationships between designers, and other stakeholders, and the concepts of creativity in design.

Together, these case studies map out the conditions of public spaces in marginal neighbourhoods, point out the shortcomings of the formal design and development processes, and outline possible future directions in which the design and development of urban neighbourhoods takes place through the participation of different stakeholders, especially the local population, rather than by using solutions that are imposed from outside.

Chapter 6

Marginal public spaces in European cities

Ali Madanipour

The public spaces at the core of European cities are considered to be their major nodes, and as such have always received much attention and investment, being embellished with artworks and perceived as landmarks in Europe's social life and cultural heritage. Cities that are attempting to recover from industrial decline are also placing much emphasis on these main public spaces. These cities are regenerating their old public spaces and creating new ones to help them project a new image that can attract new investment through tourism and relocation of firms. Often forgotten, however, are the public spaces on the margins of the European city, on the urban periphery or in the inner city. In poorer neighbourhoods, the problems of living together in extremely difficult circumstances bring to the surface the harshness of disadvantage and difference. Here, the inability of the residents to live together peacefully and the failure of the public organizations to deliver the necessary services mean that public spaces are at times major battlegrounds or residual spaces, with a reality far from the glorified image of a European urban public space.

This chapter draws on the author's ongoing research (Madanipour 2003a, b, c) and in particular on a European Commission-funded research project into neighbourhood governance and social exclusion, which involves ten teams of academic researchers from around Europe. Case studies were conducted of disadvantaged neighbourhoods in the cities of Amsterdam (the Netherlands), Athens (Greece), Cascais (Portugal), Dublin (Ireland), Helsingør (Denmark), London (the United Kingdom), Newcastle (the United Kingdom), Stockholm (Sweden), Turin (Italy) and Wuppertal (Germany). In this project, public spaces were used as one of a number of entries by which to analyse the relationships between stakeholders and their capacity to deal with the problems they were facing. Residents, professionals and others with an interest or involvement in the neighbourhood were interviewed about their views and experiences of the area's public spaces. In the context of significant political, economic and cultural differences across European cities, the aims of this chapter are to chart some of the key similarities of marginal public spaces, to explore the implications of the research findings for the design and management of cities, and to argue for the significance of marginal public spaces for social integration and for European cities as a whole.

Public space in European cities

Cities have always been the meeting point of different populations (Aristotle 1992; Southall 1998). Some central places, as best exemplified by the ancient Greek *agora*, have acted as a meeting point for these different people. The small size of ancient Greek cities meant that this central public space could simultaneously cater for political, economic and cultural needs by being a place of assembly, a marketplace and a place of rituals and ceremonies (Glotz 1929; Ward-Perkins 1974). In the modern city, however, this convergence of functions has disappeared (Carr *et al*. 1992). The public sphere is 'metatopical' – that is, it goes beyond physical spaces and is established through a variety of arenas that may never converge in space or time (Taylor 1995). The result is a loss of significance for public spaces, which have become nodes in traffic and parking lots (Sitte 1986), or monofunctional places associated with trade or tourism.

There has, however, been a recent rush of attention to public spaces in Europe; from Berlin to Birmingham and Barcelona, large investments are being made to reinvigorate dilapidated public spaces that lie at the heart of the city. Some have promoted public spaces as a vehicle of social integration, such as in Berlin's Potsdamer Platz, which is meant to heal the wounds of the dividing line that was imposed on the city for decades. Others promote public space creation as a counterpoint to the privatization push that has characterized neoliberal economic restructuring, in which private-sector production of urban environment has been encouraged and supported by public authorities (Sorkin 1992). Many, however, appear to connect their investment in public spaces clearly to city marketing, aiming to make their cities a more desirable destination for firms to relocate to and for tourists to visit. The emphasis in almost all promotion of public space is on the central, or major, public spaces of the city, which are used to project a positive image and to create new public displays for the city. The images often combine the historicity of the European city with the forward-looking sense of modernity. Rarely, however, is any attention paid to the marginal public spaces of the city, where the disadvantaged populations live. It is essential, therefore, to search for an understanding of these public spaces, whether in the inner city (in the United Kingdom) or the periphery (in mainland Europe), which are often excluded from the city marketing and public space improvement drives.

The major public spaces of the city have always had city-wide significance (Braunfels 1988; Gehl 1996; Moughtin 2003; Worpole 2000). They are used as gateways to the city, as showcases to attract investors and tourists. They are also used to support the legitimacy of the local administration, so that it can show its effectiveness in managing the city. At times, these places are seen as nodes for social cohesion, bringing different people together in public places. However, marginal public spaces rarely enjoy any of this significance. They are not on the list of priorities to be dealt with by local authorities, whether in terms of political legitimacy, the economic competitiveness and social cohesion of the city or its image and marketability.

Social marginalization and exclusion in Europe

Partly as a response to the challenges of globalization and to make Europe competitive in the global economy, the process of European integration has linked European economies together, creating a dynamic, unified space in which capital and labour move with ease. The effects of flexibility for the market, however, have had social consequences, running higher risks of inequality among the regions at the European level, and within the regions at the local level. This is why the European Union shows a particular interest in promoting social inclusion, to maintain the traditional European social model and to reduce and manage the negative side effects of heightened mobility, which could include social and spatial polarization (European Commission 1999, 2001, 2002).

The effects of increased mobility of capital and labour, new technologies, de-industrialization, and liberalization of the economy have generated new energies and economic opportunities. They have also generated severe social problems for those who are not able to compete in the new circumstances, as they lack access to resources, skills and rights. While many in the older economic sectors, especially in industrial regions, have not been able to make the transition to the new economy, the entry of new generations into the job market and the arrival of new immigrants have created new tensions and challenges for social integration.

The post-war industrial growth and reconstruction in northern and western Europe were fuelled by an invited workforce from southern Europe or former colonies. Sophisticated welfare systems were also developed to support and enable economic recovery for a war-torn continent. In southern Europe, rapid urbanization, especially in industrializing regions, attracted large numbers of people from towns and villages. Within a generation, however, industrial decline set in, and those who had not yet retired lost their jobs. Moreover, the prospect of access to similar jobs for the next generation became substantially limited. At the same time, they were joined by new waves of immigrants, asylum seekers and refugees from a wide range of countries that were going through political and economic turmoil. The combined effects of de-industrialization, liberalization of the economy and continued immigration have widened the gap between the rich and poor. The migrant poor are seen by the middle class as destabilizing and a security threat, and by the poor and unskilled workers as competitors for jobs and social support. The cultural as well as economic gaps have widened, while the welfare state as a support mechanism has been cut back, losing some of its ability to deal with the problems that the new conditions pose.

In all major cities of Europe, the most vulnerable groups – that is, the poor, the elderly, children, women and those belonging to ethnic minorities – have been exposed to the risks of social exclusion, a phenomenon that has come to the fore in understanding cities and developing policy for them (Andersen and van Kempen 2003; Woodward and Kohli 2001; Atkinson 2000). Through the mechanisms of public-sector housing and planning, and private-sector market operations, these vulnerable groups have been clustered in poor urban neighbourhoods, which now suffer from multidimensional disadvantage and stigma. They have all suffered, to varying degrees, from the combined effects of lack of access to resources, to decision making and to shared experiences and narratives (Madanipour *et al.* 2003). As a result, all the major cities of Europe have deprived neighbourhoods made up of clusters of vulnerable people suffering from multiple disadvantage (EC 1994; Room 1995). As in other parts of the world, segregation becomes the spatial expression of social polarization, and the neighbourhood assumes a special significance, both in understanding social exclusion and in combating it (Knox 1995; Kearns and Parkinson 2001; Meegan and Mitchell 2001). In December 2000 in Nice, the European Union agreed on four common objectives that could be used in national action plans to fight poverty and social exclusion. These objectives were to facilitate participation in employment and access by all to resources, rights, goods and services; to prevent the risks of exclusion; to help the most vulnerable; and to mobilize all relevant bodies (European Commission 2001, 2002).

As shown by the case studies of Britain, Ireland and Italy in our research, social exclusion is not only a feature of immigrants and ethnic minorities; the native population can also experience severe forms of social exclusion. Social exclusion is often a combination of different forms of vulnerability. Any characteristic that makes a person vulnerable can pave the way for social exclusion. The elderly, the poor, the disabled, the women, the children, the long-term unemployed among the native population can be as disadvantaged as immigrants and ethnic minorities. But it is also true that those belonging to ethnic minorities, especially the recent arrivals, suffer from the additional disadvantage of not knowing the local culture and not having access to the social capital that enables individuals to navigate the social world.

Entrapment of difference within a limited space

The residents of deprived neighbourhoods may be socially, politically and culturally different from one another; they may have come from different ethnic and religious groups, from different parts of the country or from different countries of the world. They may also be from the poor sections of the population, who have lived in the area for a long time. What connects them all is their weak economic position in society, which allocates them the space they inhabit. The city as a whole provides a framework for social differentiation and segregation on the basis of access to resources: the rich can choose where they wish to go and can create areas with distinctive cultural, social and political characters. This possibility, however, does not exist for the poor, who have to live together in the marginal spaces that are available to them. The result is a mosaic of difference that is trapped within a limited space, bearing enormous pressures from within and without, and with limited capacity to connect to the outside world. Inevitably this creates an explosive condition in which disadvantaged difference is reflected in cracks that are visible in public spaces.

Entrapment within a limited space and with limited access to resources and rights disables the population in dealing with the problems they face everyday. The cracks take the form of neglect and decline, as well as tensions along the lines of social fragmentation and stratification. As there is competition for the limited resources available, public spaces become battlegrounds. While some tend to dominate the public spaces, others are intimidated, leading to a lack of safety and withdrawal from public areas and from engagement with others.

The tensions that can be identified reflect the social fragments that coexist in the neighbourhood. The public space then becomes a display of incompatibility between these groups, which, in the absence of some supporting mechanisms, may find it hard to live together within the means that are available and the conditions that prevail. As most people in such groups are preoccupied with sorting out some of the basic problems of life, their capacity to deal with others becomes more limited.

Some of these tensions are generated by different patterns of use. For some households, the public space is an extension of the house. This may be due to the large size of the family, the small size of the dwelling, the type of dwelling (flats, where outside space is not available) and access to facilities inside the dwelling. It may also be due to some cultural patterns of using inside and outside spaces. In some countries, households are used to having access to a courtyard, which caters for a variety of activities. Some groups spend long periods hanging around public spaces, such as the unemployed, the homeless, drug abusers and street drinkers, who have nowhere else to go; teenagers, who use this space for socialization; and migrants, who may have no other forum for socialization. This causes friction with others who pass through these spaces or want to use them, and with those who are not accustomed to this pattern of behaviour and are either intimidated or made uncomfortable by it.

Another form of tension is between the newcomers and the old residents. This is not necessarily a racial and ethnic conflict. In Newcastle, it happened within the same racial group. It is the length of residence that distinguishes between those who have developed emotional links with the area and those who arrive later and are considered intruders. It is a sense of territory being invaded by unwanted newcomers. This is manifest in some forms of behaviour in public spaces and the approach to their upkeep.

Another tension is between ethnic and cultural groups, or within them. Host communities may brand all the ethnic groups living in a marginal neighbourhood as foreigners. However, some of these groups may have lived there for generations. Ethnic minorities may have come from a variety of countries with huge differences. As a minority, they may have to live with the cultural and economic minorities of the host communities. The example of the sex shops next to shopping areas used by Muslim women in Rotterdam may be just one example of how different land uses are grouped together via the mechanisms of the market or social housing allocation processes. Despite the stereotype that the members of an ethnic group are a homogeneous bunch, they may have come from different geographical, class and tribal backgrounds. They may, indeed, have been in conflict with one another in their home country, from which they may have escaped. There are also generational differences between migrants, who carry a set of ideas and identities developed elsewhere, and their children, who are born and brought up in the new countries. These create clashes in the way they use public space and generate difficulty and confusion in the minds of the professionals dealing with them. When the sense of entrapment within a limited space and limited prospect of change reaches its extreme, the result is riots in public spaces, as was the case in Overtoomse Veld, in the middle of which lies August Allebé Square, remembered for riots by young Moroccans and their clash with the police in 1998 (Figure 6.1).

6.1
The regenerated August Allebé Square, which became the site of riots by young Moroccans in 1998 (Overtoomse Veld, Amsterdam).

Competition for space: use and development

Marginal public spaces are subject to severe competition between some of the stakeholders in the neighbourhood, as each group bids to dominate and appropriate the space. Public space is a limited resource, the competition for which creates tension, fear and threat, displaying the social fragmentation that is trapped within the neighbourhood. Two types of competition can be identified for the public spaces of a neighbourhood: competition for use and competition for development. While the former is a display of incompatible public behaviour by individuals and groups, the latter is a manifestation of institutional competition for control of space.

A very serious challenge in the use of public spaces is by those who use it most, and thus tend to exclude others from it, as they are seen by others as bidding to dominate the place. The most intensive use of public spaces is perhaps made by youth, especially teenage boys. The intensive use of public spaces, together with some problem incidents caused by a minority, leads teenage boys to be blamed for a variety of problems. Teenage boys may use the public space for peaceful and legitimate purposes, such as playing football in Lisson Green, London. But by hanging around streets and at times engaging in vandalism and anti-social behaviour, if not criminality, some teenage gangs may appropriate public spaces and intimidate others, who in turn withdraw from it. This applies to ethnic minority youth (Moroccans in Amsterdam) as well as the natives (English in Newcastle, Irish in Dublin). Other groups who dominate public spaces are street drinkers and drug abusers (Stockholm, Wuppertal), who spend much of their time in public places (Figure 6.2). The result is a lack of safety for others who feel vulnerable, especially elderly people and children, a pattern that can be found in almost all the neighbourhoods studied. The problem of

6.2
Incompatible use by different groups has turned Platz der Republik into a contested public space (Ostersbaum, Wuppertal).

safety in European marginal public spaces is significant, but not yet as severe as in some disadvantaged neighbourhoods in the United States, where, for example, it is estimated that during the past two decades, 10,000 young people have died in the violence-ridden neighbourhoods of Los Angeles (Herbert 2003).

The institutional competition for public space revolves around the control of land. Where land is in high demand, public spaces may be under pressure for development, seen as luxuries that are expensive to keep and can therefore be dispensed with. Development pressures, or the difficulties experienced by public authorities (now with smaller budgets) in managing large open public spaces, tend to reduce the size of public spaces. In this sense, there is a competition over land between different stakeholders. Where deprived neighbourhoods are targeted for gentrification, their public spaces attract new attention, as they are gateways to underused land that is expected to re-enter the marketplace.

In Lisson Green, London, public spaces have been gradually reduced in size without consultation with residents; some have been attached to ground floor flats as private gardens, to rectify earlier problems. This is part of an ongoing programme of rehabilitation, which partly aims to create a normal street scene, hence involves demolishing high-level walkways. Much of the rest of the public space has been taken over by the Paddington Churches Housing Association to build new homes. The public space that is left is limited to a central park with a playground and a small football pitch. This area seems to be well used by children and young adults, although its size allows only small numbers to use it at any one time.

The prospect of development of an area and the way it is handled can lead to major tensions between stakeholders. Articulating a vision for the future of the area is a complex process, and the residents of poor neighbourhoods are in a disadvantaged position to influence the process. At times, they are seen as the problem, rather than as being able to help with the development of solutions. In Walker, Newcastle, tensions arose as a result of a major regeneration project for the East End of the city, of which this neighbourhood is a part. As a long-term, 'urban renaissance' strategy to transform this and other troubled areas of the city, the city council developed the programme Going for Growth (Newcastle City Council 2000), which involved large-scale redevelopment in these areas. The result was a rapid and angry mobilization of the residents of these predominantly public housing areas. Tensions have continued over the alternative visions for the future of the area and how it may be developed. The public spaces of the area are at times filled with tension between the residents and the council.

The neighbourhood of Ano Liosia on the outskirts of Athens houses different cultural groups: working-class Greeks; immigrants, mainly from Albania; repatriated Greeks, mainly from the ex-Soviet Black Sea region; and Roma families. Following a recent earthquake, some rebuilding activities are taking place, although the Gypsies are denied permission by the municipality to build new buildings, which has led to multiple occupancy of the existing houses. Living close to each other and to the plentiful open spaces of the area is seen as an advantage by the Roma population. However, as they feel unwanted in the neighbourhood and its public spaces, they often congregate in their courtyards and inside the houses.

Competition for space is a major source of tension, as it involves the disposition of each stakeholder in the process of spatial change. A weak disposition, as is the case with the residents of disadvantaged neighbourhoods, if not taken into account in the process of development, will be reflected in tensions and explosive events, often played out in public spaces. Rather than competition for the use of public spaces, this can be competition for the transformation of part of the area, or the entire area, with direct implications for the conditions and use by the public. Rather than competition for the use of existing spaces, this is a competition for the shape of the future, for the nature and characteristics of the public spaces and the public life of the neighbourhood.

Communication within space

In deprived neighbourhoods, where a largely diverse population may be trapped within a limited space, communication between the diverse groups who live there, and between them and the outside world, becomes a major concern. It can act as a barrier to residents' ability to live together peacefully and to solve their shared problems, and a barrier to their integration into the larger society.

The residents of Tensta, Stockholm, speak 140 different languages, creating a problem of communication and a challenge to provide education for a fast-growing, diverse population in an area with the highest level of young residents in Stockholm (40 per cent are under 25). Entrapment within a limited space also creates a distance from the rest of society. For the immigrant population, the neighbourhood of Tensta acts as a cushion. Many others there share the same experience, and it is there that government provisions for help are concentrated. At the same time, this concentration of migrants and their problems attaches a stigma to the area in the eyes of its residents, and even more so for outsiders, who see it as a place of crime, gang trouble, fights, robbery and drugs. This perception has an impact on job opportunities, insurance premiums and contact with officials. The absence of Swedish neighbours is also seen as an obstacle to integration, as the children do not have Swedish friends at school and the adults feel abandoned and neglected. The absence of some services, such as a bank and a police station, adds to this feeling (Figure 6.3).

Different groups in these neighbourhoods may enjoy similarity, but may also find a larger distance from the rest of society. If migrants are placed in proximity to the poor sections of the native society, there will be clashes and competition. On the other hand, the more affluent part of the

host society does not wish to live next door to poor people, whether local or from abroad, whether ethnic majority or minority. The problems of public spaces become problems of controlling behaviour in public places, rather than of encouraging communication and cohesion. This is why provision and management of public housing has been the subject of intense debate in the recent past. On the one hand, the liberalizing urban economies have intensified the concentration of the poor, resulting in a declining status for public housing across Europe. On the other hand, the problems caused by concentrating disadvantaged populations in particular areas have led to the promoting of social mixing through housing allocation.

The problems of communication are exacerbated not only by the diversity of language but also by the diverse forms of expression. In a number of neighbourhoods, graffiti is considered to be a major problem. However, graffiti for some is a form of self-expression, a kind of public art through which deprived youth find the possibility of expression. It is also a method of signification, which is used famously by gangs to mark their territories. Sometimes it is the work of individuals who need to express themselves and attract attention, especially as it may be their only outlet for such action. At other times, it is a mark by which to threaten others, which can be intimidating in general. For some, graffiti adds meaning to the environment, whereas for others it is a sign of disorder. It transforms the shape of the public environment, and is a constant topic of controversy.

Communication within space can, therefore, be problematic if the forms of performance and expression are not shared by all. This is a feature of the areas of social fragmentation; diverse groups have a diverse range of behaviour and performance, which can be completely incompatible. The gypsies in Ano Liosia, Athens, have an outdoor culture, but they are barred from performing their rituals, such as weddings, in the public space, which makes them feel unwanted. Public spaces are used as sites of display and performance. When public spaces allow differences to be expressed, they can contribute to a sense of well-being in the resident population. However, the performative element may be misunderstood or misused, so that local populations feel alienated from the performance. An example is Marxloh, a working-class neighbourhood in Duisburg, Germany, with a large migrant population. When local authorities wanted to celebrate the international character of the area, they set up a competition for public arts. The winner displayed statues of Native Americans, to express the social diversity and international character of an overwhelmingly Turkish population. This was a representation of difference that had a large gap with the reality of the population. In some instances, on the contrary, there is a clear attempt to remind people of the conditions and characteristics of life in a marginal neighbourhood, as is the case in inner-city Dublin. Here a monument has been set up to remember those who have died of drug abuse in the neighbourhood.

One of the key features of a marginal public space is the close physical contact it can provide between residents and their built environment. Central public spaces have often suffered from the heavy presence of motor cars. Cars have also dominated middle-class neighbourhoods where people can pass through the city at high speeds (Sennett 1994). In marginal public spaces, however, whether in the inner city or on the periphery, cars are less present, as they are not affordable. The speed of movement through the neighbourhood, therefore, is much slower, offering a greater possibility of close contact with social and physical environment. These places in marginal neighbourhoods are potentially places of interpersonal contacts. Their significance is local, and so they stand in contrast to central spaces, which are impersonal showcases of the city. Marginal public spaces are less public than those at the heart of cities, by virtue of being located within areas that are mainly accessible to, and serving, a local population, which could have a neighbourhood and community effect. This can be the case in both poor and rich areas. Another aspect of disadvantaged neighbourhoods, however, is that their residents are often tenants of public housing companies, and as such many are in a transitory condition whereby they do not expect to settle down in the area for long, hence the strength of their contact with the neighbourhood is limited. While the physical speed of cars may be less applicable here, the social speed of transition may have a similar effect.

Neglect and decline

There is intense competition between individuals and organizations for some public spaces in poorer urban neighbourhoods; at the same time, these spaces often suffer from neglect and decline. Compared to better-off neighbourhoods, or major urban sites, the public spaces of deprived neighbourhoods are often run-down, with vandalized furniture and full of litter, giving the impression that these are leftover and neglected spaces. This shows neglect by the main parties involved: by local authorities, as reflected in poor maintenance or in planning blight; and by local residents, as reflected in litter and vandalism. Furthermore, as private companies, particularly retailers, avoid these areas, the quality of public areas is negatively affected. It seems that these public spaces are not important to anyone, giving some residents the feeling of being abandoned, and displaying a poor image of the area to outsiders.

Neglect by residents is particularly reflected in widespread litter, which in all the neighbourhoods studied is a major problem and a source of irritation, especially to long-term residents. The problem is often analysed by blaming particular groups for their conduct. In Overtoomse Veld, Amsterdam, some see the large concentration of schoolchildren in the neighbourhood as the source of the problem, as they may throw the remains of their sandwich lunches or other rubbish into the streets. In Ostersbaum, Wuppertal, children, dog owners and immigrants are blamed for the spread of litter in public spaces. Some residents clean the areas around their homes, and some schools arrange for cleaning projects, one of which resulted in building a waste-monument. In Nøjsomhed, Helsingør, people complain about the lack of respect for common areas, especially when rubbish is thrown from balconies into public spaces, a practice that seems to be contagious. In Tensta, Stockholm, some residents and professionals interpret this as a cultural issue, with some individuals and cultures being seen as paying no regard to tidiness and not being bothered with what lies beyond their front door. The housing company that runs Tensta puts much effort into cleaning the public places, supplying cleaning tools, employing teenagers in the summer, and even providing cinema tickets as an incentive. One housekeeper uses children in her building and offers a visit to a Stockholm amusement park to those who help. But despite these efforts, litter soon comes back, which creates a negative image for these neighbourhoods in the city. In Via Fiesole, Turin, the absence of a sense of responsibility inside the neighbourhood is seen as a cause of its poor state of affairs. Some small areas are well cared for by individuals, while others are abandoned and dilapidated. There is a sense of lack of attachment, showing how individuals either do not care about the environment or are worried that vandals will undo their work.

Neglect by local authorities is reflected in the absence of some necessary facilities and in poor maintenance of existing ones. Public spaces in Ostersbaum, Wuppertal, suffer from insufficient lighting, waste, and inadequate repair. The poor conditions of open spaces in Via Fiesole, Turin, are partly blamed on the authorities for their indifference. There are signs of poor maintenance, untrimmed trees and uncut grass, or signs of vandalism in entrances, common spaces outside and inside buildings. Public spaces are generally viewed as unsafe and dilapidated, and remain unused, owing to the absence of facilities such as telephone boxes and benches, which could help make them useful meeting places. Via Sospello, Turin, also suffers from lack of maintenance and a bad reputation for high rates of criminal activity, even though it was developed as a high-quality residential area. The lack of maintenance, which is due to the planned redevelopment of Overtoomse Veld, Amsterdam, is causing anger and frustration. Absence of shops, playgrounds and benches explains why people do not find the public spaces inviting. The few playgrounds that do exist are out of the way and do not seem to be used even in good weather.

Private-sector neglect is another aspect of the picture, even though some marginal neighbourhoods are provided with good public facilities. In Tensta, Stockholm, there are several institutionalized public facilities in the neighbourhood: a one-stop shop, a family centre and a library provide information and advice, meeting points for households and children, and information and entertainment in a variety of languages. There is a school, a swimming pool and a lively indoor shopping centre with a range of shops and food from different countries and cultures, although some residents complain about the absence of mainstream shops. This is the sign of a wider phenomenon, which is the absence of private-sector investment in these marginal neighbourhoods. Most retailers seem to avoid poor neighbourhoods, fearing low returns on their investment, or for security reasons.

The inevitable result of neglect by residents, public authorities and the private sector is a decline in the conditions of the urban environment and a worsening of life in the neighbourhood. It may be understandable why private firms avoid an area that would not be financially rewarding for their investment. It is not clear, however, why deprived neighbourhoods should be neglected by local authorities, which in theory have to show a similar degree of concern and care for all urban areas. The unwillingness or inability of public authorities to address these problems is a sign of the changing structural parameters of European urban societies and the changing relationship between public authorities and urban populations. It is also not clear why the residents of these areas show less care towards public environments than they do towards their own private space. This lack of care is not necessarily intrinsic in low-income households, as some forms of care do not cost money. It is sometimes related to the length of residence in an area, which shows a degree of attachment and territoriality, but this is not necessarily so in all areas. Transient populations seem to pay less attention to temporary accommodation of low quality, and the public spaces around it. At other times, it is neglect by one party that triggers neglect by others: neglect spreads if the public authority or the neighbours do not look after the public environment, or if some residents effectively undo what other residents might do to care for the neighbourhood. In any case, the result of neglect by public authorities and residents is clear: a public environment that tends to be shabby and dilapidated. This degrades the quality of life in the neighbourhood, contributes to the negative image of the area, and undermines the chances of social and economic improvement.

Public space as a catalyst for change

The significance of public spaces for social cohesion and economic competitiveness is well understood. According to a former mayor of Barcelona, Pasqual Maragall, '[i]t is critical to understand that improving public space is relevant to solving social and economic problems' (quoted in Urban Task Force 1999: 5). An updated version of Stockholm's Integration Programme in 2001 (first introduced in 1997) seeks a number of features for the integrated city, including access to 'joint meeting places'. Our research showed some examples of how attention to public spaces can be a catalyst for change, through actions initiated by residents as well as by public authorities and others.

Public celebrations and group activities have been a good way to promote social integration and to fight the stigma that is often attached to disadvantaged neighbourhoods and their residents. By setting up events that can bring the people of the area together, a sense of community and confidence is promoted, while at the same time a positive image of the neighbourhood is projected to the outside world, as was the case in Walker, Newcastle, with summer festivals in the park, or the Jubilee celebrations in the streets (Figure 6.4). In Ostersbaum, Wuppertal, the staircases that connect the neighbourhood to the city centre are always littered and are considered to be dirty and dangerous. An artist's project has been set up to illuminate the Platz and the stairs by candles once a year, to show that these are areas that can be enjoyed as public spaces. In this project, institutions, professionals and residents have worked together, which has created a sense of community development.

6.4
Public celebrations have been a good way to fight stigma and bring people together (Walker, Newcastle).

In a deprived area in Coventry, the forming of a football team in the park was a catalyst for bringing conflicting groups together (BBC 2003). Some refugees were starting to use the only public open space in the area. The local young people, who had played football there all their lives, considered this to be a problematic intrusion. This was indeed a classic case of competition for use of public space, leading to several fights around the use of the park. A local man organized a football team for the refugees, and he was able to persuade some local residents to join the team. The ability of the two groups to play together enabled them to come to terms with each other better. Their football team became strong enough to defeat an established local team.

Attention to public spaces by public authorities and community groups can improve the quality of environment for local residents. In Berlin, to reintegrate the divided city, central public spaces such as Potsdamer Platz are the focus of attention, and attention to public spaces in marginal neighbourhoods has been rare. However, a community development project in the Wedding district, the Kommunales Forum, has emphasized the need for the redesign and development of the neighbourhood public spaces, to support the disadvantaged residents of the area (Figure 6.5).

Participation by residents in public space maintenance and management can be a way of improving the physical environment and developing some social capital in the neighbourhood. In Overtoomse Veld, Amsterdam, a group of Moroccan fathers organized a neighbourhood watch scheme in which they went round and tried to control the behaviour

6.5
A community development project, the Kommunales Forum, has emphasized the need for the redesign and development of the neighbourhood public spaces, to support the disadvantaged residents of the area (Wedding, Berlin).

of young people, a scheme that won national and European attention. Other specific measures have also been put in place to ensure safety, which include neighbourhood police officers, a neighbourhood concierge, a Neighbourhood Service Point and an office of Justice in the Neighbourhood. These initiatives are claimed to have stopped the growth of criminal and anti-social behaviour. A number of other initiatives were introduced, including arranging for the youth to repair what had been damaged during riots, and taking them to Morocco to see the conditions of life there. A more spontaneous example was in a deprived neighbourhood in Rotterdam. Two women put some begonias outside their house; as the flowers became vandalized by the youth, the women persisted by making new flower displays. Within two weeks, many other people in the street put flowers outside, showing solidarity with their neighbours and commitment to the neighbourhood's public environment.

In Dublin, public space improvement combined environmental improvements with job creation for the local population. St Teresa's Gardens, a small, high-density local authority complex of flats in Dublin's south-west inner city, suffered years of neglect in relation to public investment in infrastructure and the environmental regeneration of the estate, becoming an under-resourced, fragmented, alienated, isolated and marginalized community (Dublinate 2000: 1). Since its establishment in 1999, the St Teresa's Gardens Environment and Employment Project has had a significant impact through improving the quality of life of the tenants in physical, social and economic terms and creating sustainable jobs for local people. Through this project, a number of local people have been employed in improving the physical conditions of the area. The establishment of a community forum ensured that services were provided in a more efficient and integrated manner by bringing people and organizations together. Through the Environment and Employment Project, an estate management agreement has been drawn up between Dublin City Council and the residents of St Teresa's Gardens. The agreement covers such issues as maintenance of the flats and the complex in general, anti-social behaviour, future development, etc. Since the project was established, levels of anti-social behaviour, vandalism and drug dealing within St Teresa's Gardens have been greatly reduced. The level of unemployment in the area is also down.

Although many such schemes may be isolated events in the face of the massive problems these neighbourhoods are facing, they are signs of some possibilities for improvement. Public spaces can be used to bring people together to improve the quality of life and to project a positive image for a deprived neighbourhood for its residents and for the others.

These cases show how the ability to use public space in new ways, and to mobilize resources and people around their use, can bring some change in the social life of an area. As we have seen, in poor neighbourhoods, public open space is, like other resources, limited. People's ability to access other resources elsewhere is also limited, owing to lack of social and spatial mobility. With a lack of resources comes competition for them. The local poor feel threatened by the newcomers, as they have to compete for the use of limited resources. The only way to enable people to use these resources together peacefully is a framework that helps them mobilize their resources and build bridges. Public space by its nature is often neutral, which is useful in allowing different activities to take place there. However, its neutrality also means it may need extra frameworks to allow for its shared use when conflicts of interest arise.

Implications for urban design and management

Attention to the spatial qualities of the city can help in fighting some of the key urban problems. But social exclusion is a multidimensional process and these problems are caused by a host of factors, ranging from changes in the global political economy and national policies to the vulnerabilities and sensitivities of individuals. It is obvious that focusing only on the urban environment cannot be a solution to these problems, and the relative contribution of environmental factors to the fight against social exclusion should be acknowledged. At the same time, this does not mean that attention to the urban environment should be abandoned as superficial and irrelevant, as space and society are closely intertwined and the processes that shape space are at the heart of what characterizes societies.

The essential quality of public space is its accessibility: the more open and unconditional the access, the more public it becomes. This openness should include physical as well as social accessibility – access to the place and to the activities within it; without free and open access, a public space is not quite public. This open access, however, can create tensions between those who tend to use it more and the rest of the population, a potential conflict of interest and use that needs to be managed. In disadvantaged neighbourhoods, there are not many mechanisms through which to mediate and manage conflict. Although many small-scale issues are resolved through common sense, there is often a need for a system of dealing with the conflicting and incompatible uses of public spaces. The best way to achieve this is to involve the residents themselves to sort out these problems, but they may need support to set up the necessary frameworks.

Neighbourhood governance, therefore, can be improved only by developing partnerships with key stakeholders from the public, private and voluntary sectors, as well as the local residents. Good governance will be directly linked to improving the conditions of life in the neighbourhood. To ensure that public spaces are well used and well looked after, local residents need to be involved in the processes that shape the conditions of life in the neighbourhood, which can create a sense of ownership in the community. Rather than thinking that such care is someone else's responsibility, which is a widespread attitude, residents who are involved develop a sense of ownership and responsibility towards their environment. If this involvement is supported through all stages of the developing and maintaining of public spaces, it could lead to a sense of emotional attachment to the area and ensuring continuity in environmental care and quality. At the same time, it is important to emphasize that these residents are entitled to a proper level of services, equal to that enjoyed by other residents of the city.

Many disadvantaged neighbourhoods suffer from the absence of some basic services. Private-sector service providers are reluctant to enter these neighbourhoods, as the limited financial capacities of residents do not promise much return on private-sector investments. Public-sector services, while in principle equally distributed among citizens, are often under-provided in these areas. Therefore, these areas are usually in urgent need of basic services such as shops, banks, etc., which is a major challenge to neighbourhood governance. To ensure the mutual support of public spaces and public services, the two must be directly linked. By flanking public spaces, these services can contribute to the liveliness and success of the public space, while they benefit from better and safer use by residents.

The use of public arts and the staging of public events and festivals have been seen as good practice in involving local residents in their neighbourhoods, reversing the tide of stigma, creating a sense of confidence and promoting a sense of attachment to the local area. Many residents of disadvantaged neighbourhoods may feel themselves to be in transition from one place to another, without having a sense of attachment to the place where they are currently living. While this may be a general feature of city dwellers everywhere, it is a condition that is particularly hard for the socially marginal to cope with. Whether it is industrial decline or displacement that is the cause of a neighbourhood's problems, collective symbols and events in public places can inject a sense of optimism and togetherness, which is essential in the fight to turn the tide of deprivation.

This is particularly important as the challenge of integration is a long-term challenge and requires long-term solutions. It is important to acknowledge that the road to social integration often starts with economic integration. Social and cultural integration for immigrants will take a longer time, sometimes even lasting for generations, as it means adjusting to the rules and norms of a new society and for that society to learn to live with difference. Some ethnic and cultural groups wish to keep some of their distinctiveness as long as they can, rather than melting into the new society. So long as this adjustment or distinctiveness is transparent, takes place within the rule of law, follows democratic frameworks and is accompanied by full economic integration, it can add to the richness of the local society, rather than diluting it. By investing in good-quality buildings and public spaces, the city authorities facilitate this adjustment and enable some distinctions to be displayed in public. For a group to become aware of itself and to communicate with others, it is essential for it to be able to display itself in a public sphere. The public sphere, of course, goes beyond public spaces of the city; it also includes political forums and the mass media. The physical public spaces of the city, however, have their role to play.

If left to the market, the ability to pay determines where people live. This often means the poor will live in areas with lowest rent levels, resulting in a concentration of the disadvantaged population. This effect is also a result of the work of housing managers and local authority planners, who build public housing schemes or concentrate disadvantaged populations in the existing public housing areas. Throughout Europe, public housing areas have been gradually losing their initial social standing as normal housing, becoming associated with poverty and disadvantage.

Concentration of the disadvantaged households in particular parts of the city has a double-edged outcome. On the one hand, it provides the possibility that people with similar concerns and problems can relate to each other and it will be easier for the authorities to look after them in a focused way. On the other hand, the concentration of disadvantage stigmatizes a place, to the extent that other citizens and the authorities look down on these areas as trouble spots, and on their residents as second-class citizens. Sometimes it is difficult to find a job if a person's address is in the 'wrong' part of town. This can be the result of particular building styles (e.g. high-rise flats in British inner cities), sensational reporting in the popular media about particular parts of town, or the long-term presence of poverty in these areas. High-quality buildings and public spaces that do not look different, and spreading the affordable spaces across the city, can help avoid stigmatization.

Successful cities have primary public spaces that are intertwined with their general image and function. If one looks closely, however, there are also secondary public spaces that are as significant for the function and image of the city as the primary ones. In the historic cities of Europe, these secondary spaces have sometimes been embellished by monuments and have served local communities that live around them. These cities show how all neighbourhoods can be integral parts of the urban whole, and the quality of their buildings and public spaces should be as much the concern of city managers as those of the other residents of the city. A good city is good in all its aspects and not merely in its showcases.

Conclusion

Social exclusion is a multidimensional process and it needs multidimensional responses, which includes the provision of public spaces. Good-quality, well-managed public spaces can play a very important role in facilitating the social integration of the disadvantaged residents. Such places are essential in catering for the daily needs of households, providing places to meet and communicate with others, and developing a symbolic value that can create a sense of emotional attachment to the neighbourhood and the city. To function normally, many socially disadvantaged households need access to space beyond their dwellings. Most importantly, socially marginal households and individuals need places to meet others.

The acute and multidimensional vulnerabilities of weaker social groups can turn the public spaces of disadvantaged neighbourhoods into sites of conflict and disorder; at the same time, these vulnerabilities and the residents' particular needs can also be a source of strength in bringing people together and facilitating connections with the larger social environment. If urban governance functions well, public space provision and improvement should be part of an overall improvement in the management of resources in a neighbourhood. Good provision, management and maintenance of public spaces are key issues, while helping local residents to engage in their environment creates a sense of ownership and well-being. This can provide nodes for communication with others and an opportunity to display the symbols of their identity, and facilitate the feeling that they are legitimate recipients of services rather than unwelcome or abandoned inhabitants of the city. Because of their limited mobility, the residents of disadvantaged neighbourhoods are likely to use their public spaces heavily; the use of good-quality and durable designs and materials is therefore essential. So is providing institutional frameworks to reduce and resolve potential conflicts over its use. The best public spaces are the most flexible ones, which can be used for a variety of purposes. Rigid designs for single-purpose spaces are often less successful in an environment where needs vary widely.

Acknowledgements

This chapter was published in *Journal of Urban Design* (vol. 9, no. 3, pp. 267–86, October 2004), and is published here in a slightly edited form with kind permission from Taylor & Francis. An earlier version of this chapter was first presented at the AESOP/ACSP congress in Leuven in 2003. The research project on which this chapter is based was made possible through funding from the European Commission Framework 5 and the work of the following teams who have conducted the research on which this chapter is based: Eva van Kempen and Sanne Kamp (Amsterdam), Thomas Maloutas, George Kandylis and Penelope Vergou (Athens), Maria João Freitas, Joanna Feio and Catarina Matias (Cascais), Brendan Bartley and Kasey Treadwell Shine (Dublin), Gunvor Christensen and Hedvig Vestergaard (Helsingør), Judith Allen and Sheila Camp (London), Kristin Quistgard, Lina Martinson and Göran Cars (Stockholm), Liliana Padovani, Sara Carneri, Silvia Crivello and Paolo Zeppetella (Turin), Ulrich Dönitz, Christian Meyer, Stefanie Ursenbach, Ireen Stender and Vera Völker (Wuppertal), and Tanya Merridew, who worked with me on Newcastle.

Chapter 7

Gating the streets
The changing shape of public spaces in South Africa

Karina Landman

Introduction

Contemporary cities have often been referred to as 'fortress cities' (Davis 1992; Tiesdell and Oc 1998; Graham and Marvin 2001; Webster *et al.* 2002). Demand from some parts of society leads to forces that instigate major changes, leading to greater fortification and privatization in cities worldwide. It is part of a 'fortress mentality', very characteristic of many cities at the turn of the century.

The idea of urban fortification is not new. Since the earliest settlements, people have protected themselves by means of walls and gates (Mumford 1961; Kenyon 1990; Kostof 1992; Morris 1994). Yet these interventions were relatively small. The great difference between these and contemporary cities is the scale and extent of today's fortified enclaves within larger cities. The contemporary 'fortress city' is created by a combination of elements such as gated residential enclaves, shopping malls, secure office parks, gated parks and bunker-like architecture. For example, neighbourhoods or precincts are fortressed from the rest of the city through walls, gates and high-technology surveillance systems. Precincts are fortified and privatized in this way as a result of the actions of private business, large corporations, wealthier citizens and sometimes also those of local authorities (Dillion 1994; Flusty 1995; Madanipour 1996; Oc and Tiesdell 1997; Ellin 1997; Marcuse 2001; Graham and Marvin 2001). Consequently, the nature of the public realm has been changed through the privatization of public space, services and governance. Davis, referring to 'Fortress LA' and the militarization of public space in Los Angeles, describes a city in which the 'defense of luxury has given birth to an arsenal of security systems and an obsession with the policing of social boundaries through architecture' (1992: 154). In this way, gated communities contribute to the wide-scale phenomenon referred to as the loss of the public realm in contemporary cities across the world.

Similar trends are also occurring in South Africa. In response to many challenges, including high levels of crime and violence, and growing levels of fear of crime and a range of insecurities, there has been a huge growth of physical boundaries through fences and walls, burglar bars and shutters on building façades, and boomed barricades on public roads. Consequently, the urban landscape has become a tapestry of fortified and often privatized enclaves of various forms and sizes, juxtaposed with a growing number of low-income housing developments and informal settlements.

The question is whether or not this poses a problem in cities. In order to address this question, one needs to explore the relevance of public space in cities. There are many definitions of public space, highlighting different aspects such as the common ground (Carr *et al.* 1992), sharing through contact with strangers and peaceful coexistence (Walzer 1986), or free access (Tibbalds, cited in Madanipour 1996). In essence, public space can be summarized as 'space that allows all the people to have access to it and the activities within it, which is controlled by a public agency, and which is provided and managed in the public interest' (Madanipour 1996: 148).

Public space is important because it 'expresses and also conditions our public life, civic culture, everyday discourse' (Walzer, quoted in Madanipour 1996: 146). Tibbalds points out that the public realm is 'the most important part of our towns and cities. It is where the greatest amount of human contact and interaction takes place' (in Madanipour 1996: 146). It is therefore important that the development of urban public space, as part of a larger public sphere, addresses the tensions inherent in the contemporary transformation of the urban public realm and contributes to the emergence of an urbanism that promotes social integration and tolerance (Madanipour 1999: 879).

This chapter explores the transformation of public space in South Africa and its implication and meaning in that country. The first section sets the scene and explains the context of public space in the country. This is followed by a brief theoretical overview of the process of spatial transformation, introducing a conceptual framework to explain the process, and a model to interpret the nature of space in specific places. These frameworks are then applied in two case studies in South Africa, highlighting the empirical data and analysis of the findings. The penultimate section discusses the implications of these findings, paving the way for a number of conclusions related to the privatization of urban space in South Africa.

Public space in South Africa: yesterday and tomorrow

The nature and use of public space has been a contentious issue throughout the history of South Africa, since it is closely related to and can often be conceived as a product of large-scale socio-spatial engineering that goes as far back as 1656 when the Dutch settled in the Cape, and which culminated in 'high apartheid' in the second half of the twentieth century. This ideology of apartheid resulted in a struggle for the control of urban space in South African cities. As a result, planners started to carve up society into racial categories (Swilling 1991), with certain areas earmarked for specific racial groups. The apartheid policy was linked to a social system based on 'setting apart' or dividing different race groups in space. This made the power of apartheid crucially dependent on spatiality (Robinson 1996). The physical isolation of whites from other racial groups received great attention. Because of the racial dualism, the terms 'whites' and 'non-whites', evident in apartheid, were used widely, in everything from government notices to notices on park benches and public toilets. Apartheid entailed the design of a multitude of laws preventing those who were not classified as white from occupying or using declared white space (Christopher 1994). In this way, preferred social space was created and enforced through the nature of physical space.

In order to address these restricted spaces of yesterday, the present government in South Africa developed a number of policies to guide contemporary planning and design practices in the country. These include the Development Facilitation Act 1995, the Urban Development Framework (1997), and the White Paper on Spatial Planning and Land Use Management (2001) at national level and the Municipal Structures Act 1998 and Municipal Systems Act 2000 at local level. While the detail and application of these documents differ, one dominant theme emerges. All these documents support a vision for open, integrated and inclusive public spaces and include the promotion of integrated development in one way or another. This includes spatial and socio-economic integration. Spatial integration is concerned with the integration of previously disadvantaged areas with the better-performing parts of the city, and the provision of a range of facilities in underdeveloped areas. Social integration is concerned with the integration of different groups in various urban areas to allow for greater interaction and more vibrant communities, while economic integration encompasses greater accessibility to economic opportunities for all urban residents.

However, the envisioned nature of more inclusive spaces for tomorrow is currently being challenged through the proliferation of fortified spaces, fuelled by a number of drivers and pressures, including insecurity and crime. The early 1990s saw a dramatic increase in the levels of recorded crime in South Africa, to a large extent related to political violence, and this trend has continued even after the move to democracy in 1994 (Schönteich and Louw 2001). Of particular concern, though, is the high level of violence experienced, with crimes such as murder, rape and assault having among the highest incidence rates in the world (Du Plessis and Louw 2005). Despite promising decreases in the reported levels of certain crimes, they are still disturbingly high. For instance, although the murder rate decreased from almost 77 per 100,000 of the population in 1994–1995 to just under 40 in 2005–2006, it is still more than seven times the world average of 5.5 and twenty times higher than the British rate of just under 2 per 100,000 (Burger 2007). These patterns have often been attributed to a persisting 'culture of violence' in South Africa (Hamber 1999). Linked to this pervasive culture of violence is an endemic culture of fear that is prevailing in most South African cities (Dirsuweit 2002). For example, a national victim of crime survey conducted by the Institute for Security Studies (ISS) in 2003 revealed that despite the fact that South Africa's crime rates have decreased or stabilized during the past five to seven years, the public's fear of crime increased between 1998 and 2003 (Mistry 2004). As a result, urban fortification has increased tremendously in the country, including the gating of streets. This raises many questions about the nature of these changes and their impact on the urban form and function.

From space to place: a continuous process of change

According to Badenhorst (1999), those who study the relationships between social processes and spatial form are in agreement that social structure, and particularly the divisions in society, precipitate in urban structure, and that urban residential patterns act as a mirror image of the relevant society. The South African city cannot, therefore, be viewed separately from the society in which it occurs and the history of that society where it still has an impact on the present city.

Therefore, in order to understand the urban space, one has to understand the social process of urban transformation and the aspects influencing its changes. One way to understand the urban development process is to concentrate on development agencies, the structures with which they interact in the form of resources, rules and ideas, and the social and spatial contexts in which they operate (Madanipour 1996: 154). This emphasizes the close relationship between space and society: social drivers influence spatial change, leading to specific social interpretation and response.

A conceptual framework was developed in order to investigate and explain this process (Landman 2006). This framework offers a way to understand spatial transformation as a socio-spatial process. This happens through a process involving space, need, idea, order, form and meaning, and, parallel with these, the production and management of the spatial intervention in a specific context. (Space refers to the unbound natural or existing human-made space.) This does not happen randomly. It is informed by particular needs at a specific time (related to the context). The need or demand gives rise to an idea about how to address this need. This idea could relate to, for example, reigning planning or urban design trends. The idea is also the beginning of order, of structural organization to order the idea and guide form. Form is the physical manifestation of the need and idea, and takes on a particular shape, texture, size, etc., which is measurable. It reflects the character of a space and contributes to the creation of a particular place, which in turn can be modified over time. Space and place are not arbitrary. They encompass meaning. Spaces or places can therefore be 'read' and 'experienced', and can appeal to people's feelings or emotions – for example, feeling comfortable in a place, or feeling safe. In such a way, it can also influence the use of space and thus people's behavioural patterns, and consequently people can react differently to different spaces and places. Their reaction may depend on a number of predispositions, including current feelings and experiences. Places can elicit a number of responses, which in turn can add to the transformation of specific spaces if deemed appropriate by a sufficient number of supporters. This returns the cycle to the beginning, where a need arises to change existing human-made space. A range of players involved in the production and management of space influence this process, and constantly influence the need, idea, form, order and meaning in settlements. Apart from the individual blocks, the process can also be broadly divided into three key stages: existing space (context), the transformation of space, and the nature of the changed space. This is illustrated in Figure 7.1.

Although this is a highly simplified abstraction of a complex process, it offers a way to conceptualize space and place in the urban design process and understand some of the aspects involved in the process of urban transformation. It can also be argued that this is a design process that is based on an individual designer's process, and may therefore prove difficult to apply to a complex social process where many actors are involved and no one designs the outcome. While this is true, a broader interpretation will allow for a wider application, where this framework becomes a representation of multiple processes where need and demand represent a multiple range of needs, and production and management a wide range of players involved in many actions that occur simultaneously and on a constant basis. If one

7.1
A framework for investigating the making and changing of urban space.

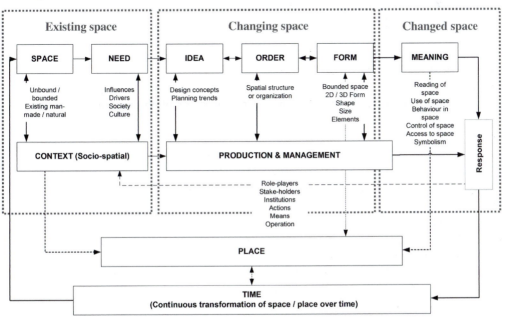

takes such a viewpoint, the framework starts to offer a way to interpret spatial transformation and design in urban areas as part of a much broader socio-spatial process, building on previous research (Boyer 1995; Liggett and Perry 1995; Madanipour 1996; Short 1996; Massey 1994, 1999).

Lastly, the framework starts to raise questions about the nature of space in cities and its relation to place. However 'amorphous' and 'intangible' our reaction whenever we feel or know space, it is typically associated with the concept of 'place' (Carmona *et al.* 2003). Therefore, places are essentially centres of meaning constructed out of lived experience (Relph 1976). By imbuing them with meaning, individuals, groups or societies change 'spaces' into 'places'; for example, Wenceslas Square is particularly meaningful to the citizens of Prague (Carmona *et al.* 2003).

Space is therefore the starting point for understanding place. For Norberg-Schultz (1980), a place is a space that has a distinct character. Relph (1976) points out that space provides the context for places, but derives its meaning from particular places. Continuous spatial transformation is a characteristic of any settlement, whether it happens relatively regularly (e.g. in large cities) or is part of a very slow process (e.g. in small rural villages) (Madanipour 1996). If the dynamism of the concept of space-time is employed, place can be understood as open and porous – 'place becomes a moment in the ever-changing social relations at all scales' (Massey, quoted in Madanipour 1996: 23).

Relph (1976) furthermore argues that 'physical setting', 'activities' and 'meaning' constitute the three basic elements of the identity of places. Building on his work, Punter and Montgomery (cited in Carmona *et al.* 2003) located the components of place and a sense of place within urban design thought (see Figure 7.2). This illustrates how urban design interventions can contribute to a sense of place. It also reflects the intricate relationship between society and space. The city, or settlement, is a stage where different actors play out their various roles (Short 1996); or, to be more specific, public space is 'the stage upon which the drama of communal life unfolds' (Carr *et al.*, quoted in Madanipour 1996: 146). These performances or interactions are socio-spatial. 'They all *take place* [emphasis in original text]. They occur in a spatial setting. Space is not just a backdrop. Space and place are crucial to what performances are given and how they are received' (Short 1996: 252).

As is pointed out in the introduction, tensions, however, emerge when over-emphasis on individual places leads to the transformation of public spaces into privatized common spaces for only a selected few through, for example, privatization and access control. This process was investigated in South Africa through the application of the conceptual framework presented above in four case studies of gated communities in Johannesburg and Pretoria. The case studies involved the use of various methods to gather empirical data, including documentation review of neighbourhood newsletters and reports from the city council, spatial analysis of

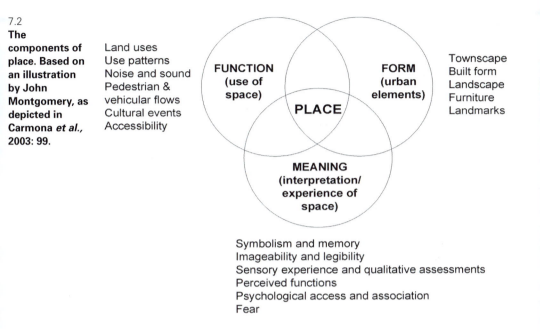

7.2
The components of place. Based on an illustration by John Montgomery, as depicted in Carmona *et al.*, 2003: 99.

Land uses
Use patterns
Noise and sound
Pedestrian &
vehicular flows
Cultural events
Accessibility

FUNCTION (use of space)

FORM (urban elements)

PLACE

Townscape
Built form
Landscape
Furniture
Landmarks

MEANING (interpretation/ experience of space)

Symbolism and memory
Imageability and legibility
Sensory experience and qualitative assessments
Perceived functions
Psychological access and association
Fear

the neighbourhoods, and semi-structured interviews with the residents, representatives from the security companies patrolling these neighbourhoods and officials from the local authority.

Transformation of public space through gated streets

The number of gated communities in South Africa, including enclosed neighbourhoods and security estates, has grown significantly in the past five years. They occur in various forms across the country and contribute to a significant transformation of the urban landscape (Landman 2003). *Large security estates* in South Africa are mostly located on the urban periphery. They offer an entire lifestyle package, including a secure environment, a range of services (garden services, refuse removal, etc.) and a variety of facilities and amenities such as golf courses, squash courts, cycle routes, hiking routes, equestrian routes and water activities. These are private developments where the entire area is developed by a private developer. These areas and buildings are physically walled or fenced off and usually have a security gate or controlled access point, with or without a security guard. The focus of this chapter, however, will be on enclosed neighbourhoods, a phrase that refers to existing neighbourhoods that have been fenced or walled in and where access is controlled or prohibited by means of gates or booms that have been erected across existing public roads. The following section briefly discusses the findings from two case studies on enclosed neighbourhoods, namely Gallo Manor in Johannesburg and Strubenkop in Pretoria, highlighting the process of transformation of public space through gating the streets.

Existing space

Physical context: existing built environment

The neighbourhood of Gallo Manor comprises 260 dwellings within the area, which is surrounded by a major sub-metropolitan road to the west, a country club with a golf course to the north and east, a secure office park to the south-east and a larger neighbourhood road to the south. The neighbourhood had ten accessible streets prior to the closure, which were mainly lower-order residential roads. The roads were laid out in a closed-road network system, with five entrance and exit points. The study area was almost entirely residential, except for a Chabad centre (Jewish place of worship), a community church and the veterinary surgery. There were no shops inside the area. There is a big shopping centre diagonally across the road.

The Strubenkop neighbourhood comprises one enclosed neighbourhood with 122 plots that are accessed from inside the enclosed area. The existing neighbourhood, north of Kings Highway (main access road into the larger residential area), was serviced by six roads. This area is almost entirely residential, except for a few small neighbourhood parks. There are no shops inside the area. There is a small shopping centre and a large sports ground just down the road.

Social context: need and idea

The most dominant need in both case-study areas was for improved safety and security. In the late 1990s, crime escalated significantly in Johannesburg, involving serious crimes such as assault, robbery and car hijackings. The fear of crime played a significant role in the community's drive for neighbourhood closure in Gallo Manor. Many residents were afraid of being hijacked as well, despite extensive target-hardening measures. As one resident explained:

> [E]specially at night, when you reversed out of your driveway and got out to open the gate, there was a certain level of nervousness about reversing into the street ... [and getting] mugged ... and after dark [if I saw a] car's headlights behind [me] and it would follow me into the area into our street, more than once I would take a drive around the blocks to see how far this car was going to follow me. But ... definitely ... you had that level of nervousness.

This is clearly indicative of the fear of crime that prevailed in the neighbourhood at that time. Residents systematically upgraded the security measures around their houses, until they came to a point where they felt they had to take additional steps to secure the neighbourhood as well. Gating the streets thus became the 'idea' to curb crime.

Incidents of crime also escalated in Pretoria in the 1990s, along with the fear of crime. There was a general perception that crime had shifted from Johannesburg to Pretoria. Consequently, the fear of crime also increased. In line with this, the most important reason given by residents for the closure in Strubenkop was safety and security. One of the older residents explained that before the closure, he had been warned not to go jogging in the evenings, since it was unsafe. He also forbade his wife to go for a stroll or even water the garden outside when he was not at home. Another resident also emphasized the crime situation and said that he was ready to move to a secure estate unless the neighbourhood streets were gated.

Apart from safety and security, residents from both case-study areas also indicated that they believed that the neighbourhood closures would benefit property prices and assist with the maintenance of public open spaces, as closing the area would reduce the number of people using the public spaces and therefore the opportunities for loitering and littering. This also reflects a need for security in a broader sense (i.e. in response to a range of insecurities) and control of neighbourhood spaces through access restriction.

Changing space
Establishment and operation
The residents in Gallo Manor made use of a specific process of community mobilization to gain support for the road closure as a means to address crime in the area. A committee was formed to address issues of crime prevention – at first to build a local police station and support the police where it could, and later to close off the roads into the area to control access. The committee prepared a budget and commissioned a traffic-impact study. At the time of the application, 90 per cent of the residents were in favour of the road closures. There were a few dissenting residents. The council received three objections to the road closure from residents staying inside the area. These residents complained about the possible traffic impact, the effectiveness of such a closure for security purposes, pedestrian access, financial obligations and the constitutionality of such an action.

The enclosed area was formally established in March 1998. In 2001, a Section 21 company was formed called the Zandfontein Farm Owners Association (Pty) Ltd. It has two directors, and the steering committee comprises seven members, each with his or her own portfolio. The committee is responsible for the ongoing management of the area and its interests. This includes financial management, membership building, park maintenance, security (including the management of the security guards) and other, related matters, for which they often have subcommittees in place. In addition, the committee also plays a lobbying role (similar to that of other Section 21 companies in Business or City Improvement Districts) by making the council aware of the needs within the area.

A similar process was followed in Strubenkop. In 1999, a group of residents came together to discuss the closure of a section of Lynnwood for security purposes. These residents registered a Section 21 company on

6 May 1999 under Section 21 of the Companies Act. The main purpose and business of the company was stated as being

> to promote the common interests of the owners and occupants of the land within the boundaries of the residents' association and to ensure the safety of the occupants by fencing and entry control and the maintenance of any electrical and communication equipment.
>
> (Report of Directors 2002: 4)

Two directors manage the company and report back to the Strubenkop Residents' Association. There were many concerns, reservations and uncertainties among the residents during the initial stages. In order to facilitate the process and address these issues, the board of trustees appointed two facilitators, who were not board members, to speak to the concerned residents. The facilitators acted as advisers as well as mediators between the newly established residents' association and the residents who had concerns about becoming members and supporting the application. After careful promotion of the idea and mobilizing community support, the residents' association managed to get 80 per cent support. The enclosed neighbourhood officially came into existence on 1 September 2001. The role of the board of trustees is to oversee the financial management and expenditure of the assets of the residents' association. In both neighbourhoods, the roads within the area are still public and remain the responsibility of the local authority to maintain and upgrade.

Changes in the physical space: fortification and access control
Three of the five entrances to Gallo Manor were closed off by gates, while two roads have controlled access points through the use of booms across the roads, which are manned by private security officers (Figure 7.3). The gates are locked permanently and prohibit entry or exit at these points. The pedestrian gates next to these gates have also been closed off for security purposes, and pedestrians are required to use either of the remaining two accessible roads. The Letaba Road entrance is retrofitted with two booms spanning both sides of the road.

Two security guards are on patrol to manage the booms and control access into the area. Two guardhouses are provided next to the entrances to serve as operational bases for the security guards. The guardhouses at the two manned entrances are temporary wooden structures located next to the road, just inside the booms. The residents' association also closed off access to the river area at both points where it crosses into the case-study area. It has since also taken responsibility for the upgrading and maintenance of the river and the park area immediately adjacent to the river, which is considered a major amenity in the area and extensively used by residents.

As mentioned before, the Strubenkop area comprises one enclosed neighbourhood with 122 plots that are accessed from inside the enclosed area. Three roads are closed off to restrict access into the neighbourhood. The result is that those plots facing inwards are located inside the enclosed area, while those facing outwards fall outside the security neighbourhood. The case-study area is bounded on the north side, where the area is adjacent to undeveloped land belonging to the University of Pretoria. A fence has been erected along the border to keep criminals out, as many incidents of crime have occurred in this area. The roads are laid out on a closed-road network system with a collection of interacting curvilinear roads.

At present, two of the three entrances are closed off by electronic gates, while Elizabeth Grove has a controlled-access point through the use of booms and gates manned by private security officers. The gates can be electronically operated by a remote control and thus prohibit entry and exit at these points. There are no pedestrian gates next to these gates, and pedestrians are required to use the main entrance. Before the closure, Protea Avenue could be accessed from two sides out of Kings Highway, on both sides of a small triangular park situated at this intersection. As part of the road closure, the left entrance and south boundary of the park have been fenced off, and electronic gates have been erected at the entrance on the right-hand side to Protea Avenue (Figure 7.4). This small park now falls within the closed-off area. This is therefore a case of privatization not only of roads but also of other public spaces. Indeed, the concern over congregation in this park seems to have been a key reason for the action in the first place. The side gates have a sign instructing pedestrians to make use of the main entrance further down the road.

7.3
**Gated street
(Jukskei Road)
in Gallo Manor.**

Changed space

Change in access to and use of neighbourhood space

Since the neighbourhood closure in Gallo Manor, a team of five security
guards works in the area at any specific time to ensure the safety of the residents in the neighbourhood. The one entrance in Satara Road is closed
during the night. The area is also serviced by a twenty-four-hour armed
patrol or reaction vehicle operated by a security guard from the security
company that mans the boomed entrances. The company also monitors and
responds to alarms at individual residences, as well as at the boom gates. In
the case of visitors, the only details recorded by the guards are the registration number, the colour and make of the car and the number of people in
the car. The reason for this is that this information can be used to provide
some independent data that the police can use in the event of a problem.

Following the neighbourhood closure, the feeling of safety
appears to be generally improved and is leading to increasing use of urban
space inside the area. Most residents agree that the neighbourhood closure
has had a positive impact on the neighbourhood's character and on the
increased use of its public spaces, as illustrated by the following remarks
made by a resident:

> The street closures and booms that were put up have made a tre-
> mendous difference to the use of the open public space. Before
> that you didn't see many people walking in the streets. You didn't
> see many couples or people [walking] with dogs. You very rarely
> saw kids playing in the street and now you see a lot of that. You

see lots of little groups of children playing in the street. In fact, about 15 metres up the road from our gate the kids are always there, and they have got little ramps for their skateboards. So there are lots more children playing, [and] you see lots more people walking around just casually.

This person stated that almost all those he referred to as using the public space were from inside the area. This meant that very few outsiders used the public space inside the neighbourhood enclosure, despite the fact that these areas officially remain public space. It indicates the extent to which one group can 'territorialize' a public area and create what is perceived as a safe environment. The closure encouraged the residents to take ownership of the common space and feel free to intervene in the management and maintenance of the spaces to some extent.

Similar trends were found in Strubenkop. Since the neighbourhood closure, the area is serviced by two security guards twenty-four hours a day. They are stationed at the main entrance and are responsible for controlling access by facilitating the entrance and exit of vehicles and pedestrians. The security guards also serve as a reaction unit and patrol the area from time to time. A patrol vehicle is stationed at the main gate for this purpose.

Residents and visitors enter the area through two different gates. Residents are issued with access discs that activate the boom at the 'residents' gate'. All visitors must complete the visitors' book unless the guard at the main gate has been notified beforehand, either in writing or by telephone, and visitors identified. Visitors are requested to complete and sign a form requiring details of the car, registration number, destination, aim of visit (i.e. 'private', 'business', 'visit', etc.). Residents are also required to make special arrangements for employees. This 'identification' takes the form of an identity card with a photograph of the employee displayed on it, as well as the details of the employer. This is despite the fact that it violates their right to freedom of access to public roads, stated in the South African Constitution. There are also strict rules regarding the removal of equipment, such as furniture, through the main gate.

Subsequent to gating the streets, the urban spaces are generally well used, even the streets, as confirmed by the residents. One resident said that he and his wife go for a walk every evening. Another resident pointed out that her children often go out into the street alone and that many children make use of the streets as extended play spaces. The transformation of the urban spaces in the neighbourhood, therefore, allows for greater use of these spaces by the residents of the neighbourhood at the expense of excluding everyone else. The neighbourhood experienced a number of changes, both in atmosphere and image, after the security access-control restrictions were implemented. One interviewee remarked, 'It is almost like a small street in the old-world countryside again. Children can really roller-skate and play ball games in the street.'

This raises the issue of the creation of a neighbourhood that reflects the characteristics of the countryside as experienced in the past. It therefore indicates the search for the creation of a rural lifestyle within the urban environment, where the community can be closer and safely gather in the streets again – a new idealization of village life within the city. Another interviewee remarked on the cleanliness of the urban spaces, and compared them to their condition before the closure, when people would leave rubbish on the pavements.

Change in urban form and function: impact on the broader environment

Gating the streets also had an impact on the broader environment. While one neighbourhood enclosure may not have a significant impact on traffic patterns, several may have, because of the ripple effect, as well as the fact that many neighbourhoods are not suited to road closure because of their layout and position within the road network system. This is evident when one considers a number of enclosed neighbourhoods in close proximity to each other. Closing off a number of neighbourhoods means that the existing urban form and road network are severely affected and transformed. Large areas are now changed into isolated and inaccessible super-blocks, with little resemblance to the original fine-grained urban form. This is evident from the case-study areas in both Johannesburg and Pretoria (Figures 7.5 and 7.6). Through traffic is also limited to a few major arterials.

Implications of spatial transformation

The previous discussion highlighted how gating urban streets in South Africa has changed the shape or form of what were previously accessible and public spaces. What also became clear is that there is a close relationship between form, function and meaning, and that changes in the form of public spaces also have direct implications for their function and meaning (Figure 7.7). This will be discussed briefly.

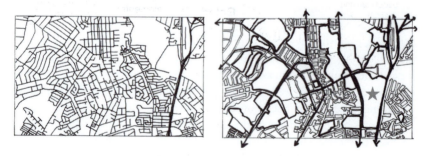

7.5
The impact of neighbourhood closures on the broader environment in northern Johannesburg (including the case-study area, marked with a star), indicating the original street pattern (left) and new urban form (right).

7.6

The impact of neighbourhood closures on the broader environment in eastern Pretoria (including the case-study area, marked with a star), indicating the existing street pattern (left) and new urban form (right).

Form

In South Africa, particular types of physical spaces were perceived to be unsafe and not suitable to a particular lifestyle, contributing to the development of new abstract concepts or ideas of what constitutes ideal space and how this would be translated to the physical realm, for example through the concept of 'gated communities'. There are various types of gated communities in South Africa, but broadly they comprise closed-off physical spaces, for example enclosed neighbourhoods created through the gating of existing streets. A number of physical elements characterize these neighbourhoods, including gates and booms, fences and walls, guardhouses and warning signs. These physical elements serve to change the existing shape of the city and transform the nature of public space on two levels related to the function (use) and meaning (visual interpretation of physical elements).

7.7
Characteristics and identity of gated places in South Africa.

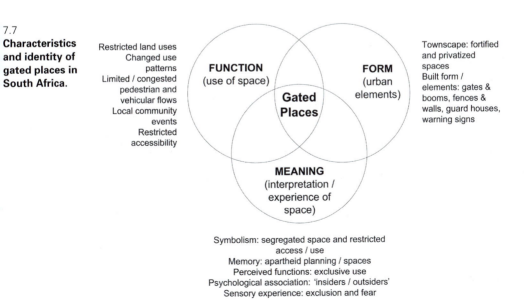

Restricted land uses
Changed use patterns
Limited / congested pedestrian and vehicular flows
Local community events
Restricted accessibility

FUNCTION (use of space)

FORM (urban elements)

Gated Places

MEANING (interpretation / experience of space)

Townscape: fortified and privatized spaces
Built form / elements: gates & booms, fences & walls, guard houses, warning signs

Symbolism: segregated space and restricted access / use
Memory: apartheid planning / spaces
Perceived functions: exclusive use
Psychological association: 'insiders / outsiders'
Sensory experience: exclusion and fear

Function

As a result of the increasing number of enclosed neighbourhoods, the physical space of the city is transformed through the creation of a series of isolated, fragmented neighbourhoods that restrict access through gated streets and limited access points, in combination with physical elements such as fences, gates and booms. This has a direct impact on use patterns for a range of affected parties. The case studies have shown that this has a severe impact on pedestrians and cyclists, as well as on traffic patterns and road maintenance. Through traffic is limited to a few major arterials, and this often leads to increased congestion and travel times. The study also indicated that pedestrian movement is often seriously affected by road closures, as not all roads provide for pedestrian movement and access (contrary to the council's policy requirements). This causes delays and increases walking distances. Gating the streets can also adversely affect access to public facilities or home-based businesses inside closed communities. The impact on pedestrians and the social impact on the larger society both raise many concerns related to the creation of more inclusive spaces for tomorrow. It also challenges the nature of the interior public space as 'free access' (a characteristic of public space, according to Tibbalds) when it is in effect hindered in practice.

In addition, larger gated neighbourhoods also contribute to problems with service delivery and the maintenance of public spaces and infrastructure inside the neighbourhood. These problems are often the result of physical changes in the road network linked to road closures, as well as difficulties in obtaining access to neighbourhoods owing to locked and unmanned gates and/or gates operated by remote control. In many instances, 'open' roads were not designed to carry the large volumes of traffic now forced onto them, which not only influences planning cycles (roads needing repairs sooner than originally planned) but also increases the maintenance cost for the city. At this stage, no provision exists for the applicants of road closures to pay the costs of the impact on the entire road network. There is also a detrimental impact on the roads within the security-restricted area, as the roads are less frequently used. Underutilized roads tend to deteriorate more rapidly, breaking up when the tar surface is not constantly compacted.

Meaning

Meaning is linked to the actual urban elements and changes in the physical space defined by order and form in the built environment. These objects emphasize perceptions or signs and significations allowing material objects to be spoken about (Lefebvre 1991). As such, they become part of the 'text' (Short 1996; Ellin 1997) of the city, allowing a multitude of readings and interpretations within the urban context. The specific physical elements associated with enclosed neighbourhoods, including the fences, gates, booms, CCTV cameras and exclusive facilities and amenities behind physical boundaries, contribute to a 'text' of exclusion within the fortress city. In this way, the 'text' refers to a series of symbols that mean something, highlighting the relationship between form, use and meaning.

Apart from the physical implications related to reduced accessibility to what legally remain public spaces, meaning also relates to the perceptions and value of places and specific typologies, such as gated neighbourhoods. It is linked to images and memory of similar applications or types in the past, representations of particular regimes, groups or actions, and even abstract perceptions of Utopia. With regard to enclosed neighbourhoods, it therefore explains the notions of 'spaces of inclusion and exclusion', 'spaces of the rich and the poor', 'new apartheid spaces' and 'idealized places' that were elicited from the responses at the public hearings on road closures that took place in both Johannesburg (in 2003) and Pretoria (in 2004). It also highlights the dilemma facing local authorities and built environment professionals regarding the appropriateness of these types of responses in contemporary South African cities.

Conclusion

The case studies have indicated that crime and insecurity give rise to increased fortification through gated streets, which in turn undermines attempts towards greater integration through the privatization of public spaces, and apparently raises the original challenge of segregation in South African cities. In this way, South African cities strongly reflect the statement by Judd (1995: 164) that 'segregation and isolation impelled by fear and anxiety are becoming fixed in urban culture'. This clearly indicates the relationship between society and physical space, as well as how various needs and ideas contribute to changes in the urban form which subsequently have different levels of meaning.

One of the main objections to enclosed neighbourhoods in South Africa is that they effectively privatize urban space and restrict access to what legally remains public space. Enclosed neighbourhoods that are based on the public approach, where streets and other facilities that are public have been enclosed, create a number of tensions in practice. The South African Constitution guarantees freedom of movement in all public space. However, it also entrenches the right to safety and security. This raises many issues around the limitations of rights of all urban residents to ensure the safety of a few within a selected geographical area. This debate remains to be challenged in the Constitutional Court, and various legal opinions have been offered, arguing both sides of the debate. Meanwhile, those whose rights are limited as a result of the changing shape of public spaces and restricted access continue to oppose the establishment of enclosed neighbourhoods in South African cities and maintain that they are changing the social space in the cities through the creation of fragmented and socially exclusive communities, as was evident from the outcry at the public hearings in both Johannesburg and Pretoria.

In summary, two issues that need consideration arise. The first debate concerns the specific persons who have suffered from gating, while the second relates to the integrity of the city as a whole and the relevance of public space that has been challenged.

Chapter 8

Public spaces within modern residential areas in Jeddah, Saudi Arabia

Khalid Nasralden Mandeli

Introduction

The decline of the public realm in cities raises salient questions about the appropriateness of public space provision within contemporary residential areas. This chapter raises these issues within the context of a country that has rapidly urbanized, highlighting the associated complexities of delivering and managing community facilities and public amenities such as public space provision. Since 1953, with the first of several economic booms after the Second World War and the beginning of commercial oil production, a diverse array of plans and strategies relating to Jeddah has been engendered, all aiming to regulate city growth and protect public spaces in the city. This accelerated development process necessitates the incorporation of modern urban planning and design concepts to meet a growing demand for new residential areas and public services. Consequently, many land subdivisions involving speculation occurred over a short period of time and pushed outward into the peripheral areas of cities. The problem is that the practice of public space provision within modern residential areas in Jeddah does not correspond well to its users and context. Such practice may succeed in providing picturesque areas that are easily constructed and maintained, but it does not create places that might contribute to the enhancement of public life. The purpose of this chapter is to seek an understanding of how the current state of public spaces within modern residential areas in Jeddah City (MRAJ) came about. My aim is to develop an analytical model that will, in the end, help shape urban design principles for the future provision of public spaces that better match the needs of those for whom they are designed.

Problems associated with contemporary public space provision

Many people have criticized the incompatibility of recent instrumental urban planning and design approaches with local communities and contexts. Many have argued that the abstraction and geometry of these approaches tend to be premised on patterns of urban environment rather on economic, social or functional arguments that generate urban settings (Lang 1996; Carmona *et al.* 2003). As is pointed out by Madanipour (2007: 4), dissenting views on producing the city in general and the fragmentary process of making spatial fabric in particular have generated 'multiple and disengaged geometries' as well as polarized urban spaces that do not pay enough attention to social and physical context. These aspects of the contemporary urban environment brought a resurgence of procedural theorizing and studies from social scientists and urban specialists, who questioned the basic assumptions that underlay previous criticisms of public space provision. While some writers linked the problem of public spaces to methods of regulating larger-scale urban developments that failed to provide social environments, others saw the problem in terms of deficiencies in micro-spatial planning and details of architecture and urban design.

Regarding the impact made by the increasing scale of development and the heterogeneity of modern residential areas, Kevin Lynch, who strongly criticized the scientific and rational approach to city planning, argued that dividing the city into a series of residential areas is 'futile' and does not support social integration (1981: 401). Punter (1991) argues that the functional separation of modern urban developments is intended to encourage spatial fragmentation and to reduce relations between people and public spaces to a bare minimum. Oscar Newman (1972) argues that spatial fragmentation not only exposes residents to higher levels of risk from traffic, noise and other urban hazards but also increases residents' perceptions of vulnerability to criminal and sub-criminal activities, as well as to actual levels of anti-social behaviour. Therefore, awareness of risk, fear of victimization and fear about the outdoor environment are heightened and rendered common in the rhythms of the daily lives of the inhabitants of residential environments. William Whyte (1956: 46–7) argued that the modern urban environment has become 'a place of boring homogeneity in which individuality was progressively eroded away and rich human interaction was lacking'. Others (e.g. Hayden 1995; Mitchell 1996; Meyers 2003) suggest that increased mobility has enabled people to move away from their communities, and that this in turn has reduced the role of public spaces as media in which individual and group identities are developed.

Other writers have highlighted the deficiency of micro-spatial planning and the issue of public space management as the main causes of decline in the public realm. Kallus (2001) argues that physical planners often focus on abstract morphological qualities of the urban environment, ignoring the urban experience and the subjective perception of urban spaces; they also disregard the different socio-cultural specificities of those who use these spaces. As a result of a misconception of the importance of public spaces, abstract landscapes following the geometric scheme of the basic layout of the land subdivision are designated as play areas and public parks that make no positive contribution to the surroundings or their users

(Trancik 1986). De-Magalhaes and Carmona (2006: 302) point out the rigid and unimaginative nature of public space provision and the fact that management has treated public spaces as 'mono-functional containers of facilities, infrastructure or movement corridors', rather than viewing them as places that promote liveability in urban areas. Furthermore, they argue that the decline of the state of public spaces can be linked to the reduction in spending on their maintenance. Consequently, these open spaces (especially the ones positioned in isolated areas) support activities such as littering, vandalism and anti-social behaviour; they have thus caused deterioration in the quality of the urban environment, as well as a general decline in the public realm.

From a socio-cultural point of view, Gehl (1987) argues that public spaces between buildings in traditional communities helped establish a sense of community. Madanipour (1992) points out that, while public spaces in traditional cities played the role of arenas for social communication and interaction, the spatial and social fragmentation of today's cities has led to a decline in the use and vitality of these spaces. Similarly, Williams (2005: 203) has stated that 'the division of space and circulatory systems in communities appeared to be the key factors influencing social interaction'. Ford (1999) likewise points out that the spatial arrangement of residential areas and street layouts and morphology are responsible for social fragmentation and work against the creation of a neighbourhood atmosphere. Others (e.g. Clayden et al. 2006; Lichtenberg et al. 2007) argue that segregation between the open spaces and residences by streets has made these spaces less accessible and more dangerous for pedestrian movement, and this in turn negatively affects the liveability and general health of residential areas. Pasaogullari and Doratli (2004) argue that public spaces lost their significance as urban planners neglected their importance in the city's public life and in increasing a sense of community and civic pride.

As stated previously, the spatial, socio-cultural and institutional changes that have occurred in western cities have had a direct impact on generating fragmented societies and residential areas with poor-quality public spaces, spreading fragmentation throughout society as whole. These issues, which impede the provision of public open spaces in western countries, are crucial for our understanding of the problems that exist for public spaces within contemporary residential areas in Saudi Arabian cities. Previous studies of Saudi cities (e.g. Bokhari 1978; Akbar 1981; Al-Hathloul 1981; Al-Nowaiser 1982; Abu-Ghazzeh 1997; Eben-Saleh 2002) show that the urbanization process and modern planning and design regulations have produced socially diverse communities with fragmented structures and free-standing buildings that invade privacy and disturb communal responsibility. Similarly, the design criteria for public space provision are mainly concerned with the objective quality of public space, proposing standards, sizes and locations for public space from a purely physical planning point of view. Such a limited scope of action and restricted understanding of urban needs combined with poor management systems has made it difficult to create attractive public spaces. As noted earlier, the purpose of the present research is to understand how the current state of public spaces within modern residential areas in Jeddah City (MRAJ) came about, dissecting different aspects concerning planning, design and management as undertaken by the stakeholders involved in public space provision. A greater understanding of the physical and non-physical properties that contribute to delivering high-quality public spaces is needed in order to enable local authorities and their professionals to play a more effective role in enhancing the quality of the public realm within this context.

Research method: case study

This study draws on an exploratory study undertaken in public spaces within three residential areas in Jeddah. In Jeddah, problems of poor-quality public spaces within modern residential areas seem to beset the public realm. Therefore, the city has been chosen in order to provide a useful lens to throw light on the subject of this research. The fieldwork took place during the period from 18 June to 10 September 2006. During this period, the decision was taken to investigate a small number of public spaces located in selected neighbourhoods and to conduct thirty in-depth interviews with residents and key actors in the different processes of public space provision. The fieldwork strategy utilized the qualitative approach and the visual perception technique in order to describe the physical attributes of the residential areas as well as the nature and allocation of public spaces within them, and to assess the problems of public space provision. In order to investigate differences in the usage patterns of public spaces, the urban tissue and building density of the selected residential areas represent existing contrasts in building densities within Jeddah's modern districts. In addition to the advantages of multiple case studies, the extreme case studies were essential to satisfy the inductive purposes of the study and to help the researcher specify the contemporary conditions of public spaces within this context, identifying commonalities and similarities among them.

The city profile

Jeddah is located in the western region of Saudi Arabia, situated on the coastal plain, called Tihama, along the Red Sea. It is the major urban centre of western Saudi Arabia and the second largest city in the country. The harbour in the city, from which pilgrim routes radiate inland to the holiest places of Islam, Makkah and Medina, has made it the primary commercial centre in the country (Figure 8.1).

For many centuries, Jeddah society remained closed and traditional. This changed with the start of Saudi rule, when Jeddah joined the kingdom in 1927. Social order in the city was homeostatic, adhering to the rules of the Islamic religion and Arab custom. Similarly, the culture, which drew upon Islamic values, was well integrated. For a long time, Jeddah

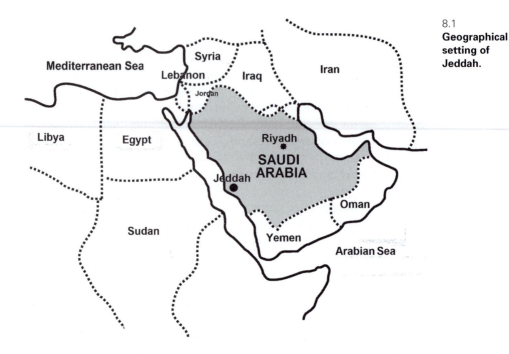

8.1
**Geographical
setting of
Jeddah.**

served as a diplomatic, commercial, distribution and service centre. Following the discovery and export of oil in 1938, the general wealth of the country increased dramatically. Jeddah grew at an amazing rate, both in population and in the extent of the urbanized area. The estimated population of the city in 1947 was about 24,000 inhabitants within the city walls. After that, a series of events coincided to lift that figure to 2.8 million by 2005 (Municipality 2006). These events included the demolition of Jeddah's outer wall, allowing the city to spread, and the sudden influx of vast oil wealth into the country.

As was the case in all major cities in the kingdom, the process of transformation of the physical environment in Jeddah was accelerated by the intensification of rural–urban migration as a result of the rapid economic boom that started after the demolition of the city walls in 1947. From that time, the dynamic of the urban growth of Jeddah changed as the city expanded. The emergence of both formal and informal settlements outside city walls occurred as a result of the massive growth of its population. In addition to demographic pressure, the availability of huge financial resources and the desire of the government to modernize the urban infrastructure led to a substantial transformation of the city. Consequently, in a short period of time the face of the city was transformed into a grid arterial network, which was a major step in laying the foundation for future expansion of the city's administrative boundary (Bokhari 1978; Daghistani 1991; Mandeli 2008).

In Jeddah, in an attempt to secure early amelioration of the most serious urban problems, such as the acute shortage of affordable housing and public amenities, traffic congestion, the unbalanced urban expansion and the proliferation of informal settlements, in 1971, after the approval of the First Five-Year National Development Plan (1970–1975), the Ministry of the Interior's Department of Municipal Affairs appointed international consultants Robert Matthew, Johnson-Marshall & Partners to prepare a comprehensive master plan for Jeddah that could be utilized as an official tool for guiding different sectoral programmes. A principal objective of the master plan was to subdivide the city into various districts separated by arterial-grid streets in order to provide formal access to land and easement for infrastructures. The implementation of the master plan's objectives was facilitated by a set of planning regulations framed under zoning ordinances and land subdivision codes (Aziz-Alrahman 1985). During this stage (1970–1980), the city had undergone widespread urban sprawl. As a consequence of rapid urban growth, Jeddah witnessed a substantial flow of new immigrants to the suburbs, where the cost of living is more affordable for newcomers. People from around the country as well as other countries have come together in a relatively short period of time to constitute a sprawling metropolis. As a result, the spatial coverage of the city expanded dramatically to an area of over 367 square kilometres in 1987 (Municipality 2004).

Although the approval of the Jeddah master plans was considered the most important step taken in planning and regulating the city's growth, it lacked the overall perspective of the urbanization process at a national level (Alkhedheiri 2002). This in turn led to imperfect buildings being constructed in inappropriate locations and the creation of undesirable urban sprawl, such as the informal housing development in hilly areas to the east of the city, which were designated at that time as areas located outside the city administrative boundary (Montgomery 1986; Mandeli 2008). Moreover, it also led to widespread subdivisions and undeveloped land as the owners speculated for higher future values (Montgomery 1986; Daghistani 1993). Today, most communities live within large metropolitan agglomerations. Meanwhile, the city continues to suffer from the transformation of the traditional urban fabric, acute social polarization, high land and property values, heavy traffic congestion and lack of urban infrastructure. The lack of urban infrastructure and the fragmentation of urban fabric of the MRAJ have resulted in a transformation in the experience of urban life that has greatly affected the quality of life of residential areas in general and the form, use and meaning of public space within this context. The following section outlines the present state of these spaces in Jeddah.

Public space within modern residential areas in Jeddah

In Jeddah, after the preparation of the first master plan in 1973, the municipality adopted building and zoning regulations as the basis for managing the social and physical developments. The unimaginative nature of master-planning and the deployment of zoning have produced new street systems and fostered the geographical separation of people into different types of residential environments. Consequently, the current state of public spaces within these residential areas has been negatively influenced by the professional preoccupation of city planners with the idea of reinforcing the grid street system and the functional dimension of the built environment. The allocation of public space for recreational purposes within residential areas typically takes place in the approval process of the land subdivision by the municipality. Principally, the professional cadre of the municipality requires 33 per cent of the subdivided land to be reserved for streets and public amenities such as parks, playgrounds, mosques and schools. Although this percentage is clearly stated in the land subdivision regulations, it is not very often respected. Consequently, this reduces the required amount of public space for recreational proposes. Additionally, looking carefully at the subdivisions of MRAJ, one can see that the majority of the public spaces are provided with a geometrical shape that is repeated many times throughout the modern residential areas. Not only do these spaces tend to be isolated from their surroundings by asphalt streets with narrow pavements, but also they are also seldom used because they are positioned in residual areas where the residents need them the least. Broadly speaking, public space allocation within the MRAJ is the result of decisions made by the officials and professionals of the municipality who were involved directly in the approval process of land subdivisions for these areas. As is elaborated in greater detail in the following sections, such involvement has raised issues of the responsiveness and appropriateness of public spaces within these areas for their users and context.

Public spaces in al-Sharafeyah district

In the 1950s, the government developed a new land subdivision and defined the urban configuration of this area. This subdivision was laid out primarily on a grid street system. The housing consists of two-storey detached villas and apartment buildings ranging from four storeys within the residential quarter up to ten along the major roads. The typical lot size was 25 × 25 metres and most blocks were 50 × 50 metres. The district is surrounded by major traffic arteries, which connect to local roads and link the district with other parts of the city. Whereas the width of east–west local roads was 10 metres, the north–south streets were 15 metres wide. Looking carefully at the subdivision of al-Sharafeyah, one can see that there is very little land allocated for public recreational space and green areas. In most cases, the available public spaces are found to be unlinked and dispersed throughout the district. During the 1980s, high-rise housing was constructed in the southern section of the district through the Ministry of Housing and Public Works. The housing units, which were mostly in the form of apartments within high-rise buildings, have been occupied since 1991. While the magnitude of the high-rise housing projects created high-density residential quarters within the district, the existing single-family housing units occupied larger land lots to create lower-density residential quarters. The major streets of the district have developed dynamic retail strips and high-rise office buildings to take advantage of the facilities offered by the major traffic arteries. Broadly, in al-Sharafeyah there are five types of public space. These are the streets, public parks, squares, linear commercial spaces and leftover areas such as the raised areas that function as protection zones for bridges and median islands for major dual carriageways.

Public space in marginalized areas

Despite the fact that the municipality attempted to tackle the lack of public space in this district by acquiring some undeveloped land designated for this purpose, its efforts were not well rewarded. It was obliged to use marginal areas and finish them with some landscape elements and children's playground equipment. These areas now form a residual space located in the northern margin of the district close to heavy traffic and noise – somewhere nobody wants to visit (Figure 8.2).

8.2
Public spaces in marginalized areas are often desolate places.

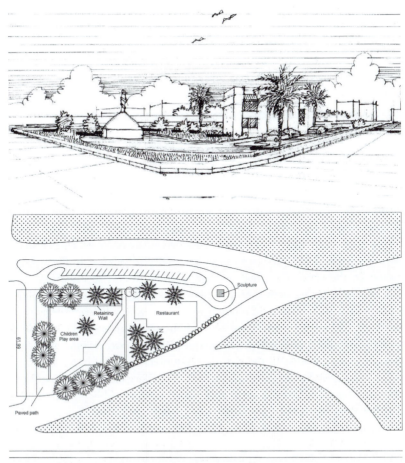

KING FAHAD STREET

This example provides clear evidence of how the allocation of space and the type of construction material used are usually determined by municipality professionals on the basis of their technical knowledge and expertise. As providers and regulators of public space, municipality officials and professionals decide what should be provided, when and where. It was clear from our interviews with residents that their role in determining the outcome of the construction process was minimal. Consequently, even if municipal constructions are of high quality, they tend to be underestimated by residents, who recognize that their outdoor environment has been designed in a way that does not correspond to their actual needs and expectations.

A visual survey of public spaces within the residential clusters throughout this district indicates that in constructing these spaces, the municipality and its contractors usually surround the space with concrete pavements, plant trees and grass, set up irrigation systems, install playground equipment and swings, construct pedestrian paths using tiles, provide concert benches for adults, and set up lighting. The lack of identification with physical space on the part of residents has influenced the way they perceive these spaces, since they think that they have no meaningful representation to reveal their aspirations and expectations for an attractive urban setting. Consequently, the construction and landscaping of observed public spaces initiated by the municipality have declined in quality.

Apartment tower park

As was noted earlier, during the 1980s the government constructed a large-scale housing project in the southern section of al-Sharafeyah district through the Ministry of Housing and Public Works. The design of the project was based on the concept of the 'superblock'. All buildings are identical in terms of design, so it is difficult to discern any differences. Within this housing project, there is a central, rectangular-shaped public space covering an area of 20,800 square metres, one of the areas on which this study draws (Figure 8.3). The design features were used to achieve an inward orientation of the space with high enclosing walls (high-rise buildings) and blank façades together with central access. Moreover, this space resembles a formal park with symmetrical relationships between its different parts. The rigidity of the axial organization of buildings, the arrangement of plant materials and the uniformity of access routes and pathways signify harmony, in sharp contrast to the chaotic residential areas in the south of the project region. In general, these features – as argued by Banerjee and Loukaitou-Sideris (1992) in their analysis of similar public spaces in Los Angeles – seem to encourage solitude and meditation rather than spontaneous human activities. To ensure safety in the project through the separation of pedestrians and cars, access roads were laid out as culs-de-sac or collector loops. Although this space is not car-oriented, since it acts as a traffic calming device, access by car is possible.

8.3
**The
monotonous
visual
appearance of
an apartment
tower park in
al-Sharafeyah.**

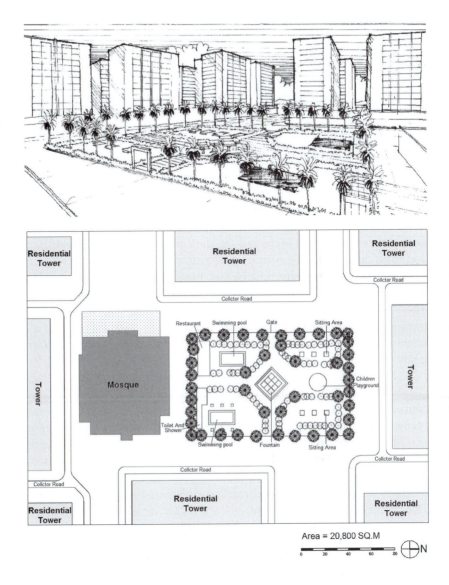

Our field observation also indicates that although the central park provides users with a relatively high-quality environment, the experience of pedestrians can become unpleasant, for several reasons. Among these is the lack of meaningful variety in the design of the apartment towers, which look exactly the same from all angles. This has given the park a monotonous visual appearance. It was intended by the designers of this project that the uniformity of the apartment towers would enrich the liveability of the park. As indicated in similar observations (e.g. Newman 1972), because the relationship between the park and the tower buildings is not clearly identified, the park becomes an open congregation area controlled by no particular group. From a social point of view, the hetero-geneity of the residents of the multi-storey apartment buildings played a significant role in reducing social interaction in terms of spontaneous sta-tionary activities such as socializing in communal spaces. Our field observa-tion also revealed that the anti-social behaviour of the users of outdoor areas is considered one of the major problems with this urban setting. Because of the lack of any natural surveillance of the surrounding outdoor areas, together with the high density and heterogeneity of the inhabitants, the park and the spaces that lie adjacent to the apartment towers become spaces given over to anti-social behaviour.

The detailed accounts given by the residents clearly indicate that fear of crime is a major contributor to the way they perceive and use the central park, or the outdoor spaces in general. One of the residents, for example, cited the blind areas and the dark places within the project site, and these, along with the deteriorating pathways, which lack natural sur-veillance or patrol security guards, and the socially mixed nature of the inhabitants, all bear a direct relationship to the inhabitants' fear of crime. These findings are not unique to this area but are supported by findings from a fairly extensive literature, which show that fear and insecurity are major factors that discourage people from gathering in outdoor places (Car-mona et al. 2003).

Interviews with the management authority indicate that the high density of the housing project makes it difficult for them to distinguish resi-dents from outsiders. This in turn fosters criminal and anti-social behaviour such as vandalism, especially in the blind areas of the project site. Addition-ally, the interviewee indicated that the management authority experiences problems with the parking habits of residents, many of whom use the public spaces or park on the pavements. In most cases, such behaviour resulted in a decline in safety measures and reduced the amount of social space avail-able. Moreover, our observation reveals that lack of maintenance is one of the major issues of this housing project. Limited financial resources to fund the maintenance process and an absence of effective management for out-door areas, together with the prevailing social atmosphere, have all resulted in the deterioration of the park and nearby outdoor areas.

Linear commercial public space

In al-Sharafeyah, there is a common attitude towards public areas adjacent to commercial developments. Although there are numerous places for the public to use for recreation, such as the pathway along the ribbon commer-cial development of the main roads, these places have been taken over by passers-by (Figure 8.4).

The undefined territories of these places have resulted in a con-flict between those who use them, and the occupiers of the adjacent residen-tial buildings, who believe their privacy is in danger from users such as passers-by and street vendors. Broadly, the potential of public spaces has

8.4
**Linear
commercial
public spaces in
al-Sharafeyah.**

not been maximized for the purposes of social interaction. The principles of designing neighbourhoods that can contribute to a high level of community interaction have been totally ignored. The stark reality of the situation was exacerbated by the straitened financial limitations, hard administrative facts, and an irresponsible attitude on the part of residents towards public environments. All these factors have resulted in the deterioration of public spaces within this district as well as in outdoor places in other districts in Jeddah.

Public spaces in al-Salamah district

The grid layout of al-Salamah district adopts a completely different pattern to that of al-Sharafeyah. A visual survey of the type of public spaces in this district indicates that compliance with the open space requirement of the land subdivision regulations was evident in the layout of the district, where there was a generous intention for the allocation of public spaces within residential blocks in accessible locations. Unlike the situation in al-Sharafeyah district, in al-Salamah these public spaces reduce block density and produce a wider organization of urban forms. Broadly speaking, most public spaces were located in a central area within the residential clusters, which most of the inhabitants can reach on foot. In al-Salamah district, there were more than thirty public spaces that were allocated for the construction of public parks within the residential blocks. These areas ranged from 1,500 to 6,000 square metres in area. Most of these spaces occurred in square or rectangular shapes and were surrounded by streets. They can be classified into two groups in terms of the density of the surrounding residential blocks: multifunctional parks, which are located within the apartment building blocks close to commercial facilities; and recreational parks, which are located within the residential blocks and remote from institutions that attract passers-by. Because of the important role that these spaces play in the quality of life in this district, the research draws on two of them which were seen to have different usage patterns.

The multi-purpose park

An example of these multifunctional public spaces is a public park located on Al-Jesser Street adjacent to ribbon commercial facilities along Ibn Sina Road, one of the major traffic arteries in the district. The park has a rectangular shape and covers an area of 5,520 square metres. It is surrounded by streets and enclosed by apartment buildings. These buildings, which are occupied by workers, not only increase the density and heterogeneity of the area but also, on account of their rigid edges and poor finish, have an unpleasant spatial character. This, in turn, has had a depressingly negative effect on the visual character of the park and the urban setting in general (Figure 8.5).

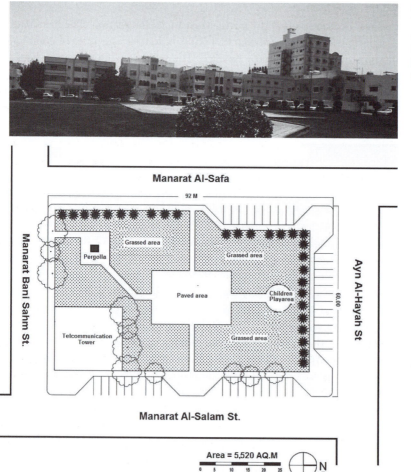

8.5
The openness of a multifunctional public space in al-Sharafeyah.

Our field observation of this park reveals that its design and construction were both carried out by the municipality contractor. Based on the prevailing design-led beautification practice of public space provision, which is rooted in the romantic tradition of the picturesque in English art and has since been applied to any public space, the park grassed over, with pathways cutting through the grass, allowing cross-circulation access (J. B. Jackson 1994; Jivan and Larkham 2003). Following the grid pattern, the geometry of the park took a rectangular shape. The axial composition of the park was reinforced by the kerbs of the surrounding asphalted streets, which are connected to cross-circulation access points. It was further reinforced by the creation of a central paved square-shaped sitting area near a circular sandy playground. In addition to the arrangement of plant materials, these features encourage solitude and meditation rather than spontaneous human activities. In broad terms, the poor-quality materials chosen by the municipality in constructing this park and the arrangement of its landscape elements do not present an aesthetically pleasing image, nor do they convey any social or cultural meaning.

Morphologically, the geometry of the park can be conceived as being isolated from the surrounding buildings rather than being a direct extension of them. This can be attributed to a lack of connection and harmony between the way the park is structured and the impoverished architectural vocabulary of the surrounding buildings. Moreover, the façades of the surrounding free-standing buildings belong to neither the street nor the park, which has in turn degraded the quality of the streetscape. Although these façades varied in shape, their inconsistent styles and poor finish were not enough to invigorate the visual appearance of the park setting in general. Additionally, although the park is aligned against the surrounding buildings, the proportion of the park to building height does not help in the creation of an enclosed space or to establish what Cullen (1971) refers to as a 'sequential experience'. In other words, the park is too open to be perceived as an enclosed public space, or to establish what Trancik (1986) called a coherent space.

The prime location of the park and its proximity to commercial activities attract inhabitants of other nearby residential areas as well as passers-by and cars. Though there is considerable private–public interaction between the park and people, the close proximity of this park to commercial facilities and the heavy traffic fumes and noise around it have contributed towards a hostile environment for those who use it. Moreover, passers-by and street vendors, who are attracted by the commercial facilities (such as garbage diggers who rummage through the bins in search of recyclable items, which they then sell at recycling centres), impaired the safety and security of the adjacent residential blocks. An interview with one resident revealed that they all suffered from frequent burglaries linked to the commercial premises. Consequently – as was made clear by the residents – a lack of sense of place and local group identity, combined with the generally elusive quality of this park, negatively affects the emotional experiences of pedestrians (Jivan and Larkham 2003). This in turn discourages them from visiting the park on a regular basis.

The residential urban park

A good example of a residential park is Basketball Park, which we have selected as another case study. This park is located within residential blocks with a rectangular shape and covers an area of 6,138 square metres (Figure 8.6).

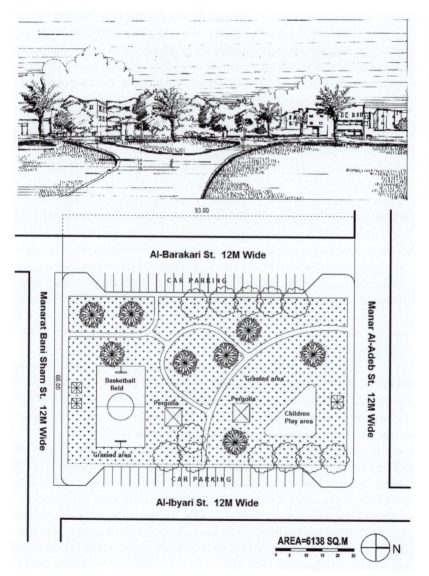

8.6
The basketball fields in al-Salamah district provide an example of residential urban parks that can be conceived of as a square isolated from the surrounding buildings.

As was the case for the multi-purpose park mentioned previously, this one is also defined by the edges of the buildings and the kerbs of the surrounding streets. In terms of design, the park is divided into smaller compartments by curvilinear pathways so that a person can move from one setting to another. Looking carefully at the way this park has been arranged, one can tell that the designer (the municipality's own contractor) did not think carefully about the intended uses of the park. More to the point, it is difficult to know whether his intention had been to create an urban park that would serve what Kevin Lynch (1981: 442) calls 'leisurely and informal activities' such as social gatherings, walking, running and sitting; or whether he planned to establish a playing field and playground that could accommodate the leisure activities of children and adults alike.

Likewise, we do not know whether the inclusion of grassed areas within this park (as discussed by Clare Marcus and Wendy Sarkissian (1986) in their analysis of similar projects) is mainly for appearance or is also meant for children. Another example is the way the footpaths are planned: it is not obvious whether the designer intended to accommodate predictable patterns of pedestrian behaviour or whether he planned to facilitate use and maintenance. Broadly speaking, the way the park is furnished with standard children's play equipment and with basketball fields and grassed areas equally does not show whether the park was originally intended to serve passive or active recreation.

Morphologically, the problem is not only related to the way the park has been designed; it may also be attributed to its location, which can be conceived as a square isolated from the surrounding buildings. The existence of the surrounding streets that reduce accessibility, the rigid edges and the poor quality of the finish of the buildings that act as a boundary to the park, the deficiency in the dimensional proportion of the size of the park when set against the height of the surrounding buildings, and the lack of symbolic references in the park composition to its context are all features that do not contribute to what Carmona and his collaborators (2003) argue is the vitality of public spaces, nor do they create a pleasant spatial character for the park. From the use of primitive plantation practices in addition to the ill-defined form of the park, one can argue that the construction of this park was an exercise in the routine aesthetic of the 'picturesque area'. Thus, it is easy to maintain, but cannot be described as a product of a coherent design process for the establishment of urban parks.

Public spaces in al-Shate'e district

According to the third Jeddah master plan, al-Shate'e district is designated as a low-density residential area. The district consists of three different land subdivisions. The layouts of these subdivisions are mainly based on the gridiron pattern, with rectangular and square lots, with the exception of the subdivision in the northern margin of the district, which was designed with a curvilinear street pattern.

According to the land subdivision of this district, there are more than forty plots designated as public spaces within the residential blocks. Most of these spaces are undeveloped. This can be attributed either to the limited resources of the municipality or to the fact that the municipality granted these lots to certain individuals. The existing constructed public spaces number fewer than ten. These public spaces can be classified into two groups in terms of their design. The first group consists of formal plazas, which are constructed with hard pavements, and the second are typical residential parks with soft landscaping and grassed areas. On the basis of this classification, two of these public spaces were selected as case studies. Although some areas have recently been improved by the municipality or the residents, most of these spaces are neglected, undeveloped, or developed inappropriately.

Walking trail in al-Shate'e

As a result of increasing public demand for recreational facilities in general and for footpaths in particular, the municipality of Jeddah recently constructed a public pathway for walking and jogging in a linear median island of Prince Faisal Bin Fahd Road. The width of this pathway ranges from 6 to 15 metres, cutting though a linear median covered with grass, and it runs to about 2 kilometres in length. To attract walkers to the area, the pathway was paved with attractive concrete tiles and the surrounding areas were furnished with sitting areas and planted with attractive palm trees (Figure 8.7). The success of this footpath, which encouraged not only the residents of this district but also those of other, adjacent districts, prompted the municipality to embark on a project to construct pathways in different parts of the city.

8.7
Walking trail in al-Shate'e district.

The formal plaza

One example of this is Al-Dahlan Plaza in the al-Hawamat subdivision in al-Shate'e district. The area of the site is about 4,100 square metres. This plaza has been developed with aid of a donation from a family in the district made in memory of their father. The park is located close to Abulrahman Fakieh Road and is surrounded on all sides by local roads that lead to the residential villas. The plaza takes a rectangular shape and is raised 1 metre above street level (Figure 8.8).

The site is divided into three sections. The first section has been set aside for car parking in the east and the west, the second was designated for a mosque, and the remaining section (about 2,200 square metres) is reserved for a seating area and children's playground. The entire terrace for the park is paved with concrete except for a small area that is covered with sand to serve as a children's play area (a total lot area of 30 square metres). The site is surrounded by a footpath covered by concrete tiles and aligned

8.8
Al-Shate'e, a formal plaza with elevated concrete terrace.

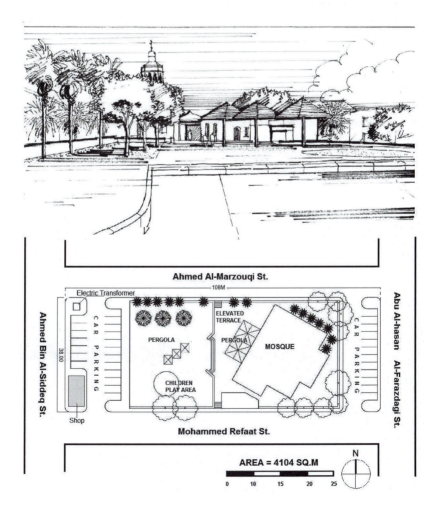

by a granite retaining wall with six steps to allow access to the seating area from three directions. Generally, the greenery is tight as the park appears to be surrounded by palm trees and some evergreen trees planted to one side to give shade to the play area and car parking. The area close to the entrance of the mosque is covered with a metal pergola. The level of the western section of the park is adjacent to the street level but set back about 8 metres and is connected to the elevated terrace by a series of steps. This level constitutes about two-thirds of the floor area of the park. About two-thirds of this terrace is open to the sky, and the remaining area, adjacent to the mosque entrance, is covered by a metal pergola.

In terms of design, the way the plaza was designed and con-structed reveals that the designer's intention was to create a supplementary area for the mosque so it could be utilized as a terrace extension for outside prayers, where worshippers might sit on special occasions, such as the Eid festivals. It could also serve as an area for social gatherings on a daily basis. A first glance at the way this space is constructed, planted and furnished gives the feeling that it is of very high quality. However, closer observation reveals that it does not have sufficient qualities to entice one to pay a second visit. Morphologically, as indicated by Clare Marcus and Wendy Sarkissian (1986) in their analysis of similar projects, the concrete terrace with the retaining wall provided a 'hard' environment, so that most of the residents perceive the seating area as impersonal, ugly and too formal. Additionally, as was the case with most of the urban parks within the MRAJ, the area can be conceived as a space set in isolation from the surrounding villas. This can be attributed to many factors, including the fact that the park was designed with little thought given to its relationship to its surroundings, it is bounded by the blank walls of the adjacent villas, there is an unbalanced dimensional proportion of the park in relation to building heights, and the formal composition of the park lacks attractive landscaping materials. Taken together, these features did not help to establish what Lynch calls experiential quality and a vivid image for the setting.

The residential urban park

The residential urban park is surrounded by villas and apartment blocks, and is adjacent to Al-Mokhtar Road. Its area is 5,280 square metres. It is one of the major parks designated as a public space in the subdivision of the district. Initially, the park was developed by the municipality but recently, with the help of donations from residents and the support of the municipal-ity, the park has improved and has been upgraded by adding some attrac-tive elements such as the basketball field and the landscaped sitting areas (Figure 8.9).

The intention of the designer (the municipality's contractor) was to construct a recreational area complete with a basketball court, play-ground equipment, seating areas, grassed areas and a small soccer field. The efforts of local authorities and the concern of the residents ended up by creating a park better than the above-mentioned formal plaza in this district. Our field observation of this park reveals that it is characterized by how it receives the direct rays of the sun. Because of this environmental factor, the park is usually used in the afternoon, one hour before sunset. Overall, the arrangement of the park has strengthened the area for public use and encouraged sociability among the children and teenagers of families from the surrounding buildings as well as the adjacent residential blocks. This can be attributed to the recent construction of the basketball court and the playing field, and the existing grassed areas, which are most appealing to people in these age groups. A wide range of behaviours was observed. Most people were usually seated near the playing fields, watching teenagers playing basketball and watching their children in the playground.

8.9
Public space in al-Shate'e developed by the residents in a way that responds to their expectations and reflects their status.

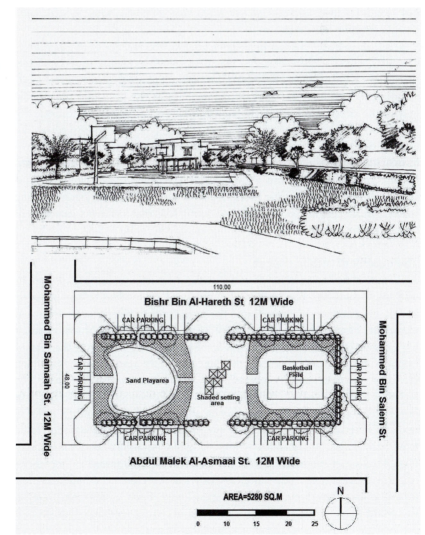

In terms of design, as is the case in most residential parks, the municipal contractor dealt with the location as an independent entity to accommodate passive recreation, based on symmetrical geometry with pathways that cut though grassed areas and are connected with the pavements of the surrounding streets. But through the intervention of the residents, who funded the improvement process, playing fields have been added to accommodate active recreation. Overall, the arrangement of different elements within the park and its general appearance had been subjected to a universal design standard. It had no identifiable character to distinguish it from other residential parks in the city. Visually, it appeared as an isolated island without any spatial definition. To tackle this issue, and in an effort to discourage fast traffic, the residents of one of the surrounding blocks paved the street next to the park with attractive concrete tiles. This direct physical intervention helped, to a certain extent, in visually connecting the park with the surrounding buildings.

Given the international styles used for the façades of the surrounding villas, none of them conveys any local symbolic significance; however, their luxury finish gives the impression of a high-quality neighbourhood. Additionally, the high standard of maintenance of the park and the cleanliness of the streets reinforce this image and help to establish an aesthetically appealing area for visitors as well as residents. This was confirmed by the qualitative research survey. For example, one male resident indicated that 'we have made all these improvements in order to show others how we really care for our children, and to show them our status'. Generally speaking, the good state of this park gives a clear indication of the importance of effective public space management as well as the significant role that residents can play in upgrading the current situation of public space within the MRAJ.

The quality of public spaces

This study aimed to examine how the quality of public spaces within modern residential areas has been negatively influenced by modern urban planning and design practices in general, and the practice of public space provision in particular. From a macro-spatial point of view, the findings of this research have shown that three major aspects seem to influence negatively the quality of public space provision. First is the huge size of the residential areas, which increases the heterogeneity of residents within the case-study areas. The second is that the existing fragmentation in urban developments does not help in the creation of well-defined territories and public spaces. And the third is that the streets are planned around the need to segregate motorized traffic from pedestrians and social activities. It could be argued that the socially diverse nature of the neighbourhoods, together with the undefined territories of public spaces, have made it difficult for residents to create a unified identity or feel a sense of community and responsibility. Such a situation played a significant role in reducing social interaction in terms of spontaneous stationary activities, such as socializing in communal spaces.

The visual survey also showed some curious differences in public space provision between the different case studies. Building density, social factors and the quality of maintenance in this respect may account for these differences. Neighbourhoods of medium density such as al-Salamah were more likely than those of either high density or low density to possess a number of features that support residents' activities in outdoor areas. This can be attributed to the proximity of public spaces to residential clusters and the moderate and socially mixed nature of the neighbourhood. It can also be attributed to the fact that high-density areas (more than 200 persons per hectare) such as al-Sharafeyah have a problem with overcrowding and have suffered from high crime rates and anti-social behaviour, whereas the low-density areas (less than 100 persons per hectare) such as al-Shate'e district suffer from some empty open spaces.

In high-density residential areas, the undefined territories within the residential areas have resulted in the emergence of an uncivilized public attitude towards the disposal of domestic waste and other activities such as littering and vandalism. Additionally, this has resulted in a conflict between those who use the areas in question and the occupants of the adjacent residential buildings, who believe their privacy is in danger from the users. Such a situation has made residents feel unable to cooperate with their neighbours to share in the creation of collective resources such as the construction and maintenance of public open spaces. Likewise, in low-density residential areas the increased distance between buildings creates tracts of widely dispersed leftover spaces that are less identifiable. Not only do the spatial characteristics of these neighbourhoods allow cars to enter, but also the way they have been designed does not allow for natural surveillance and has resulted in over-exposure to crime. This, along with the social disorder of the neighbourhood (e.g. poor maintenance, garbage and litter), reduced safety and security measures, which in turn limited both the presence of people in public spaces and the pattern of physical activities (Alfonzo *et al.* 2008).

The visual survey reveals that the practice of public space provision may succeed in providing standardized areas and abstract landscapes within residential areas that are easily constructed and maintained, but it does not provide public spaces that positively contribute to the surroundings, or promote social activities. The majority of the public spaces in the case studies have a common spatial quality, as most of them are visually isolated from surrounding residential blocks by wide streets with narrow pavements, which in turn discourages accessibility and walkability as well as other physical activities. Environmentally, the basic problem of the extreme weather conditions found in Jeddah for most of the year has not been adequately considered in the design of these spaces, most of which are often exposed to extreme heat and sun. This in turn makes them unusable during the day and affects the liveability of residential areas overall. Additionally, it could be argued that the universality of the design standards for both public spaces and their surrounding buildings does not contribute to the establishment of a sense of place and local identity. The rigidity of building edges, the uniformity of building elevations, the deficiency in the dimensional proportions of the size of public spaces when set against the height of the surrounding buildings, the lack of symbolic references to the context in the composition of these spaces, and the lack of integration in the way public spaces are constructed – all these are features that militate against a pleasant spatial character and signify a deficiency in the physical identity of the districts.

In terms of construction material, most of these spaces incorporate a large number of primitive landscape features such as trees, benches, grassed areas and paths that have been constructed in a way that discourages active recreation and does not enhance visual quality. Few of these spaces were designed to fulfil human needs, since many basic aspects of comfort, such as environmental protection and accessibility, were ignored. They are not suitable areas for families to sit in, nor are they safe for children to play in (Schmidt 2005). The study also shows that the role of local communities in constructing and maintaining processes of public spaces within their residential areas is minimal since municipality professionals and their contractors usually determine the outcome by deciding what should be provided, where and when. The lack of identification with physical space on the part of residents has influenced the way they perceive these spaces, since they think that they have no meaningful representation to reveal their aspirations and expectations for an attractive urban setting. Consequently, the construction and landscaping of the majority of public spaces within the case studies initiated by the municipality have deteriorated in quality.

The findings of this research also indicated that some public spaces are negatively influenced by the severe financial difficulties experienced by the public authorities in the provision of public services since the onset of the decline of the welfare state and the rationalization of public investments. The lack of maintenance and public investment for public spaces within the residential areas results in fewer users and makes them repel rather than attract people. The stark reality of the situation was exacerbated by an irresponsible attitude on the part of residents towards the disposal of domestic waste and other uncivilized activities such as littering and vandalism, together with the illegal use of public places. We have also seen some differences between public spaces in individual case studies. For example, while there are some spaces within al-Salamah district that have come alive and are now healthy, others such as those adjacent to commercial facilities in al-Sharafeyah and al-Salamah have been alienated from the residents and have been appropriated by street vendors.

In terms of improving public space liveability, there are many who argue that one way to achieve better public spaces is to encourage participatory planning with residents. The findings of this research support this argument for some public spaces in al-Salamah and al-Shate'e districts, where there is a remarkable level of care of outdoor areas by residents who have become aware of the importance of public spaces and have mobilized themselves to promote their development. This in turn enhances the social life of the spaces and encourages more people to interact on a daily basis. In these residential blocks within these districts, through everyday contact with each other in the mosques, residents were able to raise money in order to upgrade some public spaces within their districts. In this respect, our findings allow us to argue that the quality of public spaces within modern residential areas can be effectively enhanced by people's participation in the maintenance and management of these spaces.

Conclusion

Our research illustrates that the poor quality of public spaces within modern residential areas in Jeddah is related not only to modern land subdivision regulations regarding the designing of residential areas, but also to the way in which these spaces are constructed and maintained. Deficient design and construction, inappropriate maintenance and management together with irresponsible public attitudes led to the deterioration of these spaces within this context. As these spaces become less attractive, people are less inclined to spend time in them for social and physical activities. The findings also show that the actual practice of public space provision is to be regretted, not just on aesthetic and functional grounds but also because it is unresponsive to prevailing spatial and socio-cultural realities. All these problems raise important questions about the role of local and central authorities, as well as other stakeholders, in addressing these issues. Therefore, a clear understanding of local context, what services the community requires and why they are to be provided would reinforce attempts to deliver more satisfactory amenities, contribute to the enhancement of the public realm and address other social concerns such as anti-social behaviour and vandalism. Thus, the providers and regulators of public space within this context need to understand, first, the present situation of these spaces, and second, the relative dimensions that might affect the practice of public space provision (Madanipour 2006). More to the point, public authorities need to ensure that their intervention in regulating urban development is not based purely on technical perspectives; they need to raise the design quality of our neighbourhoods in a way that fulfils people's objective and subjective needs (Carmona *et al.* 2008).

The challenge for local and central authorities is to take into consideration the wider civic functions of public spaces. As hypothesized in the literature (e.g. Punter 2007), to improve the quality of public spaces within our neighbourhoods, full consideration should be given to how these neighbourhoods offer the potential for residents to have a greater attachment to adjacent outdoor areas; to how to encourage individuals to participate in improving their immediate surroundings; to how public spaces within residential areas become accessible, aesthetically pleasing and more sociable; and to how to reduce a sense of risk and undesirable behaviour.

Chapter 9

The design and development of public open spaces in an Iranian new town

Bahador Zamani

Public open space is fundamental to urban design. The public open spaces of many societies have played a major role in the urban environment at the neighbourhood or urban level, being meaningful settings of our social existence not only in terms of being physical entities per se but also as objects affecting the quality of our social relations and feelings towards our locality (Trancik 1986; Gehl 1987). However, in the fragmented layouts of contemporary residential communities, particularly in developing countries, public open space often has the appearance of a no man's land, depriving neighbours of places suitable for possible socialization. This is because public space in the contemporary city, in all its tidiness, is thought of as a secondary space, owned neither by the city nor by the individual (Abu-Ghazzeh 1996). This issue is deeper and more problematic in the case of Iran's new urban developments (Abbaszadegan 1999; Pakzad 2000; Golkar 2001; Poordeihimi 2003).

The background to Iran's contemporary urban development and problematic dimensions of design raise concerns about the poor characteristics of residential public open spaces, particularly in new urban settlements. Iran's new satellite towns have formed a major part of the contemporary housing environment. The housing area in this type of settlement is in turn widely recognized as a dormitory for working people. In this light, the residential streets of this area are mainly recognized as commuter routes for auto-supportive transportation; the quality of design and implementation of such spaces has been cast aside in the development process. Most Iranian research indicates that the large-scale housing projects in contemporary Iran are a quantitative response to the housing needs of people in a country with a high urbanization rate (e.g. Zanjani 1991; Tofiq 1993; Akhoundi 1996), since population growth is seen essentially as a quantitative issue. Thus, concerns about the quality of development, particularly of public open spaces, have in some instances been seen as unrealistic and therefore have not been part of the decision-making process.

Another factor in the quality of residential estates in Iran in recent years has been the car. Historically, Iranian cities were developed before vehicular traffic became pervasive, and in order to accommodate this traffic, Iran has looked to the western world for solutions. While it is appropriate to consider transferring knowledge, skills and expertise into Iran, there is much in Iranian culture and urban form that does not sit well with such a paradigm shift.

Public space: an integrated approach

Definitions of 'open spaces' deal with their roles and characteristics where, physically, open spaces are undeveloped land or water in and around urban areas (Gold 1980, cited in Woolley 2003), but are also the space and the light above this land (Tankle 1963, cited in Woolley 2003). Granz (1982, cited in Woolley 2003) argued that open spaces are wide-open areas, subject to growth. As such, urban open spaces include the city network of streets, squares, parks and green areas. Open spaces are also defined by their legal boundaries, which, as Newman (1972) has suggested, can be defined as public, semi-public (such as school playgrounds), semi-private (such as courtyards near houses) and private (gardens and homes). Free access and the term 'public' have been discussed as connoting accessibility to all, regardless of age, gender, ethnicity, physical handicap or other characteristics (Altman and Zube 1989; Light and Smith 1998).

Lynch (1992: 369) states that 'open spaces are all those regions in the environment which are open to ... freely chosen and spontaneous action'. Similarly, Rapoport emphasizes the relative freedom from obstruction or obligation that public spaces provide (1977: 119), notwithstanding the fact that some privately owned spaces are accessible to the public and vice versa (Altman and Zube 1989; Lynch 1992). Furthermore, Madanipour (2003a) argues that an accurate definition of public space may be based on the observation that public spaces in cities may be outside the boundaries of individual or small-group control, being used for a variety of functional and symbolic purposes.

Open space in public or quasi-public ownership may also be used for different activities (Gehl 1987) such as sports (Lynch 1981), and is open to spontaneous activity. More detailed notions of open space are provided by Carmona *et al.* (2003), for whom the public realm has the physical space and social activity of public life in relatively open and universal contexts. This is in contrast to private life, which is intimate, familiar and shielded (Loukaitou-Sideris *et al.* 1988). Culturally, public space often symbolizes a community and its larger society. In this regard, Francis writes that open spaces are the common ground where public culture is expressed and community life developed, reflecting the users, their private beliefs and public values (1987).

Rapoport (1986), on the other hand, proposes that urban design-ers assume not only that 'open space' means just plazas and parks but also that it refers to pedestrian activity. Yet in certain cultural contexts and for some groups, the definition of open space may be different. For example, even freeways may be used for recreation, as in recreational driving or travel. Thus, the definition of public open space is more complex and can involve factors such as culture, interest, scale, and type of activity.

'Zoning' theories of planning often resulted in socio-economic class divisions in cities, or variations in building height, and the streets around modern housing developments exemplify the rift between public and private space: access galleries, service lifts or paved space around these buildings often discourage sociability. Moreover, improvements in techno-logy and transport have changed the street beyond recognition, alienating city residents and increasing social stress, crime rates and vandalism and the associated policing costs. Clearly, any cost calculation of street renewal only in terms of fiscal effectiveness is therefore both socially and economically short-sighted.

Sennett (1994) noted the loss of confidence in public and com-munity experiences, manifested in increasing social apathy towards public life in contemporary urban societies. Loukaitou-Sideris (1988) suggested that the character of public life has also weakened, with some functions having migrated into the private sphere, leaving public space to become 'empty space' (Sennett 1994). Many argue that the modern city offers an increasingly inhospitable environment for the cultural and social uses of public space (Celik et al. 1994). Nowadays, public spaces are often residual, used for parking, or at best associated with functions such as tourism and retail (Madanipour 2003a; Celik et al. 1994).

Sharper criticism of the modernist movement can be found in Trancik's (1986) use of the term 'anti-space' and therefore 'lost space', defined as spaces that do not contribute positively to the surroundings or users. This phenomenon can be seen in North America and Europe, and Iranian new developments, though its scale is different (Abbaszadegan 1999). Trancik introduced five factors that contribute to the formation of lost spaces: automobiles, the modernist movement, zoning and renewal, the privatization of public spaces, and changing land use (1986), the first two of which have contributed most to the appearance of lost spaces in Iranian settings (Abbaszadegan 1999).

Lynch (1992) has argued for an integrated approach to the understanding of public space at the design level, with an integrated socio-spatial-symbolic understanding, which Madanipour later developed, as dis-cussed below. Benn and Gaus (1983) proposed an alternative understanding of public space, seeing it as the setting for social relations but making a dis-tinction between its private and public dimensions through the criteria of access, agency (the nature of the actions of the agents dealing with public space) and interest (whether these actions are private or public in nature).

Madanipour (2003a) suggests that this approach is too instrumental, and omits emotional and meaningful ties that allow for public spaces to be an integral part of our social and psychological existence. There is also the spatial and functional framework of how a place is organized and used, the symbolic framework of meaning and value, and how it has changed over time (ibid.). This socio-spatial-symbolic framework is the prominent theoretical underpinning of this study about public space design in newly established settlements in Iran. Following Madanipour, an integrated approach to public space is used which includes its social, physical and psychological dimensions.

This research investigates attitudes and experiences in Iranian new settlements, deals with contemporary events and concentrates on the spatial dimensions of the selected public spaces, and the attitudes of the people who inhabit them. This is the rationale behind choosing case study research (Yin 2004). This study therefore looks at the public space in three residential schemes in a new town in the Esfahan region, Pooladshahr.

To perceive how residents see and use space (the importance of which was established by Carr *et al.* (1992)), direct observation and in-depth interviews were conducted to map people's experiences in the public open spaces of new neighbourhoods, and to monitor the use of, or conflicts that emerged over the use of, these spaces. As aspirations are hard to identify by direct observation, the observation data are enhanced by semi-structured and unstructured interviews with residents.

Pooladshahr New Town

Pooladshahr (one of the three new towns in the Esfahan region) was selected as a case study in which to carry out the fieldwork and to complete the personal interviews. Several criteria were considered in selecting Esfahan as a suitable context. A high percentage of Esfahan's urban residents live in new towns, as it is where 'the new town strategy has been more vigorously applied than anywhere else in Iran' (Atash and Shirazibeheshtiha 1998). Moreover, Esfahan contains a variety of different development patterns influencing its new town development.

The new town of Pooladshahr (formerly Aryashahr), the second major contemporary company town of Iran after Abadan, was established in 1968 (PNTDC 1993). The new town of Pooladshahr was first founded for the housing of Esfahan Steel Mill factory employees and workers. After the confirmation of a comprehensive plan for the Esfahan region in 1985, the new town of Pooladshahr, with some basic changes in its construction and function, became an independent city. From 1986, the city expansion management was entrusted to its developer company (PNTDC), which was related to the Ministry of Housing and Urban Development. The town is located 25 kilometres south-west of Esfahan and has a rectangular shape extending from south-west to north-west at an angle of 45 degrees (Figure 9.1). This site is bounded by the Matbakh-Yellow Mountains, the Esfahan–Shahre-Kord highway and the lands of Felavarjan, Lenjan and some neighbouring villages, which form part of a protected area in the Esfahan comprehensive plan.

The planning and design of the town took place in two stages: first, at the time of its foundation as a company town; and second, at the time of its designation under a new government policy as a new town. At the first planning stage in 1968, Pooladshahr was designed by Iranian architects with the help of the Soviet Union for a population of 300,000 within an area measuring about 7,000 hectares (Honar va Memari 1977).

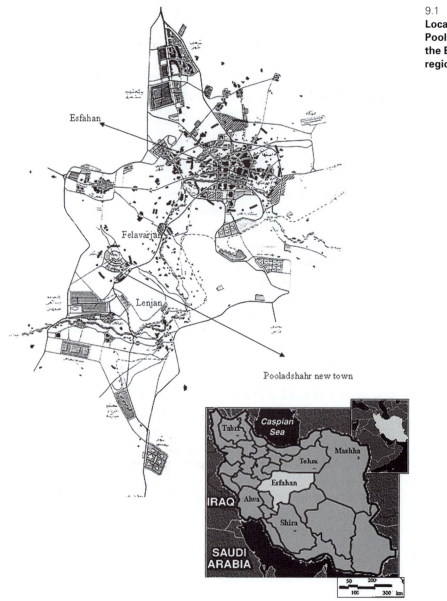

9.1
Location of Pooladshahr in the Esfahan region.

The general street pattern of the town is shaped by two networks, one in a radial and the other in a straight form, with both being integrated in a geometric order at the community level. The population of Pooladshahr had grown to about 40,000 at the time of its second planning and development stage. The city's plan was revised in 1989 under the new development policy, with the goal of converting the company town to a self-sufficient and dynamic city within the Esfahan region. To implement the new policy, the project for development and expansion of Pooladshahr New Town envisaged the incorporation of a population exceeding half a million (PNTDC 1993). Although the new policy has affected the town's role and function, it has not changed the general plan of the town except for its population density. Indeed, 200,000 more people have been accommodated within the primary site of the town in approximately the same area and design structure (ibid.). The structure of the town is based on residential neighbourhoods and a set of blocks. Generally, the town is divided into two northern zones with a chequered construction and a southern zone with a spiral construction (Figure 9.2).

9.2
Master plan for Pooladshahr.

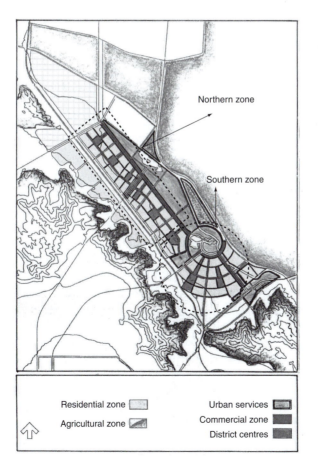

Each zone includes several districts and each district (*barzan*) includes several quarters (*mahalleh*); nine districts and fifty-five quarters were anticipated. In response to the new town's city division, the smallest units in residential areas will be populated by 5,000 persons and their daily and general needs will be provided through neighbourhood centres. Several quarters together make a residential district, which has a centre to provide for residents' substantive needs. In the comprehensive plan for Pooladshahr, in addition to the quarters' and districts' servicing centres, the city's major service centre provides services at the city level and supports the local centres. The new town of Pooladshahr now includes thirteen quarters with 18,000 residential units and a population of over 70,000 people (Talachyan 2005). At the time of this research, 70 per cent of the above quarters had been built and occupied.

At the neighbourhood scale, emphasis has been placed on the design and development of mixed dwelling types and densities, the construction of residential complexes, residential units and public facilities, as well as the construction of a street network. The residential streets are core elements used to connect, shape and harmonize the physical elements of residential neighbourhoods in the plans, whether on the scale of a small, low-density block or in the neighbourhood as a whole (PNTDC 1993).

Case-study areas: A6, B1 and B6 estates

The public spaces of three Pooladshahr neighbourhoods (A6, B1 and B6 neighbourhoods) were selected for detailed investigation. The main characteristics of these neighbourhoods will now be described.

The A6 neighbourhood was developed in the second stage of the Pooladshahr development. The neighbourhood unit of A6 (Sheikh-Bahai) was designed as a centre with a traditional pattern. However, visual observation revealed limited social interaction within its public open spaces (Figure 9.3). Strategically, the overall size of the neighbourhood was dictated by the maximum walking distance for an elderly person or a child from the neighbourhood centre to their house (PNTDC 1990). In the master plan, special attention was paid to the dwelling house and its density, the school and its distance, the neighbourhood centre and its functional centrality. There is a mixture of housing types, including two- to four-storey housing. There is also a mosque, restaurant and library in the centre, which works at the neighbourhood scale.

The B1 neighbourhood is a company (occupational) neighbourhood, which is quite complete and was designed and implemented during the first stage of the Pooladshahr development. It is located at the entrance of the town in a 58-hectare area with a population of about 8,000. This neighbourhood has mostly been populated by the engineers, technicians and workers affiliated to the Steel Mill company. This neighbourhood represents one of the best-planned neighbourhoods in the town. The low-rise buildings in the B1 neighbourhood have been accompanied by wide perspectives onto

9.3
Plan and views of the neighbourhood centre in A6.

open spaces, mostly integrated with greenery. In this neighbourhood, the service units have been located in the linear centre of the neighbourhood. The dwelling units represent two densities, including one- or two-storey units and eight- to twelve-storey free-standing blocks. In order to define the neighbourhood edges, the apartment units are located on the neighbourhood boundaries surrounding the one- or two-storey buildings. This research focuses on the neighbourhood centre and the streets and playground as its distinctive public spaces (Figure 9.4).

The B6 neighbourhood was established in 1996 to meet the housing needs of low-income residents in the southern zone of Pooladshahr. Therefore, its design was mainly concerned with the arrangement of individual dwelling blocks separated by arterial streets. This neighbourhood includes forty-seven apartment blocks, including 196 apartment units accommodating about 740 individuals. The physical structure of the neighbourhood is based on the rectangular blocks, separated by streets or green spaces (Figure 9.5).

The physical form of residential public open spaces

The open spaces at neighbourhood scale include the courts and streets between dwellings and the neighbourhood centres. In the A6 neighbourhood, public open spaces are mostly shaped in the form of square-type public gathering areas surrounded by residential blocks, and connected to the open-ended gridiron street networks. In the neighbourhood centre of A6, however, access is provided to education, recreation, religious, cultural

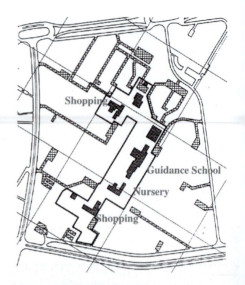

9.4
Plan and views of the neighbourhood centre in B1.

and commercial services; even substantial green spaces are provided through the established servicing centre. This shapes a special typology of public space in this neighbourhood. In the B1 neighbourhood, a neighbourhood centre with commercial, educational and recreational facilities attracts the population alongside the axes that connect two neighbourhood commercial poles. So, the neighbourhood residents use the linear paths of the neighbourhood centre to use these facilities. Apart from this centre, the public spaces also take the form of streets, playgrounds and ball game fields. In B6, because of the separated free-standing blocks, open space areas are simply left between fragmented blocks. However, an effort has been made to separate car and pedestrian routes by greenery or changes in level.

Pooladshahr's design started in the mid-1960s, and because of the length of time its development took, changes occurred to the design characteristics owing to fiscal contingencies. Although in plans Pooladshahr appears to have a very well-connected layout, the problematic phasing of the implementation process, together with inappropriate ideas that were imposed on the existing situation, led to fragmented layouts. After the revolution in 1979, with the change in political system and new government policies, the construction of Pooladshahr was no longer based on its initial plan. During the Iran–Iraq war in the 1980s, many refugees from the war

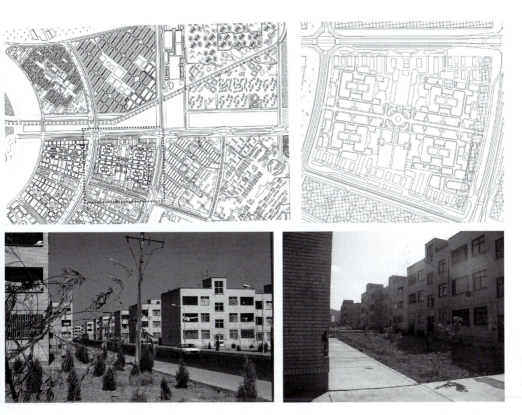

9.5
Plan and views of B6 neighbourhood.

areas came to live in this town. This accelerated the development of the town, which was again based on new ideas, giving home to many different income groups coming from various parts of the country. In the second phase of its development, the A6 neighbourhood was based on rectangular plots separated by streets which were not compatible and interconnected with the surrounding curvilinear arterial routes remaining from the first phase. Monotonous and standardized streetscape design and a low-quality implementation process have confined sociability to street spaces as the sole neighbourhood public open spaces of this neighbourhood. In B6 there is also a poor-quality community and neighbourhood-scale design; the importance of the public realm was not considered in its design process. This fact is evident through physical observation of the environmental quality of the exterior space. The objective of building more affordable residential flats led to the design of four-storey walk-up flats in brick blocks, which resulted not only in the ugliness and environmental unresponsiveness of exterior public spaces, but also in the misuse of interior public spaces. For example, because the flats are too small, residents use the staircase areas as semi-private living areas.

The appearance of buildings contributes negatively to the townscape quality of neighbourhoods in the housing estates of Pooladshahr. This is particularly visible in the case of estates that include mismatched medium-rise and low-rise buildings. The buildings' appearance and street spaces show the neglect of liveability in the public environment, resulting in a non-responsive environment. Furthermore, the lifeless and repetitive form and construction materials of exterior spaces and building appearance may undoubtedly reduce the desire of residents for social interaction.

The favourable climate and the long-term construction process mean that the Pooladshahr landscape is very rich and varied at both macro and micro levels. Our observation shows that the integration of vegetation into the residential routes has proved a considerable feature in B1, where it has created a sense of enclosure. However, one of the residents suggested that this provided teenagers with areas for anti-social behaviour. In the lay-outs such as A6, in terms of greenery, more attention has been drawn to the neighbourhood centre than to the courts or pedestrian routes. The shaping of the street landscape has mainly been achieved by means of tree planting along the verges of the street. However, in the centre of the neighbourhood the design of lawns and fountains integrated with street furniture provides users with a relatively desirable social space.

Overall, minimal or no consideration has been given to the main function of landscaping and tree planting on a street scale, or to qualities such as providing shade and protection for pedestrians and vehicles against the sun and winter winds; reducing air movement, temperature and pollution; defining spaces; providing vertical elements in the streetscape; providing screening; introducing diversity of form and colour; providing scale and identity; linking separate visual elements; providing a natural element in man-made environments; offering a sense of perspective, distance and speed; providing privacy and protection; aiding noise control; reducing the psychological impact created by an urban environment; providing a landscape corridor to conserve the original nature and wilderness of a development site; and increasing the minimal or sometimes non-existent economic value of the estate.

The traffic network in Pooladshahr is ordered generally by curvilinear and linear patterns. The main carriageway surrounds the neighbourhoods, and works as a loop in the neighbourhood. Within neighbourhoods, another traffic network gives access to the dwellings and local facilities. This network is not well connected to the main carriageways, and this fact has isolated the open space from the main network, negatively affecting the liveability of the public spaces. The pedestrian routes are commonly used by vehicles in the estates, a fact that is evidenced by the use of metal or concrete obstacles; this shows the local unacceptability of such a use of pedestrian routes. These obstacles, however, spoil the look of the streetscape of the neighbourhood.

The functional performance of public open spaces

A first glance at the documents shows that Pooladshahr seems to be of very high-quality design. However, direct observation of the town reveals limited social interaction within its public open spaces. Nevertheless, the long-term design procedure from the mid-1960s to the early 1990s created some effective physical congruities in the public realm, in the form either of streets or of other open spaces.

As stated, the idea of square-type open space, such as that in A6, shapes a special typology of public space in this neighbourhood. However, in A6 with respect to this pattern of open spaces, the presence of population in the public spaces is notably less than expected in the plan and design. This is partly because the planning for pedestrian paths was based upon the whole population, but only men are prominent users of the public space. It is worth mentioning that other parameters such as social stratification are also important in using these public centres. Furthermore, public spaces at urban district (*barzan*) and quarter (*mahalleh*) scale are not well interconnected and most of the facilities are located in a linear structure. For this reason, the quarters are understood as isolated realms because of their disconnection from other public realms at other scales.

In B6, because of the separated free-standing blocks, open spaces are left between blocks; however, an effort has been made to separate the car and pedestrian routes by greenery or changes in ground level. The central space of B1 neighbourhood has been developed in a linear form ending with two neighbourhood-scale shopping centres, which has encouraged residents to make use of this space for a range of activities including walking, cycling, sitting, chatting, playing and shopping. The rich greenery of the route between the two shopping centres, and the linear form of the centre and the establishment of various urban services along the linear pathway, have created a space with a multifunctional character, enhancing social interaction by tempting people from different age groups to shop, to play or just to be there. Moreover, being surrounded by residential dwellings creates a sense of enclosure in the centre and in turn maintains the sense of locality and privacy to some extent. The two shopping centres attract people from all over the neighbourhood and play a very important role in the liveability of the centre during the day. The spaces between the buildings are connected to the centre by the curving pedestrian-ways that interconnect the whole of the neighbourhood.

The open spaces between apartments in zones one and four in B1 were livelier than the in-between spaces of the villa houses, which is mainly due to the larger population of apartment areas. As mentioned before, the neighbourhood centre of B1 is used by different age groups owing to its multifunctionality and responses to different social activities, whereas the space between buildings in B1 is mostly used by children for playing or cycling owing to its lack of facilities, its mono-functionality and the incongruence between residents' lifestyle and the design patterns of the spaces. Although in the B1 neighbourhood the buildings have enough distance between them, there is a problem of unwanted observation into the dwellings from the passages, which intrudes on the privacy of residents, which is extremely disliked in Islamic culture. This is because the pathways penetrate the dwelling areas without any hierarchy for public, semi-public and private spaces. Residents have reacted to the sense of intrusion and lack of safety arising from this problem by keeping their curtains closed most of the time or by adding fences around their property and in effect 'privatizing' parts of the public realm. Indeed, the existing reality in this community demonstrates a negative feature of the personalization concept as developed by Bentley *et al.* (1985), and as applied by others in the urban design profession.

Another conflict observed in apartment units concerns the streetscapes. It seems that the apartment units are not occupied by the size of family unit they have been designed for. As a result of the large population in the units, the residents have changed the function of their balcony to make it part of their indoor space, which has a very negative impact on the façades of the block, and consequently on the streetscape observed from the public realm. Roofing part of the public space and using it for parking, and dividing the two-storey (duplex) villa houses into two separated units for two households with an exposed staircase in public spaces, was another change made as a result of economic demands.

The more frequently observed physical-spatial features and characteristic problems related to mass housing schemes concerning – directly or indirectly – qualitative aspects of the external built environment include confusing legibility of layout, uniformity, isolation from urban context, badly maintained semi-public and semi-private outdoor spaces, monotony, anonymity, and also being alien to users' culture and values. The repercussion of the number of standardized projects with similar problems, in its urban context, looked as damaging to neighbourhood residents as to the town as a whole. Uniformity and homogeneity among the blocks, and identical visual aspects, have been reported as affecting orientation in the scheme, sometimes making things difficult for visitors not familiar with the area.

People and neighbourhood space interrelation

In response to the question about physical condition of current neighbourhoods, residents strongly expressed the view that their neighbourhood was good in terms of urban form and spatial patterns but that these forms were also cold and isolating. The responses tended to be more abstract regarding this question, and their complaints regarding their neighbourhood tended to pinpoint government policies or performance or the technicalities of life in the neighbourhood. One resident in the A6 neighbourhood pointed out that the grid layout is good for car movement, utilities and the organization of public services. However, in his opinion the municipality or the authority should pay attention to some of the problems in terms of traffic volumes and direction, establish different-type yards and streets, and establish an identity system for the different residential districts. Also, they should be concerned about the social problems in the buildings with regard to privacy, walking distances and the provision of safe playgrounds for children's activities.

From another interviewee's point of view, the sense of isolation is partly attributed to increasing heterogeneity and population mobility. Residents also noted the loss of socio-cultural values in their districts, commenting that

> the material quality in these modern districts is pretty good. The new building materials used in the houses, in the streets, and in the utilities are practical for daily use and durable over time. However, they complain that the socio-cultural implication of the contemporary setting pattern definitely does not fit their cultural values or what they used to have before. Nevertheless, such deficiency would not prevent them from living in these districts because the times have changed and they live in the new setting with some sacrifice. This is why you see numerous conflicts, namely doing religious rites in the desert-like streets. Such ceremonies used to be done in certain open spaces called *hosseinyyeh* in the past.

This notion was confirmed in the remarks of one of the interviewees, who, although he admired the physical forms of the contemporary neighbourhood and spoke admiringly about the modernity of the neighbourhoods and their facilities, cleanliness and prestige, believed that the socio-cultural norms in his previous area were more desirable:

> I thought of moving out of this district because of the lack of strong social ties to the community. These districts are clean, spacious but from the socio-cultural standpoint the neighbourhood where I lived before coming here was superior. We knew each other and used to gather together in front of the local shops in the afternoon and talk about different issues.

The results pointed to the social relations among residents in all cases as one of the major weaknesses of these urban environments. In other words, life in the selected clusters and related public open spaces brought a feeling of status and physical well-being, accompanied by feelings of social distance and alienation.

After investigating residents' general sense and concerns about their living places, they were asked a series of questions to reveal their perception of public open spaces and how they evaluated the public open spaces of their area, and what aspects they felt were important. These interviews showed overwhelming support for the overall aims of public open space areas as perceived by respondents. When asked why they cared about public open spaces around their living places, they articulated a range of reasons addressing their social, physical and psychological needs relating to these spaces, using phrases such as 'spirit and life generators' or 'an integral part of my daily life'. As a resident commented, 'compared with houses in this neighbourhood which have boring spaces we need open spaces to refresh our spirits'. Therefore, in spite of the existing inadequacies of design and conflicts over use of the spaces, the residential public spaces are still of great importance for local residents and are noticeably being used and patronized by different user groups.

Neighbourhood public spaces and human use

Regarding the street spaces and other, related public open spaces around the home, the residents' comments indicate that transport activities, particularly by motor vehicles, are the main functions served by streets. However, the existence of other activities, such as children playing and social interactions, is also mentioned. Indeed, as was stated by many respondents, residents use the street spaces for as many of their needs as can be accommodated by the street layout and development features.

The distribution of street space use can be classified into two groups. The first group includes those activities done on a daily basis, such as parking, family activities, children playing, social activities and interaction, walking around, jogging and enjoying the fresh air, looking at various activities taking place in the street, coming and going. The second group is those done on a seasonal or annual basis, which are programmed by the city or defined by traditions or religion. In this case, the commemoration ceremony for the martyrdom of the third imam of the Shi'ite Muslims and the celebration of the birthday of the twelfth imam, which are usually held in public open spaces, are notable examples. In this type of event, people engage in a communal activity and perform certain ceremonial procedures. Therefore, activity follows a certain predicted and well-planned programme, but with the addition of individual and collective feelings and emotions through which space takes on its identity and meaning.

In general, the statements made by residents regarding the use of street space as the main public open space indicate that motor vehicle parking and movement are the main functions served by streets. For most of the residents in all cases, the street is the main space used for parking their motor vehicles. However, according to residents' responses, a large number of residents were indifferent to the use of streets for the movement and parking of motor vehicles. In addition, according to further investigation by local planning authorities, developers and residents' representatives, nobody complained about the use of local roads for parking and vehicular movement. In response to enquiries concerning the possible cause for this opinion, residents said that the streets had been mainly designed and implemented for cars and car-related activities (Figure 9.6).

9.6

Covering the area with asphalt as the last and most important phase of developing public spaces in housing clusters for serving cars.

Within the estates, public spaces concentrate leisure and sport activities close to home. Observations revealed that these were mainly used by children. Interviews revealed that their layout and design partially catered for the different needs of users. Most respondents stated that they like to meet friends or neighbours in these areas. However, adults and elderly people complained about areas, not pavements. Parents commented that they prefer to have their children playing nearby, owing to the perceived threats of accidents in the streets and injury within the playground areas.

While children and youngsters use the streets for playing, mainly on the carriageways, pavements also become a space for adults. The fact that children play outside encourages adults to go out as well. In most urban environments, it can be observed that when children are playing outside, at some point their parents also go out to watch them. This is also a reason for adults to go out to the public space and use the street and the pavement for social interaction rather than movement. In many streets, adults often go out to sit outside on the pavement on a daily basis, and more so at weekends. They sit on the pavement while their children are playing outside; they say that they sit there to watch the children, but they like to gossip and exchange their experiences (Figure 9.7).

The idea of having a public space where users could find physical features with natural beauty is described as desirable by a majority of the residents. For most of them, the type of public open space they most like is a green space for relaxation. When they were asked about the reason for this, it was found that green spaces represent not only spaces significant for their beauty, but also as places to refresh their spirit. 'I know some elderly men who come out every day and walk along the estate court park regularly

9.7
Socializing on pavements. In many streets, adults often go out, especially when the weather is good, to sit outside on the pavement.

at a certain time. It seems that it is an integral part of their life being here in the park, without which they cannot imagine being alive at all!', stated one of the residents in A6 neighbourhood. Additionally from the point of view of the settlers, neighbourhood parks and green spaces are associated with improving social interaction. Elderly people usually take care of the plants, getting involved in tidying up or watering the plants, activities that help them socialize as well as being enjoyable.

A kind of conflict exists between the usability of street spaces as determined by their layout and construction configurations, and their actual use as stated by residents. Walkability is the first area of conflict in the areas where the actual physical context was not suitable for walking. The widths and construction quality, particularly on the verges of local streets and on most of the pedestrian routes, were the main elements that caused this conflict.

The second type of conflict derives from the land-use and zoning characteristics of residential street blocks. The majority of residents desire to obtain their daily needs from places very near to their homes, particularly in the immediate local streets, and therefore do not like to go to the main community facility and recreation centres to satisfy these needs. Residents, neighbourhood members and association members demand a mixed use of micro-scale residential areas and local street-based facilities. As supported by the literature, the types of land use and zoning in most of the traditional neighbourhoods of Iranian cities show a mixed pattern at the neighbour-hood level, which is associated with vibrancy of the neighbourhoods (e.g. Naqsh-e Jahan Pars 1991).

Conclusion

The public spaces in Pooladshahr new town's residential neighbourhoods do not seem to be suitable for public life. First, the creation of large housing estate projects has not been the result of long-term planning. Most have been shaped by the pressure of population growth, in response to housing needs. Additionally, the use of modern urban planning and design ideas in Iranian new towns is not in line with the residents' way of life in, and use of, public spaces. Therefore, streets as the main public spaces in new urban environments have been used as the basis of urban development in a mechanical and socially insensitive manner. Because of this, the external spaces of dwelling places in residential neighbourhoods are not suitable for living.

Generally speaking, as a result of the rapid growth of population and rapid urbanization, the current urban planning paradigm in Iran can be characterized as a quantity-oriented one. This means that the main concern of the planning agencies is the quantifiable characteristics of the settings, which is usually expressed in a naive 'functionalist' approach with too much emphasis on the provision of motor-vehicular circulatory networks. Indeed, the urban design qualities, particularly the experiential qualities of public spaces, are virtually neglected, as the designs are concerned only with two-dimensional plans – that is, land use and the street network plan – rather than with the three- or four-dimensional phenomenon of perceived urban environment. Furthermore, looking at the ordinances and codes, which are currently the only tools to control the third dimension of urban spaces, makes it clear that these codes are mostly quantity oriented, devoid of adequate urban design and architectural meaning, and can be summed up in issues such as floor area ratio, coverage ratio, and the like.

Moreover, as was explained and demonstrated, modern urban planning and design in Iran has been unsympathetic, with very little regard for the non-physical (socio-symbolic) importance of public places. Such urban design (i.e. urban design without regard to place), by spreading monotonous, standardized and soulless urban spaces in the new developments, has led to the emergence of environmentally and socio-culturally unresponsive environments in the newly developed areas. As a result of unsympathetic physical consideration, another urban design issue raised is a total disregard for the associational and social meanings of the public places on the part of 'modernist' town planners. For the 'modernist' planners, the town and its districts have been a set of geometric 'spaces' rather than meaningful 'places' as experienced by the residents, and the failure of master plans can be partially explained on the basis of this tendency in Iranian new towns.

In sum, the need to reform the present situation, with an emphasis on pedestrian-oriented street space, the involvement of residents' views in the design and development process, and the necessity for a new neighbourhood design paradigm, is evident. Throughout this research, the importance and necessity of an integrated approach in housing environment design in the case of Iranian new towns have been underlined. Such an approach as this is inherent in the traditional housing design, but designers of new housing environments seem to ignore it.

This study investigated the characteristics of public spaces as the most tangible outcome of urban design in new neighbourhoods and addressed the socio-spatial aspects of these spaces in the daily life of users. Obviously, turning back the clock is impossible. However, modernity has affected different aspects of the residents' lifestyle. The success of the traditional forms of neighbourhood and housing environment lies in the fact that they deal successfully with their users' socio-cultural values (Hester 1984). In this regard, understanding users' socio-cultural needs is essential when establishing new housing environments.

Chapter 10

Making public space in low-income neighbourhoods in Mexico

Mauricio Hernández Bonilla

Introduction

> People made a mistake here. We managed to get into the public works programme of the municipality in 1996. The municipality was going to pave our street and we had to contribute with around 100,000 pesos. They had given us the opportunity to pay it in five instalments. We had to pay the first one of 15,000. The municipal architect came several times to negotiate with us; we had the meetings on the street and everybody came. We talked about the project, about the budget and everybody was aware of everything. However, some people agreed and some others did not; some said that it was too expensive. In this street, there are a lot of construction workers and they are supposed to know the real cost of materials and so on, so some of them started to disapprove of the budget and then other residents followed them. Finally, everybody stepped back – and look at the street, it is still unpaved; it is a shame.
>
> (Señora Yolanda, Colonia Revolución, Xalapa, Mexico)

Urban environments are produced and constructed through social processes formed by different relations between actors, negotiation strategies and decision-making occasions, resources, rules of action and ideas (Jacobs and Appleyard 1996). In any democratic urban context, negotiations between different individuals and groups occur in order to encourage urban transformation and improvement. However, the different interests and points of view of those involved can either move urban development forward, or slow down and restrict it. This public arena of social actions and relations brings about a political-democratic dimension within public space development processes, and since individuals think differently and have different interests, backgrounds, cultures and powers, oppositions and conflicts often emerge (Berman 1986; Francis 1989). Generally, there are contrasting economic, socio-political and symbolic interests and views; and from these differences, disagreements about how cities and their urban elements should be created arise (Bentley 1999). Mitchell (1995) recognizes that the struggle to maintain public spaces is also part of politics, and these struggles occur over the parks, squares, streets and pavements in our cities and towns, and they are fought through ordinary people's actions in the everyday spaces in which we live (Mitchell 1995; Cope 1996). Hence, public space is always a space of conflict; it represents a struggle over who controls it and who has access to it, who determines its make-up and how it is reproduced (Deusen 2002: 150).

In low-income urban environments in the Mexican context, residents and local authorities are immersed in socio-spatial processes in which everybody discusses the appropriateness of improvements to be carried out. What Yolanda describes, in the epigraph that starts this chapter, tells us about the opposing and contradictory opinions related to public space upgrading in a low-income peripheral neighbourhood in Mexico. It reflects the complex social interactions that occur among actors in order to achieve urban space development. Moreover, such an account demonstrates that consensus and collaboration are a vital element in making urban development possible. However, in democratic societies, when concurrence among those involved does not occur, owing to the existence of different views regarding urban improvement, transformation does not take place either. In the transformation of the urban space, different groups with different interests and roles can find themselves in tension and conflict with each other. There are contradictory opinions and actions in regard to the planning, design, construction, use and appropriation of the urban space. However, during processes of development, these contradictions often give rise to conflicts and tensions among those involved.

From this point of view, the purpose of this chapter is to discuss the conflictive social dynamics that occur in the transformation of public space in low-income urban neighbourhoods in the city of Xalapa, Mexico. Tensions emerge over the land available for public development; conflicts arise when actors discuss what they think is right for development, and the kind of interventions that should be carried out. Finally, competition occurs over the use and appropriation of the space. As a result, public space development processes are highly contested socially, spatially and symbolically.

Low-income neighbourhoods in Mexico

In Latin America, most low-income peripheral neighbourhoods are initially developed through people's spontaneous and often illegal actions of appropriation on peripheral land around consolidated urban cores. These neighbourhoods are first characterized by precarious living conditions, without any urban infrastructure, or services, or the necessary facilities for human development. In Mexico, these settlements have been called '*colonias populares*'[1] (people's neighbourhoods).

In the past few decades, large numbers of neighbourhoods have experienced gradual improvement and upgrading due to social participation and inhabitants coming together, and to the changing attitudes towards these settlements on the part of planning officials and authorities. The government has recognized the weakness of the state in providing accommodation for the new urban population, and therefore tolerates 'illegal' settlements as a way to provide housing for the poor in urban areas. Therefore, property regularization[2] and urban upgrading programmes[3] have been part of most government projects in Latin America.

Nowadays, settlements established some twenty to thirty years ago have been absorbed by continuous urban growth and have obtained ownership for the inhabitants. The vast majority of houses have reached high levels of consolidation, changing from flimsy and temporary materials to permanent, well-finished structures made from materials such as concrete. Urban services and infrastructure have been introduced and many streets have been paved. Moreover, the development of public facilities has played an important role in urban consolidation strategies.

Nevertheless, consolidation and integration have not been completely attained, especially with regard to communal open spaces. In many neighbourhoods, the spaces allocated for neighbourhood gardens, parks or playgrounds show little improvement, or are still empty and undeveloped. In spite of this, public space is a rich arena of social action where residents interact in different ways to discuss and make decisions about urban development, socialize with their neighbours on a daily basis, and celebrate people's festivities. And since there are different viewpoints regarding the use and development of the public space among neighbours and other external agents, there are usually situations that involve disagreement.

Public space research approaches in low-income urbanization

Since the 1980s, there have been studies that have dealt with the public environment in low-income neighbourhoods. In the 1980s, Vogel (1981) and Riaño (1990) focused their studies on social practices and public space appropriation in Brazil and Colombia respectively. A pioneering study of public space in low-income neighbourhoods in Latin America was carried out by Matas *et al.* (1988), who investigated the *barrios* (low-income neighbourhoods) of Santiago de Chile regarding the morphological, visual and perceptual dimensions of their neighbourhood parks and streets. Later on, in the 1990s, Riaño (1990, 1996, 1998) studied appropriation and self-build practices in public spaces for sports and recreation in the barrios of Colombia and Ecuador. Viviescas (1997), Saldarriaga (1997) and more recently Ceballos (2005) have also offered various interpretations of public space in Colombia. Rojas and Guerrero (1997) and Niño and Chaparro (1997) in Bogotá contributed with ethnographical studies of the streets and the culture of public spaces of the *barrios*. Moreover, in Chile, Segovia (1997) studied the uses and appropriation of public space in low-income neighbourhoods from a gender perspective. Bolívar (1990) as well as Pérez Valecillos (2000) in their studies in Venezuela have given us some hints about public space, affirming that there is insufficient land in the *barrios*, and open spaces for the recreation of children and the relaxation of adults have rarely been left. Only the streets serve for small meetings, which leaves a great shortage of spaces for sports and family recreation. More recently, Segovia (Segovia and Oviedo 2000; Segovia 2001) has also focused her research on public space in tackling themes about production processes, development and people's participation. Finally, Ceballos (2005) has explored the defence of public space as a meeting place for individuals and as the pre-eminent place to develop citizenship, and finally as the structuring component of urban spatiality in the Colombian planning context.

In general, these studies have made a significant contribution to the study of public space development in popular environments and take into account the prominent role of inhabitants in the development process (Figure 10.1). However, integrated approaches combining public space dynamics of development and transformation, combining social, spatial and symbolic dimensions, and examining participatory practices in public space production and consumption, have been lacking in research on low-income peripheral urban environments.

Research approach and methodology

In these circumstances, the investigation into public space development and transformation in low-income neighbourhoods in Xalapa, Mexico, is part of a doctoral research project studying the production and consumption of public space in low-income urban environments. The study is based on four interrelated notions: the physical, psychological and social dimensions; tracing the process of public space development as a social process; addressing

10.1
Public space: a street in a *barrio popular* in Bogotá, Colombia.

both individual actions and the structures that frame these actions; as well as addressing the social and physical contexts in which it takes place, as suggested by Madanipour (1996) regarding study of the urban environment. Under this conceptual umbrella, the research analyses the transformation of communal spaces in various neighbourhoods into public places through the actors' competing social relations, roles, interests and actions, carried out in the development of parks and streets (planning and design, construction and management, use and appropriation).

The investigation was carried out through a qualitative multi-method strategy based on case studies and ethnographical approaches, which involved a variety of research techniques such as interviews, participant observation, documental analysis and visual methods. The interview format was either unstructured and informal or semi-structured, conducted with agents involved in the processes of production such as ordinary users, community leaders, municipal authorities and professionals working in the city's management and development. The questions making up the interviews were explorative in nature and related to the various issues concerning urban transformation and development such as participants' roles, activities and people's opinions, physical changes in the environment, and concerning the difficulties and challenges experienced in pursuing the construction of public spaces. Participant observation was used to find out about the nature of interaction and negotiation between participants in the process of development, and moreover to find out about people's actions and attitudes towards the use, protection and maintenance of public places. Another important source of information was provided by various documents such as newspaper articles and inhabitants' official letters and photographs, which all provided important data about public space development since neighbourhoods were established. Furthermore, old and new photographs of urban spaces in the neighbourhoods were used in interviews to help us to elicit comments, memories and discussion in the course of interviews.[4]

The research setting

The research was carried out in the city of Xalapa, which is an intermediate-sized city with a population of 413,136 (INEGI[5] 2005) in south-east Mexico. During the twentieth century, the city became consolidated as the modern capital city of the state of Veracruz, becoming a centre of economic, cultural and government activities with great influence in the central region of the state. This city was selected to carry out the empirical fieldwork because little urban research had been done there and the city had grown following the patterns of urbanization previously described. In 1950, the area of the city was estimated to be about 643.9 hectares and it had a population of 51,109; at the end of the 1980s, the area of the city had reached 4,090.9 hectares and there were 317,598 inhabitants. By this time, 75 per cent of the urban fabric of Xalapa had already occupied peripheral agricultural communal land through the creation of informal and spontaneous *colonias populares* (Rodríguez 1993).

The research focused on five neighbourhoods in the city (1. Colonia Revolución; 2. Colonia Ferrocarrilera; 3. Colonia Constituyentes; 4. Colonia Los Pinos; 5. Colonia Tres de Mayo), which were mostly created through informal processes (Figure 10.2). Nowadays, these neighbourhoods are no longer peripheral and have reached high levels of urban integration and consolidation. Integrated and highly improved *colonias populares* were selected, with the purpose of tracing back the processes of public space throughout the settlements' history and thereby providing a wider vision of public space dynamics. This allowed the research to uncover different disputed situations in the production and consumption of public spaces during the urban consolidation process. More similarities than differences were found in the case studies, and these are discussed in the sections that follow. First, the process of public space development is described. After that, the challenging situations over communal areas are discussed. Then the focus moves to the tensions and conflicts in the development, use and maintenance of public spaces in the *colonias*. Finally, some conclusions are discussed.

The development process

From beginning to end, the development of public spaces takes place through individual or collective interventions during neighbourhood consolidation This can be through spontaneous or planned actions, and through temporary or permanent interventions, depending on the social, economic and political capital available to *colonias*' residents. First, the residents of *colonias* identify the different needs, problems and threats that

10.2
Public space in peripheral neighbourhoods in Xalapa, Mexico.

impinge on their immediate public space. The lack of physical public space for the development of an adequate public life (circulation, entertainment and social exchange) requires residents to carry out actions and interventions of improvement; however, most of these are temporary and limited. Residents' improvement activities in communal areas start when these are threatened by illegal occupation; actions can include building footpaths, cleaning, and planting trees. In the streets of the *colonias*, residents initiate the development process by levelling the carriageway and building pavements, as a solution to the need for good accessibility. In many neighbourhoods, the street is the sole public space; as a result, the street is a space not only of movement but also of socialization, and therefore its development is very high on the residents' agenda for urban consolidation. At this point, residents become aware of the significance of the outdoor space within the neighbourhood environment. Therefore, the development of alliances and partnerships with different agents both within and outside the *colonias* takes places in search of public space transformation.

Community organization represents a very important aspect if residents want consolidated public spaces. The achievement of a positive community organization can lead to a transitional stage of movement from a temporary to a permanent development, within which long-lasting solutions can be found. As the definitive permanent development of public space in the strict sense cannot be carried out by the community itself, the city council intervenes in the process. At this stage, negotiations between the local authority and the *colonias*' residents take place about the costs, form and design, construction and all other aspects involved in the development. The organization of the community, the positive relations between the actors, and the consensus and agreements reached in this interaction lead to improvements in public space; without these, no development of public space could take place (Figure 10.3).

10.3
Negotiations for public space.

Promoting privatization of public areas

In general, formal and informal urbanization focuses its interest on obtaining maximum economic profits, assigning great value to private property; therefore, the urbanized land allocated for public use is usually kept to a minimum. In most Mexican cities, it is evident that there are large expanses of built-up areas, with very little land allocated for public recreational space, and few green areas. Moreover, since there is a high demand for land for housing and private use, the land available in low-income neighbourhoods is commonly a subject of dispute. In most cases, no land is set aside in these settlements for public use, and even where land has been allocated, these spaces are illegally invaded, or somehow privately occupied, and are likely to disappear. There are different interests and actions that compete for the space; however, those residents who understand and acknowledge the significance of the spaces for collective use resist the different kinds of private appropriation, defending the spaces and undertaking a struggle to maintain the public and communal nature of the areas. Under these conditions, public space development can be restricted by a process of struggle, which often lasts for many years.

There are different agents promoting the illegal appropriation of communal open spaces in low-income neighbourhoods. Political groups and parties may encourage privatization in exchange for political support.[6] In other cases, inhabitants have encouraged relatives and friends to occupy the land illegally. For example, a resident called Elena arrived in Colonia Revolución with her daughter to live with her brother and lived with him for sixteen years until she was able to get a plot by privatizing an empty communal space of the *colonia*. She was encouraged to occupy the space by her brother and some neighbours, who knew that the space was not owned by anybody, that it was a communal public space and that, in any case, sooner or later it would be taken by someone else. As a result, the land was suddenly appropriated by Elena, her daughter and another six families, who subdivided the land into eight plots. In a single day, they built their dwellings with the help and support of the rest of the neighbours, who assisted them in setting up the dwellings and in accessing shared water and electricity, which allowed them to make a living space in the communal space allocated to that street.

Neighbourhood leaders can be the ones promoting the disappearance of spaces meant for collective use by selling them to newcomers. In Colonia Los Pinos, it was the neighbourhood leader, as the one in charge of managing the creation of the settlement, who sold the communal space. When the *colonia* was created in 1991, an area of 1,017 square metres was allocated for public space. However, little by little the area was reduced to a third of this size through the allocation of four more plots for housing. In this *colonia*, the neighbourhood leader sold the plots not only to newcomers, but also to residents already living in the *colonia* who wished to build another dwelling or simply wanted to extend their existing one.

Other agents promoting the privatization of public space are the local authorities,[7] which, according to their different interests in the development of the city, authorize the occupation of the few spaces allocated for public use in the *colonias populares*, through granting the land to individuals. In some cases, the land is granted to squatters who have settled in dangerous and risky areas of the city, and therefore are relocated into the communal spaces of *colonias populares*, as happened in Colonia Revolución. Another way to privatize public spaces is to grant it to individuals, as happened in Colonia Los Pinos, where the communal area was granted to an individual in exchange for an expropriated property that the council needed for public works (Figure 10.4).

Contesting privatization of communal spaces

The different methods of privatization are a threat identified by residents, a threat that motivates them to start spatial improvements, thus triggering the development process. Alongside invasion and attempts at privatization or illegal occupation of public spaces, confrontation, resistance and defence of the public space take place in the *colonias populares*. In many cases, those trying illegally to privatize the space face resistance from those residents who know and acknowledge the significance of the spaces for collective use. In the context of invasion and defence, the interaction between those who wish to keep the land for public use and those who want it for private use becomes a very difficult one. The public spaces of the *colonias*, therefore, become a battleground in which the different interests and actions compete, carrying out a struggle, which takes place in the public space, for the public nature of that space to continue, and for its permanence to be assured. In Colonia Los Pinos, when the communal area was privatized and the 'owner'

10.4
Privatization of a public place in the *colonias* of Xalapa, Mexico.

tried to start building a house, the residents defended the public space. The atmosphere became volatile; clashes occurred during the dispute over the space, and even the safety of residents was threatened. The police had to be sent to the *colonia* to calm down the clash between the person intending to occupy the space and the residents, who claimed that the space was an important public place for their recreation and for public development.

The defence of the space has to be carried out collectively by many members of the neighbourhood. Residents of the *colonias* organize themselves, establishing networks within, and even outside, the neighbourhood to carry out collective resistance. The creation of 'community boards' is a mechanism used by residents of *colonias populares* to defend their communal space. In Colonia Revolución, residents organized themselves into a committee to defend the neighbourhood communal spaces. They created 'the council of defence of the green areas and streets of Colonia Revolución'. The activities of this group were focused exclusively on defending the spaces that were considered to be legal urban facilities. Through this group, the residents of the *colonia* worked together in the different spaces, cleaning and improving them. They faced a different kind of invasion by squatters, and the members of the council negotiated and explained to these occupiers that these areas were designated for communal use, and that although they were currently empty, the intention was to develop them with parks, gardens and different communal services for the benefit of the *colonia*'s residents. In this way, the council for defence of the green areas and streets in Colonia Revolución was legally registered as a committee before the authorities in 1996, and it managed to protect and recover five communal spaces from the ten allocated initially in the *colonia*.

> We had problems with the people who had built their huts here, we force them to clear the area, and they [squatters] threatened us. However, this space was already designated for a green area; they did not have any reason to argue or fight against us.... This happened when many other areas around were invaded. We organized ourselves; we were a lot of people who were defending the communal areas.
>
> (Juanita, a resident of Colonia Revolución)

In many low-income neighbourhoods of Xalapa, residents have defended, protected and initiated the development process of their communal spaces through their actions of transformation and improvement. Little by little, residents, making use of the few resources available to them, have protected and maintained the spaces as public areas (Figure 10.5).

Conflicts in public space development processes

In urban development processes, groups and individuals are divided through having different interests and priorities, which bring about a conflictive

10.5

Public space protection through actions of improvement.

environment in the decision-making arena of public space transformation. Berman (1986) affirms that the desire for diverse and often competing groups to control the design and management of a public place, such as a plaza or park, will increase the amount of conflict in the development and management process (cited in Francis 1989: 165). In low-income neighbourhoods, negotiation moments among actors take place under the structure of the community boards for urban improvement. Agreements and disagreements occur among residents, and between residents and the local authorities, regarding the way the public space should be developed. Private interests can constrain the community boards in the *colonias*; the diversity of objectives, ideas, and ways of thinking among members of the community gives rise to different attitudes towards the collective effort. For example, in the 'council of defence of the public space of Colonia Revolución', some residents joined the organization with the intention of persuading the community to allow them to occupy one of the communal spaces for housing. In Colonia Constituyentes, a conflictive moment occurred when the organization for the defence and protection of a communal space was affected by clashes between the residents about who should be president of the community board. In this case, issues of power and leadership within the community organization led to fragmentation and abandonment of the main goals of the community. No agreement was reached, and the group initially working for the permanence of the space disappeared.

As seen at the beginning of this chapter in Yolanda's account in Colonia Revolución, the community has to agree and negotiate with the city council about the budget[8] for the works to be developed. A consensus has to be reached about the amount of money residents must contribute to the development. This part of the process is a very difficult one; if residents do not reach any agreement with the local authority on this point, they risk losing the development of their public space. The community board has to gather the economic contribution from the *colonia*. However, there are often residents who are not willing to pay because they argue that it is the government's obligation to provide for the development of public space. Within these scenarios, the community board commonly faces difficult and conflictive interactions. Moreover, when local authorities realize that the residents are not willing to pay their share, and that it is going to be difficult to reach agreement about the cost of the development, they simply step back. This is disappointing, especially in light of all the efforts made to attract the attention of the local authority within the development process.

The development process also turns conflictive and becomes a place of tension, dispute and struggle when each actor tries to impose on, and dominate, the process for their own benefit. For example, in Colonia Tres de Mayo there were diverse opinions concerning the development of its park; this brought about a struggle between different groups about the form and use of the space. Until 2001, the space available for public use was a big empty area and it had been used for many years by the youngsters of the *colonia* for football matches. There was even a group of people who had organized a football league.

The space was a main sports area for Colonia Tres de Mayo and the neighbouring *colonias*. However, later on, the ecclesiastical group of the *colonia* became interested in the space in order to develop it as a multifunctional public place for the whole neighbourhood. The ecclesiastical group invited residents to participate in the meetings and also used questionnaires to determine the real needs of the people. In the meetings and question-naires, the majority of the residents stated that the main needs of the zone were for public spaces for recreation and sports, and for a day-care centre. However, not everyone agreed with the idea of building all these amenities in the space available. Those using the space for football matches com-pletely disagreed with the new ideas for the space, and a conflict occurred between the two different groups. Even though football pitches were being considered in the new development, the football league tried to block the ideas of the wider community as represented by the ecclesiastical group. In the main, the football players did not agree with the idea of losing control of the space. They argued that they had been given the space by the previ-ous municipal authority; however, they did not have any documents to prove this, and therefore nobody believed them. They also stated that the proposed ideas were uninteresting, that the space was already allocated for football matches only, and that therefore they did not want anything else happening in the space. Furthermore, they argued that there was no need for a day-care centre, because one already existed close to the *colonia*. In this way, the football players tried to impose their views in order to keep the space purely for their own needs. The ecclesiastical group tried to defend its members' ideas by communicating the results of the questionnaires in which the majority had expressed their needs. As these disagreements persisted, the ecclesiastical group carried out the development of a project that included a football pitch with stands, a playground, a building for the day-care centre and a library. Additionally, the design integrated the surrounding urban space through pedestrian areas and green spaces.

In order to promote the project with the local authorities, the residents concerned formed a community board, and in 2002 they managed to attract the authorities' attention. However, once the local authorities intervened, they also tried to give priority to their own interests, and to dominate the development process. In these interactions, residents also faced situations of conflict resulting from differing points of view. The city council took control of the development process of the public space and it told the residents that the construction of the park would be carried out. However, it would not be done as the residents had proposed. The pedestrian areas were replaced by roads with traffic (according to the city's development plan[9]), and the stands were eliminated. Also, very little space was left for the football pitch and the playground, and almost no space for the day-care centre and library, which residents were planning to run. All these changes provoked clashes between the stakeholders. The ecclesiastical group was very disappointed by all the changes to the project, and argued that its proposals were based on the real needs of the *colonia*'s people. It also appealed against the decisions of the local authority, mainly in an attempt to gain more space for the day-care centre and the library. Also, at this stage the football players intervened when they realized that the city council was going to build a very small football pitch; they advocated a larger pitch. However, the municipal architects told them that everything was already decided, and nothing could be changed. The residents had no choice but to accept the development the way the local authorities had determined. They were afraid of losing the construction of their park if they failed to agree with the authorities' decision.

Negotiation also takes place between the local authorities and the community about the kinds of materials to be used in carrying out the construction of the public space. Negotiations about materials are usually conflictive and contested, especially since the local authority commonly tries to do the most that it can with very few economic resources. Frequently, the municipality prefers 'quantity rather than quality', and in their turn, the *colonias*' residents fight back in support of durability and long-term interventions. The community often resist local authorities' impositions, as happened in Orozco Street in Colonia Revolución, where residents did not accept the development of their street. The municipality offered to pave the street with asphalt; however, the residents wanted to have the street paved with hydraulic concrete, for its durability and better image. Since residents had to pay an economic contribution to the development, they argued that if they had to pay money, it was better to pay a bit more and invest in something worthwhile. The city council in turn argued that asphalt was the best option to avoid expensive costs in the development. Residents strongly rejected the authorities' proposal; some residents argued that the local authority always tried to impose its will without taking into account people's opinion. The lack of agreement in this negotiation resulted in the authorities telling the residents of this street, 'If you do not accept the project, if you do not want your street to be developed, we'll take it to another *colonia*; take it or leave it.' Facing this kind of ultimatum, the residents of Orozco Street reflected on the effect that the rejection of the city's council proposal would have on their street. They realized that if they did not accept the local authority's proposal for the development, their street would remain undeveloped for many years, and therefore they accepted the development. In contrast to what happened in this case and in the park of Colonia Tres de Mayo, there have been cases where residents have totally refused the development, and have preferred to wait a couple of years for a new municipal administration in order to negotiate again. 'We are citizens and we deserve opportunity and choice; we have the right to defend our opinion. However, they [the authorities] do not respect it' (community board in Colonia Tres de Mayo).

Conflicts over the use of public space

In *colonias populares*, some people view the public space as a place of freedom, where anything can be done. Others believe that the space must be controlled and regulated, and people should follow certain social rules in the way they behave. Diverse users claim different territories through different acts and attitudes of use and appropriation. The space of conflict is shaped by different behaviours influenced by gender, age, group and culture. The conflict is usually between ordinary users and those residents who participate in the management and maintenance of the public space. This situation gives rise to a series of frequently competing social interactions, which impinges on the physical and social life of *colonias*' public space. For example, empty plots are often dirty and full of weeds and rubbish, and are very dark at night. These bad conditions create a very unpleasant and insecure environment, so that these spaces are open to littering and anti-social behaviour. They are frequented by alcoholics and drug addicts, who often hang around continually bothering pedestrians, and harassing women and children in particular. This makes residents worried about their public space, and encourages them to take control over their immediate public environment. Residents launch different strategies of improvement and transformation, according to the resources at hand. In the *colonias* studied, the wide range of effective strategies used to throw out undesirables have included cleaning activities, the introduction of lighting, the construction of pavements, and even the construction of shrines to the Virgin of Guadalupe.[10] Another very common strategy to protect neighbourhood parks and green areas in the *colonias* is to put up metal fences around the spaces. Having experienced illegal appropriations, people put up these fences to secure the permanence of communal areas and to keep conditions there in good order. Fences are an effective way to control the use of neighbourhood parks at night and to avoid conflicts over use, such as anti-social behaviour. Nevertheless, there are cases where communal spaces that have already been transformed into neighbourhood parks have still been appropriated by anti-social behaviour. Conflicts arise between those under the banner of 'protection' and 'right use' of the space and those not willing to follow rules of communality. The misuse of playground equipment is a very common aspect of confrontation. This situation takes place in most neighbourhood parks, with adults and adolescents using equipment that is only suitable for young children, and sometimes even vandalizing and destroying it. In these circumstances, control of the use of public space is an important aspect of the life of the community. Promoters of public space struggle to keep spaces in good condition. They argue that there is a lack of education about how to use and how to behave properly in public, and a lack of respect for others. A resident involved in public space maintenance argues, 'All public spaces of the city centre are respected because there is control and rules to follow; why not in the public space of the periphery?'

Another way of controlling mistreatment is by putting up signs. These are set up around the space, at the park entrance and on the playground equipment, as has been done by the promoters of Villahermosa Park in Colonia Ferrocarrilera. They have set up various signs instructing people about how to behave in the park, thereby aiming to control people's behaviour in the space, and inviting them to take care of the plants, trees and equipment. In this way, the residents in charge of the park have achieved a mutual understanding with most users.

> We tried very hard, struggling, fighting, lots of fighting. Many people got angry; they were not from the *colonia*. They usually said to us, 'Is the park yours? Then why don't you close it?' And we answered them, 'We are not fighting because you come to the park, we are fighting because you are destroying it; the place is not for destruction.'
>
> (Señor Modesto in Colonia Ferrocarrilera)

After much struggle, the residents of Colonia Ferrocarrilera have successfully controlled and moulded people's behaviour in their communal area. Both park users and residents have reached a shared appreciation about what is correct behaviour in the park and about how to use it and behave in it in such a way as to foster a socially and physically healthy public space.

Conflicts about the way public spaces are controlled have also taken place in neighbourhood parks, which has also given place to tensions among neighbours. Excessive control by those taking care of the spaces has also occurred. For example, in Colonia Revolución a resident taking care of a small public green space decided to fence it in with a metallic wire mesh, thereby preventing pedestrians from passing through any more. This situation provoked conflicts between the resident controlling the space and the rest of the community, leading to a confrontation among neighbours. Most people felt that privatization and illegal appropriation was taking place. Finally, the local authorities removed the fence, allowing people to use the space freely once again. Another conflict took place in Colonia Revolución concerning the times of day at which children and youngsters were playing in a park. If the youngsters remained in the park after 8 p.m., residents living nearby called the police, so that officers came to take them out. In this way, children and teenagers were often ejected from the park. Eventually, many residents responded by no longer visiting the park. According to a resident, 'The playground used to be full of children, but now not many people come to the park because we threw them out so many times.'

Education is necessary for those managing and controlling public space uses; too much protection creates an idea of privatization of the space. Those taking care of parks sometimes seem to forget that the space is public and that it should be treated and controlled in the light of its public nature. The character of publicness of these community spaces is challenged by those who over-control the space, to the detriment of the community. Freedom in public spaces is one of their inherent characteristics. An urban space that is freely used and that provides the chance of interesting encounters is an invaluable asset for the development of any community. However, freedom must be negotiated, and users and managers should find a common understanding that brings about both freedom of use and also respect for other people's rights. Lynch and Carr (1990: 415) describe this balance in the following terms: '[N]egotiating acceptable divisions of ground, providing the subtle markers that allow groups to find their places, teaching tolerance to those who operate the space, and controlling unobtrusively are keys to free use.' This means responsible management and responsible use. Moreover, in this control and use, both managers and users should keep in mind that public interests must come before private interests; this is key for successful public involvement, as it allows permanence and liveability for public spaces.

Moreover, the lack of public spaces deprives the community of the opportunity for acquiring a collective education, and learning social and community values. Public spaces in the *colonias* have even become spaces of stigmatization. There are some residents who regard green areas and parks as places that are always appropriated by anti-social behaviour, abandonment and insecurity. They argue that green areas and neighbourhood parks are not necessary in the neighbourhood environment, and that housing or other facilities should be built instead.[11] Señora María Paz of Colonia Revolución thinks in this way:

> We don't want green areas or parks; why would we want them? They are just spaces for youth gangs and they use them to con-

> sume alcohol and drugs. Nobody cares about those spaces, really. It is better to have something else; we don't want parks or green areas here.

This argument is worrying, as indifference towards public spaces has reached such a point that some people are unable to recognize the significance of public spaces for their neighbourhood environment. This is an important issue to take into account when considering the permanence of public space, and public participation in their development.

Maintenance of public space

Neighbourhood parks have been maintained by the commitment of those involved in their defence, improvement and transformation. However, these people can become discouraged by the different conflicting uses, practices and situations that affect the life of the parks. The different kinds of confrontations with users, residents and youngsters, and the lack of support from local authorities, have discouraged committee members of communal areas from taking care of parks and green areas. The result is a fragmentation of the organization for public space maintenance. Today, some parks are well kept and others are abandoned. There are residents who are committed to maintenance and others who do not care at all. For example, in the neighbourhood park of Colonia Revolución, the basketball court is maintained by a group of boys who play on the court every day; on the other hand, the playground is run down and has uncut grass because it is in front of the house of a resident who does not care about the park. This kind of situation also takes place in other neighbourhood parks and gardens in other *colonias*. Moreover, local authorities show very little interest in maintaining the public spaces of the neighbourhoods in the periphery. Residents argue that the public spaces of the peripheral *colonias* are only visited by the authorities at the inauguration ceremony. Again, Yolanda of Colonia Revolución argues:

> The parks and the avenues of the city centre are always being protected, well cared for and maintained, but what happens with the public space of our *colonias*? They never come; we have to call them many times. There is no support at all.

In these circumstances, residents' involvement in the maintenance of public spaces is an important issue. Villahermosa Park in Colonia Ferrocarrilera represents a significant example of the commitment of the main promoters to the maintenance of the space. In this park, a group of enthusiastic residents keep the space in good condition. They clean the space, sweep it every day and paint benches, playground equipment and fences regularly. Similarly, another park in Colonia Revolución has also been maintained by the residents living nearby. The park in Colonia Los Pinos is also well maintained by the residents, especially by the children, who also clean the space on a daily basis. It is important to remark that in those spaces where residents pay attention to the maintenance, the spaces are very well used, as visitors have realized that the residents are protecting the spaces and taking care of them. Visitors interpret the maintenance in a positive and welcoming way. These cases tell us about the great importance of public participation in the management and maintenance of public space.

Who is responsible for the maintenance of public space? Who should assume a sense of responsibility for public spaces in the *colonia* environment? Little recognition is given by the local authorities to the sense of responsibility undertaken by those involved in public space improvement and maintenance in the *colonias*. Municipal officials often argue that there is very little public participation and that people do not assume responsibility for the maintenance of their public spaces. However, most people in the *colonias* recognize that they are responsible for the maintenance of their public environment. They recognize that nobody else is going to take care of their public space. But if that is the case, why do few people participate in the neighbourhood parks? Something is unclear here; on the one hand, people recognize their responsibility, yet on the other hand they do not participate. This could be explained on the basis that the residents of *colonias* also argue that both local government and the wider society must share the responsibility for the maintenance of the public environment. Furthermore, they also argue that there is very little support, encouragement or incentives from the local authority to maintain the public space. It is important to reassess these positions in order to achieve a real sense of responsibility towards the maintenance of public space on the part of both authorities and the residents of *colonias*. Local authorities grant almost no recognition to residents' efforts concerning, for example, Villahermosa, Jovita, Mascarenas or Constituyentes Parks. Moreover, the local authorities have even tried to privatize them by granting the space to individuals. This leads to disappointment for those who have participated, and discourages community initiatives, which eventually affects the sense of responsibility, as happened in Solidaridad Park. The majority of participants interviewed in this research recognized the importance of public space,[12] as indicated in some of their remarks: 'we need parks', 'there are no spaces for children', 'there are no trees' and 'there are no places for youth'. However, the majority also recognized that both community and authorities should participate. There are many who embrace a sense of responsibility; there are also those who do not. A sense of responsibility needs to be promoted, encouraged, supported and redirected towards true involvement (Figure 10.6).

Contesting collective memory

Meanings are defined along the path of public space transformation. Meanings are created through the interaction of persons and the environment through which individuals and groups reproduce their social and symbolic

identity in the public spaces of the *colonias*. Symbolism and identity cannot be imposed, but this aspect has been a conflictive issue in the *colonias* between residents and the local authorities. In this case, meaning is attached to public spaces through the names that users give to a public space. These are usually related to memories and to life experiences, which bring about the creation of meaningful public spaces. In Colonia Revolución, the name 'Jovita' for a park was decided on by the residents in honour of the main promoter of its development. For the residents, this name involves remembering the person who promoted the progress of their public space. The name depicts an event, a fact, a person and an image that the community wants to remember, and identify with, and represents their collective memory. However, residents went through a struggle to defend the chosen name with the authorities, who, after having intervened in the improvement and transformation, decided to change the name of the park to David Ramírez in honour of a bright intellectual of the city. Residents did not know this person, and they could not accept the fact that the name of the place would be changed. People became very angry and they complained furiously. The local authorities even intended to put up a plaque with the new name, but the residents did not allow it. They even threatened to break any plaque the authorities put up in the park; so the authorities backed down. Legally the park is called Parque David Ramírez; however, everybody knows it as Parque Jovita; in spite of what was imposed by the local authorities, the residents keep the name they have chosen. Neither identity nor collective memory can be imposed on a social group. The built environment and the intangible elements that complement its symbolic value and character are intimately entwined with the people who produce and consume it.

Conclusion

Public spaces in the *colonias* of Xalapa are highly contested socially, spatially and symbolically. Processes of production and consumption take place in an environment of competing and opposing views, values, social and spatial actions. The *colonias*' residents initiate the production process of public spaces by carrying out actions concerned with protection, improvement, development and transformation; without these actions, the few public spaces in the low-income neighbourhoods of Mexican cities simply would not exist. Residents of the *colonias* want public spaces of quality that solve and satisfy not only functional or environmental problems but also their needs for beauty and durability; however, often the local authorities and other actors overlook these needs. The people of the *colonias* compete with various agents to achieve the permanent consolidation of their spaces, in an interaction where issues of power, knowledge, culture and capital come into play to dominate the development process and the resulting form of the space.

In low-income urban environments in Mexico, the achieving of public space occurs through a process that is full of limitations, constraints and barriers, and the process embodies great significance in people's life. The ingredients for achieving public space development are the struggle and hard work of the *colonias*' inhabitants. Through struggle and competition, residents develop a sense of belonging and attachment, and learn to value their achievements. These cases show us that public spaces are places where conflicts occur but where agreements and consensus can also be reached. Moreover, the existence of public spaces is essential for the sake of a viable, participative and integrative urban environment. In any case, the vitality, identity and character of our cities are highly sustained by people's interactions, activities and participation in the creation and transformation of public spaces. Public spaces that bring communities together have great importance for the sustainable development of our cities.

Notes

1 Informal settlements have been given different names in different countries of Latin America. For example, in Colombia they have been called *barrios populares*, in Brazil *favelas* and in Venezuela *ranchos*.
2 Several government bodies were set up to deal with this problem. In Mexico, the Commission for the Regularization of Land Tenure (*Comisión para la Regularización de la Tenencia de la Tierra*, CORETT) was created in the 1970s at federal level. Since then, it has worked throughout the country, legalizing the land of informal urban neighbourhoods and granting property titles for housing to the people of *colonias*.
3 In Mexico, the administration of President Carlos Salinas de Gortari (1988–1994) implemented a programme called *Solidaridad*.
4 This technique is known as 'photo-elicitation' (Caldarola 1985).
5 National Institute of Statistics, Geography and Informatics.
6 Authorities and politicians have regarded these settlements as political arenas where political support can be obtained, taking advantage of the urban needs of the population and the social organization behind the urbanization process.

7 Interestingly, in constrained urban environments of the 'developed world' where the availability of housing is scarce, communal lots are also threatened by local authorities who wish to allow new buildings to be erected, and conflict arises between those concerned with public space and those promoting privatization, as happened in the struggle regarding community gardens in New York (Staeheli and Thompson 1997; Staeheli et al. 2002).

8 Residents and the city council share the cost of development. This is city council policy in many Mexican cities in order to maximize resources for more ambitious goals in the public works programme.

9 Plan de Ordenamiento Urbano del Area Metropolitana (Xalapa–Banderilla–Coatepec–Emiliano Zapata–San Andrés Tlalnehuayocan, Veracruz), Secretaria de Desarrollo Urbano de Veracruz (Desarrollo Urbano de Veracruz 1998).

10 The Virgin of Guadalupe is a representation of the Virgin Mary adored by Mexican Catholics.

11 Gomes (2002: 34), in her research in the *favelas* of Rio de Janeiro in Brazil, tells a similar story. First, *favela* residents are more concerned with using the free open spaces for housing to satisfy the high demand; and second, residents argue that public spaces for sports are appropriated by delinquents and can become sites for drug consumption, therefore becoming unsafe and useless.

12 Recognition of the significance of public space varies among different cultures. For example, in a study of public space in Hong Kong (Xue et al. 2001) the majority of interviewees showed no concern about the amount of public space or the existence of greenery within neighbourhoods.

Chapter 11

Co-production of public space in Nord-Pas-de-Calais

Redefinition of social meaning

Paola Michialino

Introduction

This chapter reports the experience of a study of the planning and implementation processes of urban design projects undertaken within the framework of the *Politique de la Ville*, a national policy for an integrated urban and social development established in the 1980s in France by President Mitterrand and developed with several changes over the years. This chapter particularly investigates the potential of the planning and implementation processes (as well as the completed projects) to contribute to social reform and the development of new forms of democracy.

The experiences presented were first studied with the objective of evaluating the benefits of co-production of public space through the use of participative laboratories as a catalyst of urban and social development (Michialino 2006). The participative laboratory approach was introduced as a strategy through which it would be possible positively to engage citizens and other stakeholders at the local level in public space projects under the *Politique de la Ville*, and to overcome its inconsistencies and paradoxes. The term 'co-production', influenced by Lefebvre's theoretical concept of 'production of space' (2000), was adopted to refer to the participative approach and the collective development of processes and projects; the term 'laboratories' appropriately expresses the experimental purpose of this strategic approach.

The cases studied: context and issues

The cases analysed in this chapter are part of a series of seven participative laboratories carried out in France in the region Nord-Pas-de-Calais in a pilot project driven by the 'Habitat and Development' research team of the Université Catholique de Louvain, of which the author was a member (Declève *et al.* 2002).

The main intention of the pilot project was to develop a new strategic approach to enhance the planning and design of public spaces in accordance with the *Politique de la Ville*. The purpose of the project was to redefine both the design and the decision-making process, to give social meaning a primary role in the development of public space.

The participative laboratories were set up with the political, administrative and financial support of the French government, the region and local municipalities. Their principal objective was to establish local processes of co-production of public space in a new urban design strategy leading to redefinition of urban development and social identity. Most cases appear to have been successful in applying the principles of the *Politique de la Ville*, realizing effective social and urban development and establishing local dynamics engaging citizens in new forms of (participative) democracy. However, two of the seven cases were unsuccessful in establishing such processes (Michialino 2006).

This chapter outlines four cases (one of them unsuccessful) representing a varied spectrum of the experiences involved in the pilot study, including Haubourdin Petit Belgique, Saint Pol sur Mer, Avion and Bruay-la-Buissière. Other experiences were implemented at Haubourdin Centre, Tourcoing, and at the Communauté de Communes du Val de Sambre (Figure 11.1).

Although the areas involved in the project had experienced economic and social problems, and obtained support and funding within the *Politique de la Ville* from the national and regional levels, the local urban issues were very different, and each project was tailored to suit local needs and characteristics. Haubourdin Petit Belgique, on the outskirts of Lille, is

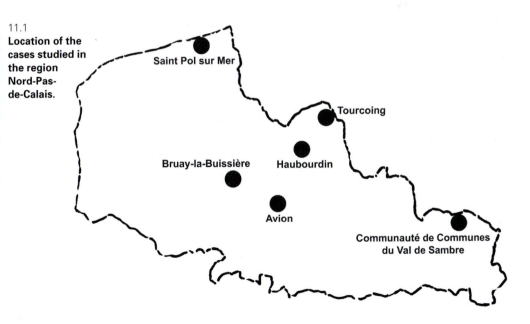

11.1
Location of the cases studied in the region Nord-Pas-de-Calais.

an ancient neighbourhood that was becoming progressively overwhelmed by heavy truck traffic. The laboratory worked on more than thirty projects, at different scales but all essentially intending to improve living conditions for the residents, local activities and traffic by using the central roads as connections at the local and regional level. Avion and Saint Pol sur Mer have large, concentrated areas of public housing, with public spaces of very low quality. The main objective of both laboratories was the improvement of public spaces and their social use. Bruay-la-Buissière is an old mining area, with housing built for miners in the 1920s, and brownfield sites resulting from the abandoned mine.

The political context: the *Politique de la Ville* as the national framework supporting local processes

The primary policy objectives of the *Politique de la Ville* were the resolution of unrest in disadvantaged (mostly residential) areas across France through the participation and broad partnership of all the stakeholders, including the inhabitants. Although the methodological approach for the implementation of the general framework of the *Politique de la Ville* followed a top-down logic of organization of state policies, this framework opened new methodological opportunities to develop an authentic bottom-up process at the local level, empowerment of civil society, broad partnerships and more extensive negotiation of local issues. The *Politique de la Ville*, and its structural funding, allowed the launch of broader 'transversal' practices aimed at developing decentralized and comprehensive approaches to local urban, social and economic problems of the city (Négrier 1999), and at coordinating the various political and administrative levels of power (Anderson and Vieillard-Baron 2000). Critics consider that such decentralization multiplied the centres of decision making, producing a paradoxical situation of increasing politicization of local affairs that directly contradicted the purposes of decentralization (Villars 1986).

The strategy of the *Politique de la Ville* was first used in relatively limited neighbourhoods and then, in subsequent plans, it successively enlarged both the areas and the complexity of its objectives up to urban communities, and including several towns within given geographic, economic and social contexts (Chaline 1998). The failure of such ambitions was probably inevitable (Donzelot and Mongin 2004); however, the *Politique de la Ville* can claim interesting and successful achievements.

The *contrats de ville* signed between each town, region and state for supporting local initiatives within the general strategy of the *Politique de la Ville* were established as strategies for implementation of its general principles at the local level. The cases of participative laboratories presented in this chapter were established, within the *contrats de ville*, to develop particular local initiatives for promoting the co-production of projects concerning local public spaces. The concept of co-production of local public spaces refers to the definition of the production of space as the social production and redevelopment of social relationships, in which the uniqueness of the local community produces an original project based on local uses of the space, individual representations (meanings) of the space, and definition of identity with the space (Hannerz 1980: 280–96; Gottdiener 1994: 110–56; Lefebvre 2000: 40–3). In this respect, the participative laboratory approach to the local public space projects embraced two main aspects. The first concerns the social processes involved in the realization of participative laboratories as public forums, including large panels of stakeholders, elected representatives, public servants, professional experts and inhabitants. The second aspect concerns the conceptual and technical approach to the design process of local public spaces and, in some cases, the physical development of new public spaces. This chapter discusses whether the participative laboratories achieved both the social and the urban outcomes.

The participative laboratories were organized as public forums in which conflicting perceptions were given a positive role, allowing recognition and legitimacy of the various participants, new structures of authority, the formation of collective identities, and the negotiation of spatial solutions (Burke 1979: 158–74; Healey 1997: 83–7). Conceptually, this idea of participative association brings with it the idea that the system of representative democracy can evolve towards a different democracy, one open to a larger base (Ricoeur 1985).

In this respect, participation in the laboratories and the realization of new structures of authority (and associated changes in the decision-making processes) appear to have introduced a shift from a 'democracy by consensus', reflecting Habermas's concept of *deliberative democracy* (Kapoor 2002), to a 'democracy by participation', reflecting Foucault's theory of situational ethics in a context-dependent dialectic, recognizing individual differences (Flyvbjerg 1998). This conceptual change emerges as a shift from a separation between the 'public sphere' and the 'private sphere' (Habermas 1978) to a mobilization of the 'private sphere' with relevant interests and 'passions', to participation in the democratic process (Carr *et al.* 1992: 22–7; Mouffe 1999). The uniqueness of the 'public sphere' thus appears to be challenged by the multiplicity of 'publics', often with conflicting interests, participating in democratic action, and by the interactions of these different 'publics' (Fraser 1997: 80–5) towards increased influence of the 'private sphere' over the 'public sphere' (Mouffe 1999).

The challenge for the *Politique de la Ville* was to provide the capability of identifying various objectives at the different levels, from local to state, and of developing appropriate strategies at the various levels for achieving those objectives within the prevailing political agenda of providing priority to the weakest areas, and of achieving increased social mix, economic and territorial integration, and solidarity (Chaline 1998: 53). It was evident, however, that the national agenda of the *Politique de la Ville* and the objectives of the various levels, from local to state, challenged the state-centred organizational method and the mechanisms of the democratic deliberation of the majority. It also challenged a management system based on rational principles with universal and anonymous values, the principles that were the foundations of the French state (Worms 1994) and could not be achieved solely by organizational restructuring.

The participation of the inhabitants was a key ingredient of the *Politique de la Ville* and an essential means of defining objectives and strategies for the achievement of the national agenda (Blanc 1995). The *contrat de ville* therefore included provision for mobilizing local stakeholders, including the inhabitants, and for the negotiation of local objectives and priorities for achieving them. This approach, in turn, required a negotiated social construction of the rules of action, one that projected and reinforced the image of a local society, and that was capable of reducing the conflicts by creating common criteria for decision making, and by giving a consensual social meaning to local programmes of actions and outcomes (Maury 1995: 56–7; Comité Technique Régional 1999).

Haubourdin Petit Belgique

The town of Haubourdin, in the *département* of Nord, is an old centre on the periphery of Lille, part of the Communauté Urbaine de Lille (Urban Community of Lille). The Petit Belgique quarter is situated to the southwest of the city centre, separated from it by the railway and delineated by the River Deûle, and is structured along two principal axes, rue Roger Salengro and rue Général Dame (Figure 11.2).

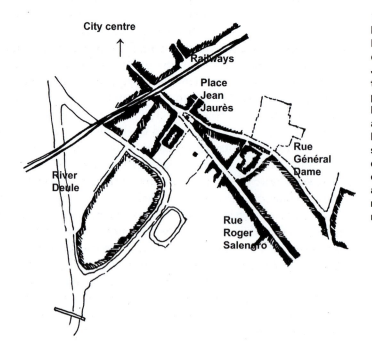

11.2
Map of the Petit Belgique quarter: place Jean Jaurès is the starting point of rue Roger Salengro and rue Général Dame to the south, and connects to the city centre across the railway to the north.

The typological characteristics of the quarter are those of an *old intra-urban area* (Chaline 1998: 27–9), with the presence of both active and abandoned industrial areas, and of some heritage elements, specifically the old house of the doctor of the former village, and the private park pertaining to the castle that used to belong to the lord of the town. As Lescieux-Macou (2001: 14–15) observes, the quarter of Petit Belgique was subject to multiple territorial definitions, as different types of boundaries defined by differing logics defined it within the regional territorial structure. Among these boundaries were physical boundaries, defining the space limited by the railway track, a channel diverted from the River Deûle, and a main highway; economic boundaries, defining the establishment of an industrial area along the banks of the River Deûle; and administrative boundaries defined by the administrative organization of the territory and/or inclusion in particular political and social strategies (for example, territories defined by the national educational programme, by the National Institute for the Statistics and for Economic Studies (INSEE), by the electoral areas, by the Family Allowance Office (*Caisse d'Allocations Familiales*, CAF), by the *Politique de la Ville*, by the landlord companies of social housing, and several others).

The set-up of the participative laboratory

The participative laboratory established within the context of the *contrat de ville* for the town of Haubourdin was in action from 1997 to 2000, and followed the principle of participation previously experienced in the 'Quartier du Parc', which had been the result of local social initiatives. The establishment of the participative laboratory was based on two theoretical hypotheses. The first was that urban planning, particularly in relation to public space projects, was a privileged domain for experimenting with new forms of community action and reflection, and for experimenting with possible new forms of local participative democracy at the boundaries between representative and direct democracy. The second hypothesis was that inhabitant participation was not meant to appear to decision makers as an imposed negative constraint, but rather as a positive opportunity to improve transparency and democracy in their approaches to decision making.

From the start, the participative laboratory adopted seven 'rules of the game', which were discussed, approved and adopted by all participants: (1) voluntary involvement of inhabitants, professional experts, public servants and elected representatives; (2) freedom of expression and participation; (3) recognition and acknowledgement of the competencies of all those involved; (4) internal coordination to ensure local organization, mobilization of the participants, and regular archiving of the records and memory of the experience; (5) external facilitation responsible for pedagogical, technical and political mediation; (6) development of a process of reciprocal education; and (7) creation of a creative environment for the generating of proposals.

Definition of the project

Support for the definition of programmes and the follow-up of projects involving the development of public space and social infrastructures followed. The projects had six main themes, including both the development of proposals and, in some cases, the implementation of complete projects for rue Roger Salengro, rue Général Dame, place Jean Jaurès (Jean Jaurès Square), Maison de la Petite Enfance, Salle Polyvalente and public spaces in the vicinity of a social housing estate. The work of the laboratory therefore focused on structural urban issues and the development of public spaces, infrastructures and social facilities. It was approached through a programme of twenty-five actions intended to support decision making and implementation of the projects.

The participative laboratory was involved in all stages of the project, from preliminary consultation, through diagnosis, definition of criteria for each project, the launch of a competition for architects to design a particular project, selection of the preferred proposal, to implementation of micro-projects such as planting in public gardens, and the painting of the fence bordering a social housing estate in order to distinguish the housing courtyard from the public space (Declève *et al.* 1999: 15 and section 2).

A number of key actions in particular prompted the direct and active involvement of the inhabitants, allowing, first, the actions to be carried out, and second, the participants to acquire particular skills needed in the specific action.

Surveys were undertaken with the participation of the entire group, and three main surveys were produced. The first addressed the traffic in the quarter and made an evaluation of the circulation flows, and was undertaken with the participation of students from the Université Catholique de Louvain (Contrat de Ville Haubourdin Petit Belgique – Atelier d'Urbanisme Participatif, 1998). The second addressed the needs for child care, and was undertaken within the context of the organization of the 'Contrat Enfance' (Contract for Childhood) (Declève *et al.* 1999: action 2). The third addressed the uses of public spaces in the vicinity of social housing, and was undertaken within the context of a project for redevelopment of those public spaces (Declève *et al.* 1999: action 17) (Figures 11.3 and 11.4).

Various actions were undertaken with the intention of reinforcing the urban management and revitalization structures. The function of the laboratory itself was focused on the objective of mobilizing increasing numbers of participants. The success of the laboratory induced a lengthy reflection on the future of the group after the conclusion of the *contrat de ville*, and led to the creation of an independent local association, the 'Petit Belgique Initiatives' (Declève *et al.* 1999: action 7).

The 'roundabout project' at the entry point to the quarter constituted the first important challenge for the participative laboratory. That project was already at an advanced planning stage as a result of work

11.3
**Preparation of
the traffic
survey.**

11.4
**Carrying out the
traffic survey.**

undertaken by the Communauté Urbaine de Lille (Urban Community of Lille) when the participative laboratory was set up, and the potential implications led to a major reconsideration of the project. The challenge of developing a new proposal, based on different criteria and more respectful of the local life in the quarter, engendered a need for detailed analysis of the public space.

Place Jean Jaurès appeared to be the principal 'hinge' around which the quarter functioned, the heart of the quarter, and therefore became the central focus of the participative laboratory. Although the square was located at one extremity of the quarter, near the city centre, it was clearly perceived as the quarter's urban and social centre. A specific project for the redefinition of place Jean Jaurès was launched within a proposal for readapting the square and transforming the 'Doctor's House' (previously earmarked for demolition) into a kindergarten and day-care centre. Through a competition, an architect was selected to develop the project in collaboration with the participative laboratory. The works were completed between 1999 and 2000 (Declève *et al.* 1999: actions 2 and 3).

Several other actions enhanced by the participative laboratory concerned a rearrangement and reorganization of the two main streets important to the structure of the quarter, rue Roger Salengro and rue Général Dame, which converged onto place Jaurès (Declève *et al.* 1999: actions 4, 5, 12, 16 and 19). These projects, including the renewal of place Jean Jaurès, the transformation of the 'Doctor's House' into a kindergarten and day-care centre, and the renewal of rue Roger Salengro and rue Général Dame, were realized within two to three years, with inhabitant participation and a method of co-production that changed both the process of decision making and the process of implementing the project.

Local evaluation of the process and of the project

The participants noted that the number and variety of projects and proposals addressed by the participative laboratory seemed to be dependent on the development of strong positive relationships within the participative laboratory, and between the various stakeholders and the town council, and particularly with the mayor, who strongly supported the initiative. The organization of several proposals and projects for the development of the urban structure and of a new image for the quarter seemed to emphasize the capacity of strategic planning at the urban level within the laboratory (Declève *et al.* 2000), which led to twenty-five actions and an allocated budget of 22 million French francs (about 3.35 million) (Declève *et al.* 2002: 30).

The achievements of the laboratory in terms of construction of territory and identity were particularly emphasized by the inhabitants in relation to the processes and methods of participation; these were identified as the key to effective change in spatio-temporal perceptions, manifestation in territorial and identity definitions, and influence over decision making (Lescieux-Macou 2001: 87–8). The transformation of the public space therefore acquired multiple meanings. The improvement of the space's physical image enhanced the perception of the public space as a place for public activity, as a space where social relationships could flourish and as a space of symbolic representation of individual and community identities and histories (Goffman 1959; Jacobs 1961; Lescieux-Macou 2001: 88–90).

The success of the initiative at Petit Belgique, and the commitment of the elected representatives, particularly the mayor, persuaded the municipality to initiate and support a second initiative with the participation of the inhabitants, this time focused on the city centre, which was beyond the boundaries and funding of the *Politique de la Ville*, and to give longer-term support to the initiative at Petit Belgique, to well beyond the timeframe of the *contrat de ville*.

Saint Pol sur Mer

The town of Saint Pol sur Mer is situated at the extreme north-east of the *département* of Nord in the conurbation of the city of Dunkerque (Dunkirk), facing the Northern Canal. The town has an urban structure of two parts. The eastern part includes the first settlement of the town, and the western part includes a series of public housing estates owned by several social housing landlord companies and accounting for 60 per cent of the housing of the entire town (Goyens and Michialino 1998). The two parts of the town, therefore, appear completely separate from each other. The only point of conjunction is the square facing the town hall. A kiosk located in the centre of the town hall square appeared to be the sole symbolic element representing a common perception of identity and gathering for the inhabitants from the two parts of the town in particular social events, such as the carnival.

The set-up of the participative laboratory

The initial focus of the participative laboratory was to set up the laboratory itself, define the methodological approach, negotiate the 'rules of the game' and identify local priorities, including objectives and actions to be undertaken. The strategy adopted a gradual approach to the urban and technical problems, starting from small-scale actions that were assured of immediate effectiveness and were intended to mobilize the participative laboratory in preparation for other, larger-scale objectives that would require considerable budgetary investments. The experience of the participative laboratory was characterized by sub-groups, each developing particular projects. As the scale and the typology of the projects were micro-local, the inhabitants involved in each project were essentially those more directly affected by the proximity of the project.

Definition of the project

After the completion of the small projects, the participative laboratory undertook a much bigger project for the development of a park. The scale of the project and the proximity of several housing groups and a local high school (the Collège Deconinck) expanded the challenge of the participative laboratory, involved a larger number of stakeholders and increased the visibility of the laboratory and the influence of its work to the rest of the town. A project for new social housing was already in progress in the area where the participative laboratory proposed to develop the park, and negotiations were therefore established between the town council and the landlord company to reduce the scale of the new housing, and to dedicate some space to the park (Declève *et al.* 2002: 48).

With the agreement of the elected representatives and with the external facilitation support of a team from the local planning agency (AGUR), the participative laboratory reached a negotiated solution for the development of the park, and a final draft of the park project was approved and adopted. However, it proved very abstract and difficult for the participants to understand the translations from personal perceptions of the (three-dimensional) existing space, through graphic (two-dimensional) representations of the space perceived, and then to a representation of the project's outcomes drawn on paper.

The implementation of the park project required a comparatively complex administrative organization in the background, to prepare the budget for the works, to launch tenders for building contractors and to follow the formal steps required by the administrative and technical machinery. From definition of the project to the beginning of the works, the management of the local social processes proved very difficult for the local teams of social facilitators because of the unrealistic expectations of the inhabitants (in terms of timing) and their persistent fears of disillusionment.

After the park had been completed successfully, it again proved difficult to establish strategies and initiatives to increase the use of the park by the inhabitants, and also to extend the park's social impact to include people living in the town centre. This was due to resistance at the political level to support for the promotion of further specific social initiatives (Michialino 2006).

Local evaluation of the process and of the project

The inhabitants observed that it was very difficult to move from perception of the three-dimensional reality of the space to the two-dimensional representation of the proposals on paper. However, the full-scale representation of the park allowed a completely different appreciation of the project, a better understanding of the issues and more realistic discussions within the participative laboratory.

Oral communication also presented a challenge, as the technical and administrative jargon appeared obscure to the inhabitants. Negotiation about the project, as well as follow-up of the administrative procedure for its completion, needed patient and extensive 'translation' of technical and administrative jargon into everyday language. In the evaluation, the public servants, and particularly the local facilitation team, stressed the necessity to adopt tools and language adapted to the public, and not vice versa.

The lapse of time necessary for the administrative and technical organization of the project of the park, from approval of the project to the completion of the works and the establishment of the park, created considerable difficulties for the local facilitation team in their dealings with the inhabitants. The perception of the length of time required, as viewed by the public servants, who were used to the timing and the procedures of such projects, was very different from the perceptions of the inhabitants, for whom understanding and acceptance of what they considered excessive delays presented a particular difficulty (Declève *et al.* 2002: 48). The public servants found difficulty in meeting both the administrative and technical lead times and the expectations of the inhabitants, for whom delays were perceived as serious threats that the project could be abandoned. A strategy adopted to 'inform' the expectations of the inhabitants was the publication of a local bulletin of the participative laboratory (*La Lettre de l'ATU*) explaining the programme and progress of the process.

However, despite all these difficulties, the laboratory proved successful both in influencing the decision making, and therefore enabling the realization of the park, and in supporting local social development, with the achievement of more conscious citizenship and direct resident participation at all levels of the project's process.

Avion

The town of Avion is situated in the *département* of Pas-de-Calais, on the periphery of the town of Lens. The area in which the participative laboratory was established was the Quartier de la République, which consists mainly of public housing. The quarter is separated from the town centre in both the physical/urban and the social sense. The railway and the station maintained physical/urban separation; social separation was reinforced by negative images of the social housing, and the labels 'distressed' and 'problematic' that were applied to the quarter (Comité de Pilotage de l'Aménagement du Quartier de la République, 1999). The housing mainly comprised large social housing estates built during the 1960s and the 1970s. The presence of a number of large low-quality public spaces distributed across the quarter further reinforced the negative image, insecurity, and lack of connection with the urban structure.

The set-up of the participative laboratory

The participative experience at Avion started with a small group of unemployed people and volunteers, who, under the guidance of two educators, undertook the construction of a scale model of the quarter. This led to various outcomes that were subsequently exploited by the participative laboratory, including, principally, capability of working in a group; capability of constructing a model; understanding of the principles of scale representation; abstract representation of the quarter in a model, including details of the built environment such as housing, infrastructure and public spaces; and capability of developing urban and architectural analyses. The group then integrated with other people, and was established as a participative laboratory within the context of the *contrat de ville*, with the objective of producing a diagnosis and project proposals for the local public spaces.

In order to collectively approach both the diagnosis and the elaboration of the analysis, and in order to enhance the involvement of other people, the participative laboratory developed two strategies: a 'sensory' approach, involving critical 'promenades' through the quarter; and an analytical approach, involving work with drawings, plans and models. The work of the participative laboratory achieved this first phase by mounting an interactive exhibition, organized by the municipality in the spring of 2000, which provided the foundations for a broader forum concerning the future of the quarter. The success of this first phase encouraged the municipality to repeat the experience and to involve the inhabitants further.

Definition of the project

During the first phase, the laboratory produced a model of the quarter and a proposal for a park to be developed on part of the abandoned land. The implementation of this project enthused the laboratory and motivated it to continue the experience, to extend the project to various other spaces and to address the social problems of the quarter. The participative laboratory, after identifying both the spatial and social issues, provided an analysis articulating them as different aspects (although not the only ones) of the general problems of the quarter. The laboratory then elaborated proposals for an integrated approach in which the two aspects were interrelated.

Among the various public spaces of the quarter, the attention of the laboratory was particularly focused on connective spaces: the central avenue, which served as an infrastructure spine, and various types of circulation. The principal social issues concerning these spaces were street security, connections to facilitate exchanges between the quarter and the town centre, renewal of the housing, and quality of life and environment.

For improving the quality of life, the laboratory identified the need to improve the image of the quarter, both internally and externally, through development of the quality of the landscape; installation of shops and local public services; realization of a plan for street lighting; and development of a strategy for management of vegetation and improvement of the urban furniture. A major proposal was for the construction of a residents' community hall at the centre of the quarter, allocated to the various associations of inhabitants. This last proposal included a programme and functional diagram of the building, and a proposal for its location.

A need to improve the existing housing was also identified, including demolition of key obsolete buildings, construction of bigger apartments with direct access at the ground floor level, diversification of the typology of housing, and inclusion of individual houses. The proposals of the laboratory for the renewal of the buildings also included proposals for the rehabilitation of residual land adjoining the housing blocks, with creation of private gardens adjacent to ground floor apartments, and small public spaces with playgrounds and varied facilities.

The mission of the laboratory was completed with the exhibition and public evaluation of these proposals. The work on the projects and the elaboration of proposals were accepted by the elected representatives, and essential parts of the proposals, including particularly the community hall, were included in the town programme, to be realized in the following year and financed in the context of the *Grand Projet de Ville* (Grand Project for Cities) (Figures 11.5 and 11.6).

Local evaluation of the process and of the project

The public evaluation of the laboratory by the participants, in accordance with the principles of the *Politique de la Ville*, focused both on the methodological approach and on particular local objectives for the development

11.5
The model made by the laboratory.

11.6
The laboratory at work, with the model in the background.

of various projects and proposals. The perception of the inhabitants was that their engagement was successful and that their proposals were effectively implemented. The participants acknowledged that the participative process had proved both feasible and successful, sustained by a strong political will to promote a process of co-production. Analysis of the work of the participative laboratory showed it to have been sensitive and professional, and to have provided real interest for all the stakeholders, who expressed a wish for the laboratory to be extended to address new themes. From a methodological point of view, it was acknowledged that the laboratory achieved genuine co-production, overcoming the limitations of simple consultation of the inhabitants.

In the perception of urban planners who were involved in the role of external facilitators, the experience appeared extremely positive, allowing the production of valid projects, the development of a new role of mediation, and the use of new methodological techniques. The positive political attitude towards the participative laboratory extended to allowing the material realization of the laboratory, including allocation of funds to the laboratory itself (e.g. for the salary of local and external facilitators, and operating costs) and to enhancing the dialogue with the inhabitants, accepting the proposals of the laboratory and sustaining realization of the proposals (such as the park). This positive attitude was a principal reason for the work of the laboratory being eventually transformed into realities that changed the public space and the social image of the quarter.

Bruay-la-Buissière

The town of Bruay-la-Buissière is also situated in the *département* of Pas-de-Calais. The town emerged between the two world wars as an important mining centre. The mine supported the local economy but also left a legacy to the landscape in the form of waste heaps, mine structures and housing for the mineworkers. Various quarters had been built during the development of the mining industry to accommodate the mineworkers, some of whom came from the countryside and some from other European countries such as Poland, Italy, Spain and Portugal (Rygiel 2000).

These quarters, built mainly during the 1920s and 1930s, had features that were common to housing for industrial workers and mineworkers across northern France (Chaline 1998: 27–9). The housing was composed mainly of uniform terraced houses with red brick façades and small private gardens, following the standards of the time. Some of the housing had been renovated according to current hygienic and comfort standards; the remainder was in need of extensive renovation.

The housing was originally owned by the mine company and allocated to the families of mineworkers. The collapse of the company induced a collapse of the local economy, with consequent problems for both the residents and the housing in the mine quarters, because of the withdrawal of funding for maintenance and renovation of the housing. The company remained the owner of the quarters (except for a few houses that were sold to their inhabitants), however. With the original concessions for exploiting the mines, the mine companies had also bought the land on which the housing was built. The ownership of the land created conflicts between the company and the municipality in relation to the definition of 'public' space and the responsibility for its maintenance, which increased with the collapse of the company and the withdrawal of funding for maintenance of company-owned spaces.

The Quartier des Terrasses, where the participative laboratory was attempted, had been established relatively recently as a political regrouping of two former neighbourhoods, adjacent but with differing urban and social characteristics: the former mine quarter, identified with the number of the pit (Cité du 4 – City of the 4), which had been only partially improved in the previous two decades, and a more recent area of public housing. The embankment of the railway serving the pit physically separated the two parts of the newly named Quartier des Terrasses. Although the railway embankment had been removed during the 1990s, and the space that it occupied had been flattened, it was still perceived by the inhabitants as an internal barrier between the two parts of the quarter, rather than as a public space reunifying it.

The physical separation (due to the – now flattened – railway embankment) was reflected in social and psychological separation within the quarter, and in social differences, which were particularly marked in the differing age profiles of the inhabitants. The inhabitants of the older mine housing were mineworkers and their families, predominantly of advanced age and with the right to occupy the housing for life. With the progressive decline in the number of elderly mineworkers and their families, a generational shift in the population was changing the identity of the quarter, with the older families of mineworkers being replaced by a younger, heterogeneous population, giving new meaning to the identity of the quarter and of the public spaces (De Craeke *et al.* 1996). The inhabitants of the social housing were generally younger, with different vocational backgrounds, and were often unemployed. This imbalance, however, was expected to change significantly in the following few years because of the mortality rates and demographic changes in the quarter (Figure 11.7).

The set-up of the participative laboratory

The establishment of a participative laboratory at Bruay-la-Buissière arose not from a voluntary approach by the elected representatives of the municipality, nor at the request of the inhabitants, but from the direct invitation of the regional council and the state (represented by the relevant *départements*) to participate in this pilot project. For the regional council and for the state, it was desirable that the pilot project should include sites with a wide range of urban and social problems, and distributed geographically across both *départements* constituting the region. In this respect, the case of Bruay-la-Buissière

227

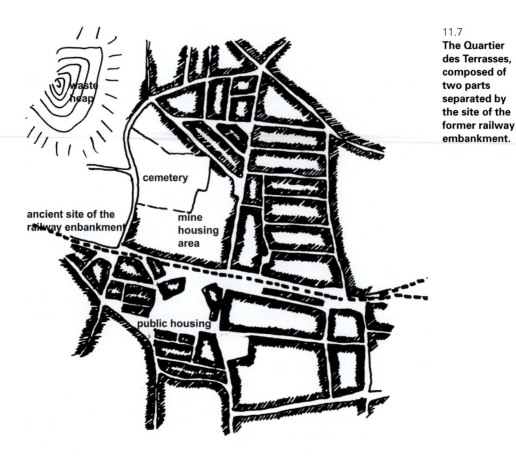

ancient site of the
railway enbankment

cemetery

mine
housing
area

public housing

waste
heap

11.7
**The Quartier
des Terrasses,
composed of
two parts
separated by
the site of the
former railway
embankment.**

represented the problems characteristic of mining centres, and was the first
site within the *département* of Pas-de-Calais to be involved at the start of the
pilot project.

In this case, therefore, the invitation to participate in the pilot
project generated a new local initiative, and required support for the com-
mencement and building up of a participative laboratory. One elected representative of the town welcomed the invitation and supported it, together
with the local facilitator. Although participation in the pilot project was
publicized in the local press, the cautious rhetoric used in public communi-
cations suggested a preoccupation with ensuring the 'benignness' of the participative laboratory in terms of decision making (*La Voix du Nord* 1998).
Involvement in the pilot project required the creation of a participative laboratory to develop a collective project and process concerning a public
space.

Definition of the project

Initially, the urban issue proposed by the elected representative and the
local facilitator was a study of ways of linking the Quartier des Terrasses
with the city centre. This first proposal was derived from two political aims:

the need to address problems and conflicts generated by social change in the Quartier des Terrasses, and the opportunity to address the development of a large public space resulting from the removal of the railway embankment that physically separated the two parts of the Quartier des Terrasses (the former mine housing and the more recently renovated social housing).

As soon as the inhabitants began to participate, however, there was a displacement of the theme of work, because the urban and social issues that most concerned the residents were the existence of both 'visible' and 'invisible' separation between the two parts of the quarter itself. The 'visible' separation was the large grassy plain, with newly planted trees, that resulted from the elimination of the former railway embankment; the 'invisible' separation resulted from social difference between the inhabitants of the two parts, with particular reference to their different histories and to the generation gap. The inhabitants of the mine housing had a history of long-term settlement in the quarter, closely linked with the history of work in the mine. The inhabitants of the renovated public housing, however, had a much briefer experience of the history of the quarter, commencing after the closure of the mine and linked with unemployment problems. The younger generations particularly pointed out the problems of the generation gap, and the absence in the quarter (and also in the town) of infrastructure and attractions for sport and entertainment.

The principal issues raised concerned conflicts of uses and perceptions, particularly in relation to small spaces where differing ownerships and problems of boundaries between public and private space created local conflicts, but were considered to have great potential for the development of positive images and for improvement of the urban quality of the quarter.

Despite almost self-generating participation by the inhabitants, and the development of ideas and proposals for the public spaces, part of the quarter was renovated and some public spaces were transformed, but without taking into consideration the possible contribution of the inhabitants, and dismissing the proposals of the laboratory.

Local evaluation of the process and of the project

The experience of the participative laboratory concluded with a public evaluation undertaken by the participants, focusing on the achievements of the laboratory in terms of the principles of the *Politique de la Ville*, particularly from the point of view of the methodological approach for developing a local participative dynamic and generating political responses, and from the point of view of development of structured proposals for a series of small projects across the quarter to solicit town council support for a new programme for the development of the quarter.

Particular successes of the participative laboratory at the Quartier des Terrasses were considered to be its achievements in local mobilization and the extensive participation of inhabitants, public servants and professional experts without the benefit of a precedent structure in this locality, and with a limited contribution from the local facilitator, who was allocated only limited time and energy to invest in the quarter.

However, a limited political will to achieve real participation can be seen in the limited commitment and involvement of the elected representatives. Only one participated in several meetings. It also appeared that the role of the elected representatives and the place they were asked to take in the structure of the participative laboratory were not clear to them, limiting their interaction with the laboratory and the development of a new municipal strategy for the involvement of the inhabitants in the decision-making processes, particularly with respect to projects for public space. The reticence on the part of local politicians towards authentic participation, and so to co-production, appears to show the difficulties experienced by the *Politique de la Ville* in introducing new democratic procedures and challenging the established authority structures and decision-making processes. Also, it emphasizes the need for political will at all levels in order to achieve effective results.

Some renovations of parts of the area were realized by the municipality, completely dismissing the contributions and the proposals of the laboratory, disillusioning the residents, who had invested time and energy on the project, and representing a failure in terms of the principles of the *Politique de la Ville*.

Evaluation of the cases studied

This section compares the success of the various cases in achieving the objectives of the pilot project for participation and co-production, the realization of the urban projects, and the objectives and principles of the *Politique de la Ville*.

The pilot project was designed to develop a new strategic approach to enhance planning and design of public spaces, with a particular focus on the implementation of design and decision-making processes for giving social meaning a primary role in the development of public space. In the context of the strategies identified within the *Politique de la Ville*, and as a consequence of decentralization as regards the establishment of new forms of (local) democracy, participation was a principal objective (Triantafillou and Risbjerg Nielsen 2001). The success of the pilot project in itself, therefore, depends on the success of each laboratory in achieving the various levels of objectives, from local participation and co-production, to urban redevelopment, to change in the decision-making process and the establishment of new forms of democracy. The analysis of the extent to which participation occurred at the various levels of the design and project processes shows that the degree of success varied in the different cases studied.

The first element of evaluation is the achievement of participation, change in the decision-making process, and authentic co-production at the local level. The participative laboratory of Haubourdin Petit Belgique was successful in achieving authentic participation in the local community and overcoming the paradox of recentralized power. The decision-making process appears to have been more transparent and the reasons and criteria for decisions were defined on a negotiated basis, founded on strategic planning proposals and documented analysis undertaken by the participative laboratory. The participative laboratory of Saint Pol sur Mer was successful in authentic participation, renovation of urban structure and social development, and also in enhancing local economic development and reducing unemployment. The participative laboratory of the Quartier de la République at Avion achieved authentic participation by the local community and stakeholders in the participative laboratory and overcame the paradox of recentralized power by bringing change to both processes: the political decision-making process and the process of urban planning in relation to projects of public spaces.

The experience of Bruay-la-Buissière was partially successful in establishing a participative laboratory with a large panel of stakeholders, and authentic participation within the laboratory in the formulation of a diagnosis of the urban problems. However, it was not successful in terms of achieving authentic participation in the decision-making processes. That is, the *internal* participation in the laboratory was not followed by a participation of the laboratory in the *external* levels of the decision-making processes. In this respect, while the participative laboratory achieved the project's steps of diagnosis and analysis (Declève *et al.* 2002: 73), a parallel (traditional) project process was undertaken by the town council, which engaged professional experts charged with the definition of strategies of intervention and with making project proposals for the public spaces in the quarter. This parallel (traditional) project process did not include interaction with the participative laboratory, so that the results in terms of change in decision making were not achieved, and the projects were realized without authentic participation. In this respect also, the fact that the professional experts participating in the laboratory were not those engaged to develop the project is further evidence of lack of political will to commit any stage of the project to a more participative decision-making approach.

It appears that in the successful cases, authentic participation also promoted a change in the decision-making process and achieved social development in various ways, although managing the expectations of residents was a challenge. The unsuccessful case of Bruay-la-Buissière shows that residents were ready to engage with the laboratory and to invest time and energy in the project, but the lack of political will jeopardized the entire process.

The second element of evaluation is the realization of the urban public space projects. The various cases presented different types of projects, with different degrees of success. Haubourdin Petit Belgique was successful in the realization of several projects undertaken by the participative laboratory. Among the most important achievements, in terms of their impact and economic investment, were the renovation of place Jean Jaurès, with the redesign of a neighbourhood square instead of proceeding with the round-about proposal; the renovation of the two main streets of the quarter, rue Roger Salengro and rue Général Dame; the transformation of the disused swimming pool into a multi-purpose hall; and the renovation and change of function of the Doctor's House.

Saint Pol sur Mer was also successful in achieving the realization of several micro-projects and one large project, the park, which were made possible through the achievement of the administrative and technical pro-cedural requirements for the funding and realization of the project. At Avion, the mission of the laboratory was completed with an exhibition and public evaluation of its proposals. The work on the projects and the elabo-ration of proposals were accepted by the elected representatives, and essen-tial parts of the proposals, including particularly the park and the community hall, were included in the town programme, to be realized in the following year and financed in the context of the *Grand Projet de Ville* (Grand Project for Cities). The positive political attitude towards the partic-ipative laboratory was the principal reason for the successful implementa-tion of the work of the laboratory.

The original project set in the agenda by the city council of Bruay-la-Buissière (that is, creating a stronger urban and structural link between the Quartier des Terrasses and the city centre) was too vague to allow the development of serious proposals, and was perceived as a false agenda by the inhabitants; moreover, no funding was allocated for the real-ization of the project. Proposals from the participative laboratory did not appear on the agenda of the town council, and the participative laboratory therefore focused on specific places (e.g. the railway embankment), but without the possibility of achieving any concrete results beyond developing an analysis of the urban and social problems of the quarter. Even though the analysis indicated specific issues and allowed the formulation of ideas regarding the future of the quarter, there has been no follow-up, and there-fore the initiative was aborted without achieving any effective contribution to the design of the place.

The success in terms of commitment of the participants to the laboratory and to the development of new local social community was not accompanied by any recognition of the participative laboratory as part of the decision-making process. Nor was the participative laboratory encour-aged to contribute to the projects elaborated by professional experts and adopted autocratically by the town council. In this context, the completed urban development projects cannot be considered as part of a process including the wider and contextual social, urban and economic develop-ment that was the basis of the *Politique de la Ville*. The need for economic development appeared patently urgent, but the records of the participative laboratory of Bruay-la-Buissière contain no evidence of achievements in this direction.

In sum, it appears that it was mostly in the cases that had achieved authentic participation that either projects for achieving better public spaces were completed, or there was a strong commitment towards creating the conditions for their completion. In addition, these cases were successful in implementing projects of various types and scales, from micro-projects to local interventions, to projects that involved several administrative and political levels of decision, and consistent financial investments, proving that the political will to achieve authentic participation also allowed effectiveness in achieving change at the urban level. The case that proved unsuccessful in achieving authentic participation was also unable to change the urban spaces in accordance with the wishes of the residents.

Finally, this section analyses the success of the cases studied in achieving the objectives and principles of the *Politique de la Ville*. It appears that, in most cases, the achievement of local authentic participation and the realization of projects for the improvement of local public spaces also led to achievement of the general objectives of the *Politique de la Ville*, demonstrating effective social and urban development. Furthermore, attaining the different levels of achievement from authentic local participation to improvement of public spaces to effective social and urban development also allowed the achievement of the theoretical principles of the *Politique de la Ville* through establishing local dynamics that engaged citizens in the decision-making processes and through establishing new forms of (participative) democracy.

In the case of Haubourdin Petit Belgique, the political objectives of the *Politique de la Ville* were achieved, particularly in terms of authentic participation in the decision-making processes, and integrated social, urban and economic development. The change in the political approach to decision making allowed the development of a new model of democracy that embodied a shift from the Habermasian model of deliberative democracy to the Foucauldian model based on situational ethics. Also, a cultural change appears evident in the characteristic of continuity that the participative laboratory has maintained across several years of existence, and its progressive evolution as a permanent interlocutor in the local processes of decision making. This appears coherent with the strong political will to support and enhance participation, and in the understanding of the necessity for both internal and external facilitation teams, which enabled the development of authentic change in the decision-making processes.

The participative laboratory at Saint Pol sur Mer was also successful in addressing the national objectives of the *Politique de la Ville*, particularly in terms of authentic participation in the decision-making processes, and integrated social, urban and economic development. The strategies for increasing participation also brought about education of the various participants, in terms of changed perception of the space, housing and community, and in terms of development of communication strategies and technical skills for reciprocal understanding among inhabitants, elected representatives, public servants and experts, and therefore establishing new social power relations among the participants.

The participative laboratory of the Quartier de la République at Avion was successful in achieving authentic participation of the local community and stakeholders in the participative laboratory, and overcame the paradox of recentralized power with change in both processes: the political decision-making process and the process of urban planning in relation to projects of public spaces. It might be concluded that both the political will and the authentic participation contributed to the achievement of co-production and that the facilitation process was essential to achieving and maintaining *both* the political will *and* the authentic participation. That is, positive political will, effective facilitation and authentic participation were inseparable, and essential to the successful outcomes in this case.

Bruay-la-Buissière did not achieve either of the political objectives identified in the framework of the *Politique de la Ville* in terms of authentic participation in the decision-making processes or of integrated social, urban and economic development. Participation in the decision-making processes was not only 'not achieved', but was clearly opposed by the town councillors, as appears evident from various press articles and in the need for the *chef de projet* to reassure the town council about the 'benignness' of the participative laboratory.

The establishment of the participative laboratory and the almost self-generating participation of the inhabitants could be considered as evidence of a partial success in achievement of social development. However, limited participation by elected representatives and lack of authentic participation in decision-making produced two perverse consequences: first, that the engagement and commitment of individuals in the participative laboratory generated frustrated expectations and confirmed, in the eyes of the inhabitants, the ultimate uselessness of trying to move towards having a more proactive attitude as citizens; second, it reinforced expectations at local government level (e.g. the town council) that local politicians could continue to exploit 'the system' (e.g. the *contrat de ville*) for special funding without accepting any change in their approach to the management of power authority. The will, enthusiasm and commitment of inhabitants, public servants and some professional experts to bring about a change of culture appeared successful at the individual level, but the conservative attitude of the elected representatives jeopardized the entire experience and prevented achievement of any change in terms of social culture and political processes.

In summary, the experiences that were successful in achieving the local objectives of authentic participation and development of public space also addressed the objectives and principles of the *Politique de la Ville*. In contrast, the experience of the participative laboratory of Bruay-la-Buissière raised expectations among the inhabitants that were ignored at the political levels, generating an adverse feeling of disillusionment among the participants. This also shows that the objectives of the laboratories, as conceived and organized within the pilot project, were appropriate for addressing at the local level the objectives and principles set at the national level.

Conclusion

Comparing the outcomes of the various experiences, it appears that in some cases there was notable success in achieving social reform and the development of new forms of democracy in processes of planning and implementation of projects of local urban spaces. In most cases, the local participative laboratories, established as part of the pilot study, were successful in catalysing urban and social development, and in facilitating the achievement of the political objectives of the *Politique de la Ville*. Direct involvement of the elected representatives, the capacity to address the conflicts of perception and elaborating compromises adapted to the specific situation and context, and the capacity of the participants to adapt their institutional, professional or situational approach to the context of a participative laboratory with negotiated rules and appropriate internal and external facilitation appear to be essential factors in the achievement of these objectives.

The evaluation of the various cases shows that strong political support and commitment is the most essential element of success. The unsuccessful cases, such as Bruay-la-Buissière, prove that the lack of political support deprives the participative laboratory of any meaning. When successful, the participative processes allowed an effective change of perspective for the decision makers, the introduction of new criteria for the project with the active involvement of all stakeholders, and a different perception of the realization.

The programme's objectives for each participative laboratory were realized, at various scales and to various degrees, once each laboratory's proposal for the development of local public spaces was adopted and the projects elaborated within the laboratory were accomplished. The bringing to reality of the projects and the proposed local urban development schemes represents the tangible fulfilment of the local programmes, and the achievement of the objectives of the laboratories.

The multidisciplinary approach to the design process also provided an increased *and shared* awareness in all participants of the extent and complexity of the planning and logistics framework surrounding urban management, planning and redevelopment, and (reciprocally) of the extent and complexity of the impact of management, planning and redevelopment decisions on the social and cultural fabric, as is particularly evident in the case of Saint Pol sur Mer. This increased shared awareness allows all participants (including politicians, bureaucrats, professional experts and lay citizens) to redefine their individual positions and contributions, and thus to progress in both material development and the advancement of the quality of urban life.

235

The laboratories, by achieving authentic participation and social development, also established *authentic* educational processes and effective co-production of space, and accomplished education in citizenship; the establishment of local groups of residents and stakeholders; participation in the political and strategic decisions; social development and integration, thus achieving the political objectives of the *Politique de la Ville*; and realizing, within their experience, a change of culture and a shift towards new forms of democracy.

Chapter 12

Whose public space?

Ali Madanipour

After investigating these cases from around the world, through the theoretical frameworks of place and process, can we now answer the question that was posed as the title of this book, and identify to whom public spaces belong? The complexity of the urban design, development and management processes in these cases, and of the configuration of urban societies in which they are located, makes it impossible to find simple answers. But across the cases, we are able to identify a recurring theme whereby individuals, social groups and organizations make or withdraw claims over space, thereby implicitly or explicitly contesting the claim of others, instigating a process of inclusion and exclusion, creating spaces with overlapping meanings. We can see how public spaces are significant for all urban societies, no matter what the size of the city, its economic basis or its political and cultural configurations. Public spaces, as significant material and social components of cities, are therefore subject to intense processes of social interaction through which their quality and character are determined.

Claims could be made by powerful individuals and institutions, such as a supermarket chain or a shopping mall in England, a local authority in France, a local prince in Nigeria, or housing designers and developers in Saudi Arabia and Iran. Claims could also be made by individuals or informal groups of people who try to shape the space, such as youth subcultures in the United Kingdom, public housing residents in the Netherlands, street drinkers in Germany, low-income households in Mexico, local businessmen in Taiwan, or middle-class South Africans, each with widely different views and outcomes. Depending on their level of political, economic and cultural power and influence, these individuals and organizations can shape and determine some of the features of the urban space, creating the structural conditions within which others live and use the city. Their resources allow the more powerful individuals and institutions to make substantial physical and institutional changes in cities, while the claims by the less powerful groups may take softer, temporary forms. Each individual, group or organization may try to shape the city in their own image, creating spaces that would enable them to feel safe and in control, with or without consideration of what others may need. Public spaces, even in their most public forms, therefore, tend to find particular flavours, a different character associated with particular combination of groups and interests, under pressure to find a fixed identity within a particular fragment of society.

Public spaces are shaped not only by claims, but also by the absence of claims, by withdrawal from the public sphere. Withdrawal from public space may be due to a fear of crime, mistrust of other social groups, and intensified social polarization. This withdrawal is reflected in neglect and decline, poor maintenance, accumulation of waste and refuse, or lack of care and attention. Neglect of public spaces may be a result of exaggerated preferences for vehicular movement, which was the dominant theme in shaping cities for much of the industrial era. Such neglect may also reflect the absence of local governance – that is, coordinating mechanisms to facilitate negotiation between different claims over space. Public spaces provide linkages between private spheres, and represent the character and quality of a city as a whole. The decline of public space reflects a breakdown in social and spatial linkages and a deterioration of the city as a whole.

The case studies presented in this book map out the changing nature of public space. Public open spaces are changing from being embedded in the social fabric of the city to being a part of more impersonal and fragmented urban environments. The various chapters show how public spaces are changing alongside the changing nature of cities and urban societies: from places embedded in particular communal traditions and routines to impersonal spaces produced by economic, political, technical and management considerations – in other words, they are undergoing a transition from an expressive to an instrumental character. Public spaces that once were meaningful places are becoming a mere part of a transportation network dominated by cars. They are also at risk of being taken over by minority interests, being privatized in the name of safety or exclusivity, further fragmenting the urban society and space.

The particular characters of public spaces may be instrumental or expressive. As instrumental spaces, they are used as a means to an end, such as the development of a public bus station, or the pedestrianization of a street for the purpose of gaining commercial profit for businesses, or the gating of streets for the perceived safety of resident groups. Instrumental use can also be made for an essential need, such as the public spaces in low-income neighbourhoods in Mexico or small towns in France, where the quality of urban life is closely connected with the process of urban development and the provision of public spaces. As expressive spaces, they may be used to project and explore identity, such as the gathering of youth subcultures or international migrants in a European city, or a festival space in a traditional African city. The inclusive and participatory development of a common good such as public spaces can help combine instrumental and expressive concerns, creating places that people use and can identify with, while reinvigorating society through collective action.

Urban spaces may physically change very slowly, but socially they may embody new beliefs and behaviours. Society's economic and social configuration may change from agrarian to industrial to services, and these changes may leave some spaces intact, but the pattern of their use and the nature of their meaning for the urban populations will have changed dramatically. The design and development processes may therefore result in substantial changes that introduce new beliefs and practices, undermining the established patterns, liberating some groups from their inferior positions, but also abandoning built environment that reflected those traditions. Public spaces may retain some of the symbols and festivals, but these lose their original meanings, turning into aesthetic practices carrying only a fading trace of their economic and political content.

The city is often shaped at the intersection of these claims and characters. Each claim may shape one part of the city, or one aspect of a place, and the interaction among these claims and counterclaims shapes the complex city of people and places. Resistance, transgression and contest are as much a signifying character of these places as the claims to establish a fixed or abstract identity for them. The aims of designers to control the character of a housing scheme and its spaces may be met by a different use of the place, one that they did not envisage or approve. The intentions of local authorities to formalize development and promote a sanitized identity for the city may be met by the colonization of space by groups that threaten that image. The traditional authority and status of a place may be undermined by the growth of population around it and the expansion of places and activities. Actions may have more unintended consequences and challenges than there were intended outcomes.

City design and development becomes a continuous process of projection and contestation, in which some groups project an identity for a place and others accept or contest that identity, either by consciously transgressing the boundaries that this process sets, or by ignoring it – knowingly or unknowingly. Even those who admit the claims of the projected identity of places, and therefore appear to fall in with the planned character and routines, may undermine and transform these claims by performing new activities, or by forgetting or ignoring the intended routines and practices. The place takes on a life of its own, one that may be very different from what was intended, through conformity, accident or defiance.

How can the complex and fluid process of urban design and development be led so as to ensure the place is as public as possible, serving as many people as possible, rather than being at the service of a privileged few? If the design and development of cities lies at the intersection of different claims, how can these claims all be taken into account? There will be many occasions when the conflict is so powerful that no bridge can be built between different positions and interest groups. The choice appears to be between battling it out and trying to negotiate to find a solution. Such negotiation can only take place through an inclusive process of city design and development in which as many views as possible need to be involved. Desire for exclusivity goes hand in hand with social inequality, and so it is only through inclusive processes that the possibility of creating accessible and shared places increases.

There is a large degree of overlap between the book's chapters across its two parts. Overall, they show the gaps that exist between different perspectives and how the tension tends to be resolved in favour of more powerful groups. The power resides with the designer who shapes the place, the developer who initiates and coordinates the production of space, the investor who brings forward financial resources, the public-sector agencies that promote and regulate the transformation of the place, the homeowner who wishes to be in control of the neighbourhood, the male domination that prevents women from entering public arenas, the higher-income groups that demand exclusive places, the majority populations who keep minorities and subcultures out – and so on. Those who do not control resources and have no voice in political representation, those who remain silent in the process of spatial transformation, or those who are physically weak can be at the receiving end, and potentially lose out in a contest over the use and control of space. This is an interdependent process, with no one party in full control, although the degree of power and influence of agencies varies according to their economic and political capital or their relations with the others around them.

The ascendency of the market paradigm in city building, which shifted the initiative for investment to the private sector, has had a clear impact on how the process of urban design and development may be influenced. By encouraging private investors, either through partnerships or through reducing regulatory pressures on them, the urban development process has been bent towards their expectations. This shift of power towards the market is perhaps the defining feature of many urban development schemes in recent decades, with the unavoidable outcome that the market determines the character of the outcome, which often means producing places that facilitate monetary exchange. The prevalence of economic justification for public spaces, therefore, becomes the norm rather than the exception. It becomes an integral part of the logic of place making; anybody who questions this logic may be accused of naivety or lack of economic awareness. As the aim of the urban development process is often economic regeneration, place finds an instrumental value, as a tool through which economic vibrancy can be delivered. Developers and local authorities may both look for quantity rather than quality.

Public space, urban regeneration and economic development, therefore, are closely entwined. In some cases, the only way that public spaces can be developed and maintained is through engaging private-sector resources. So, the solution is not to exclude private investment from the process, and thus argue for poorer places and more deprived cities. The argument is that individual interests should not be given free rein. The aim is to allow the character and quality of places to be established through a variety of criteria and at the intersection of different voices, giving ultimate primacy to the public and its different layers. Powerful groups inevitably try to exert a stronger influence in the process, and negotiations never become altruistic dialogues, which is why participation, inclusivity and transparency become essential.

Urban sprawl has put pressure on both urban centres and their peripheries. While urbanization in much of the developing world is still ongoing, suburbanization in the developed world is a primary feature, both trends leading to rapid and fragmented expansion of the city into the surrounding areas. In the outward growth of cities, city centres and their public spaces have lost much of their significance, even though the urban showcases are still in the centre, where the pressure of competition for space is still prevalent. Hollowing out of the centre, which is a feature of car-based urban growth, has been experienced in most of our case studies. Marginal areas, meanwhile, have suffered from the shortage of public spaces, both in rich suburbs and in poor inner-city or peripheral neighbourhoods, albeit at different levels. Public spaces are closely associated with the degree of urbanization in a city, and when urbanization suffers through suburbanization and individualization, public spaces also suffer from neglect and loss of meaning.

The key issue is to have a clear sense of what is gained and what is lost, as an inevitable component of any development process, and have some control over this balance in favour of a wider range of people than many plans may suggest. Images of busy and lively public spaces abound in the promotional material put out by city authorities, developers and designers to show the attractiveness of their cities, the success of their schemes or the desirable places that they aim to create. Inherent in these images is the notion of happy shoppers and joyous lifestyles, which would cause no problem if these developments did not exclude many people with limited financial means or people who were forced out of their places to make space for the new arrangement. A place, therefore, should not be seen as a cosy tool to facilitate the supply and demand of consumer goods and lifestyles. An urban place has many more layers, which should be taken into account in its design and development.

A primary concern in the production and use of a place is the intention by some agencies to narrow and control participation so as to ensure particular outcomes, namely creating places that ensure a return on investment, that support and facilitate commercial operations and consumerist lifestyles, and that can be used as brands and promotional vehicles to attract more investors and visitors. Another reductive pressure on public space is the assumptions made by the designers, developers and local decision makers concerning who people are and what they need. These assumptions may be biased in favour of particular social classes, cultural groups, individual tastes and aesthetic considerations, different concepts of order and disorder, and different historic periods, often reflective of those who make them. Designers and developers may decide to allocate the worst part of a scheme to public spaces, designating the leftover areas as public spaces. They may impose an abstract geometry without paying attention to the patterns of lived experience among the users, creating lines on the map rather than places defined by physical enclosures and supported by a range of activities.

How can these competing claims over space be assessed? Each group may be able to justify its claim on the basis of its needs and requirements. But if the impact on others is exclusionary, such justification may lose its legitimacy. The principle by which the claims are evaluated and the character of public spaces examined should be the principle of equality. If a place is equally accessible to everyone, irrespective of their physical abilities, age, gender, ethnicity, income level and social status, it can be called a public space. It is on this basis that public spaces should be designed and developed, as places that embody the principles of equality, by being accessible places made through inclusive and democratic processes. Democratic and inclusive processes that create public space as a common good appear to be the best way of ensuring a better physical environment with social and psychological significance for the citizens. Where everyday needs for public spaces are met through participative processes, the result is both physical improvement and social development, laying the foundations for further enhancement of democratic practices.

References

Abbaszadegan, M. (1999) *An Examination of Certain Characteristics of Urban Open Spaces and Their Relation with User Behaviour in Iranian Cities*, Sheffield: University of Sheffield.

Abdullahi, R. (1986) *Self-Concept and Cultural Change among the Hausa*, Ibadan, Nigeria: Ibadan University Press.

Abu-Ghazzeh, T. M. (1996) 'Reclaiming public space: the ecology of neighbourhood open spaces in the town of Abu-Nuseir, Jordan', *Landscape and Urban Planning*, 36: 197–216.

Abu-Ghazzeh, T. M. (1997) 'Vernacular architecture education in the Islamic society of Saudi Arabia: towards the development of an authentic contemporary built environment', *Habitat*, 21 (2): 229–53.

Akbar, J. (1981) 'Responsibility and the traditional Muslim built environment', unpublished thesis, MIT, Cambridge, MA.

Akhoundi, A. (1996) 'Siasat-ha-ye tose'a maskan dar Iran' (Housing policies in Iran), *Iran*, 1 (490): 9–12.

Akkar, M. (2005a) 'The changing "publicness" of contemporary public spaces: a case study of the Grey's Monument area, Newcastle upon Tyne', *Urban Design International*, 10 (2): 95–113.

Akkar, M. (2005b) 'Questioning the inclusivity of public spaces in post-industrial cities: the case of Haymarket Bus Station, Newcastle upon Tyne', *METU Journal of the Faculty of Architecture*, 22 (2): 1–24.

Alfonzo, M., Boarnet, M. G., Day, K., Macmillan, T. and Anderson, C. L. (2008) 'The relationship of neighbourhood built environment features and adult parents' walking', *Journal of Urban Design*, 13 (1): 29–51.

Al-Hathloul, S. (1981) 'Tradition, continuity and change in the physical environment', unpublished thesis, MIT, Cambridge, MA.

Alkhedheiri, A. A. (2002) *The Role of Secondary Cities in National Development Process of Saudi Arabia*, Riyadh: Abdulaziz A. Alkhedheiri.

Allen, J. and Pryke, M. (1994) 'The production of service space', *Environment and Planning D: Society and Space*, 12: 453–75.

References

Al-Nowaiser, M. (1982) 'The role of traditional and modern residential rural settlements on the quality of environmental experience: a case study of Unyzeh and new Alkabra in Saudi Arabia', unpublished thesis, University of Southern California, Los Angeles.

Altman, I. and Zube, E. (eds) (1989) *Public Places and Spaces (Human Behavior and Environment)*, New York: Plenum Press.

Amin, A., Massey, D. and Thrift, N. (2000) *Cities for the Many Not the Few*, Bristol: Policy Press.

Andersen, H. T. and van Kempen, R. (2003) 'New trends in urban policies in Europe', *Cities*, 20 (2): 77–86.

Anderson, A. and Vieillard-Baron, H. (2000) *La Politique de la ville. Histoire et organisation*, Paris: Editions ASH.

Anon. (1994) 'Debate in store', *The Journal* (Newcastle upon Tyne), 8 June: 9.

Anon. (2001a) 'Employment change in Tyne and Wear 1998', Newcastle: Tyne and Wear Research and Information. Online, available at: www.tyne-wear-research.gov.uk/TWRI.nsf/0/7b42cca74bfcfacc80256b2500574cb5/$FILE/Employment%20Change91-98(p).pdf (accessed 8 August 2004).

Anon. (2001b) 'Plan to change face of the city', *Evening Chronicle* (Newcastle upon Tyne), 26 July. Online, available at: http://icnewcastle.icnetwork.co.uk/0100news/0100local/page.cfm?objectid=11184921&method=full&sitei d=50081 (accessed 7 August 2004).

Anon. (2003) 'Developers lay out the Square deal over revamp', *The Journal* (Newcastle upon Tyne), 3 December 2003. Online, available at: http://icnewcastle.icnetwork.co.uk/0100news/thejournal/thejournal/page.cfm?objecti d=13685949&method=full&siteid=50081 (accessed 7 August 2004).

Arendt, H. (1958) *The Human Condition*, Chicago: University of Chicago Press.

Atash, F. and Shirazibeheshtiha, Y. S. (1998) 'New towns and their practical challenges: the experience of Poolad Shahr in Iran', *Habitat International*, 22: 1–13.

Atkinson, R. (2000) 'Combating social exclusion in Europe', *Urban Studies*, 37: 1037–55.

Aristotle (1992) *The Politics*, London: Penguin Books.

Aziz-Alrahman, H. (1985) 'Review and Analysis of Land Use Regulations in Jeddah, Saudi Arabia', unpublished MS thesis, University of Wales, Cardiff.

Badenhorst, M. S. (1999) 'The South African City: a study in socio-spatial engineering', paper presented at the Third International Urban Planning and Environment Association Symposium, Pretoria, 5–9 April.

Banerjee, T. and Loukaitou-Sideris, A. (1992) *Private Production of Downtown Public Open Space: Experience of Los Angeles and San Francisco*, Los Angeles: School of Urban and Regional Planning, University of Southern California.

BBC (2003) *Britain My Britain*, documentary broadcast on Thursday 1 May 2003 at 11.20 p.m. Third in a series of four, London: British Broadcasting Corporation.

Benn, S. I. and Gaus, G. F. (1983) 'The public and the private: concepts and action', in S. I. Benn and G. F. Gaus (eds) *Public and Private in Social Life*, London: Croom Helm; New York: St Martin's Press.

Bentley, I. (1999) *Urban Transformations: Power, People and Urban Design*, London: Routledge.

Bentley, I., Alcock, A., Murrain, P., McGlynn, S. and Smith, G. (1985) *Responsive Environments: A Manual for Designers*, Oxford: Butterworth Architecture.

Berman, M. (1986) 'Take it to the streets: conflict and community in public space', *Dissent*, Fall (33): 478–85.

Blanc M. (1995) 'Politique de la ville et démocratie locale', *Les Annales de la Recherche Urbaine*, 68–69: 99–106.

Bokhari, A. (1978) 'Jeddah: a study in urban formation', unpublished thesis, University of Pennsylvania.

Bolívar, T. (1990) 'Los barrios: nueva forma de urbanización contemporánea', in M. Bassand and J.-C. Bolay (eds) *International Colloquium: Creative Habitat, Culture and Participation*, Lausanne: Institut de Recherche sur l'Environnement Construit, Commission Nationale Suisse pour l'UNESCO.

Boyer, M. C. (1992) 'Cities for sale: merchandising history at South Street Seaport', in M. Sorkin (ed.) *Variations on a Theme Park*, New York: Noonday Press.

Boyer, M. C. (1993) 'The city of illusion: New York's public places', in P. Knox (ed.) *The Restless Urban Landscape*, Englewood Cliffs, NJ: Prentice Hall.

Boyer, M. C. (1995) 'The great frame-up: fantastic appearances in contemporary spatial politics', in H. Liggett and D. C. Perry (eds) *Critical Explorations in Social/Spatial Theory*, Thousand Oaks, CA: Sage.

Braunfels, W. (1988) *Urban Design in Western Europe*, Chicago: University of Chicago Press.

Bromley, R., Hall, M. and Thomas, C. (2003) 'The impact of environmental improvement on town centre regeneration', *Town Planning Review*, 74 (2): 143–64.

Broomfield, D. (2000) Emails on Haymarket development from David Broomfield, the representative of M&S, 25 May and 26 June.

Brown, L. (ed.) (1993) *The New Shorter Oxford English Dictionary*, Oxford: Clarendon Press.

Burger, J. (2007) 'Security arrangements for the 2010 FIFA Soccer World Cup', *SA Crime Quarterly* (Pretoria), 19 (March).

Burke, E. M. (1979) *A Participatory Approach to Urban Planning*, New York: Human Sciences Press.

Caldarola, V. (1985) 'Visual contexts: a photographic research method in anthropology', *Studies in Visual Communication*, 11 (3): 33–53.

Calhoun, C. (ed.) (1992) *Habermas and the Public Sphere*, Cambridge, MA: MIT Press.

Cameron, S. and Doling, J. (1994) 'Housing neighbourhoods and urban regeneration', *Urban Studies*, 31 (7): 1211–23.

Carmona, M., Heath, T., Oc, T. and Tiesdell, S. (eds) (2003) *Public Places – Urban Spaces: The Dimensions of Urban Design*, Oxford: Architectural Press.

Carmona, M., De-Magalhaes, C. and Hammond, L. (2008) *Public Space: The Management Dimension*, London: Routledge.

References

Carr, S. M., Francis, M., Rivlin, L. G. and Stone, A. M. (1992) *Public Space*, Cambridge: Cambridge University Press.

Castells, M. (1977) *The Urban Question*, trans. A. Sheridan, London: Edward Arnold.

Ceballos, O. (2005) 'La evolución del planeamiento urbano en la configuración del espacio público del área periférica de Bogotá', *Bitácora Urbano/Territorial*, 9 (1): 17–26.

Celik, Z., Favro, D. and Ingersoll, R. (1994) *Streets: Critical Perspectives on Public Space*, Berkeley: University of California Press.

Chaline, C. (1998) *Les Politiques de la ville*, 2nd edn, Paris: Presses Universitaires de France.

Christopher, A. J. (1994) *The Atlas of Apartheid Space*, London: Routledge.

Clayden, A., McKoy, K. and Wild, A. (2006) 'Improving residential liveability in the UK: home zones and alternative approaches', *Journal of Urban Design*, 11 (1): 55–71.

Cloke, P. and Jones, O. (2005) ' "Unclaimed territory": childhood and disordered space(s)', *Social and Cultural Geography*, 6 (3): 311–33.

Collard, W. (1971) *Architectural and Picturesque Views in Newcastle upon Tyne*, Wakefield, UK: S.R. Publishers.

Comité de Pilotage de l'Aménagement du Quartier de la République (1999) 'Convention territoriale, Comité de pilotage du 08 septembre 1999', dossier, Archives of Ville d'Avion, unpublished.

Comité Technique Régional (1999) 'Préparation des contrats de ville 2000–2006. Documents d'aide méthodologique à l'usage des sites politiques de la ville en région Nord-Pas-de-Calais', unpublished, Archives of Région Nord-Pas-de-Calais, Conseil Régional.

Commission for Architecture and the Built Environment (CABE) and Office of the Deputy Prime Minister (ODPM) (2002) *Paving the Way: How We Achieve Clean, Safe and Attractive Streets*, London: Thomas Telford.

Contrat de Ville Haubourdin Petit Belgique – Atelier d'Urbanisme Participatif (1998) 'Enquête rue Général Dame–rue Roger Salengro', 20 February, unpublished, Archives of Ville de Haubourdin, France.

Cope, M. (1996) 'Weaving the everyday: identity, space and power in Lawrence, Massachusetts, 1920–1939', *Urban Geography*, 17 (2): 179–204.

Cousins, J. (1994) Letter on Haymarket development from Jim Cousins to the NCC, 29 June, NCC files: DET/01/0625/94.

Crilley, D. (1993) 'Megastructures and urban change: aesthetics, ideology and design', in P. L. Knox (ed.) *The Restless Urban Landscape*, Englewood Cliffs, NJ: Prentice Hall.

Crowther, J. (ed.) (1995) *Oxford Advanced Learner's Dictionary*, Oxford: University Press.

Cullen, G. (1971) *The Concise Townscape*, New York: Van Nostrand Reinhold.

Daghistani, A. (1991) 'Urban growth management in Jeddah', *Planning Outlook*, 34 (1): 2–9.

Daghistani, A. (1993) 'A case study in planning implementation', Working Paper 32, Newcastle University.

Davis, M. (1992) 'Fortress Los Angeles: the militarization of urban space', in M. Sorkin (ed.) *Variations on a Theme Park: Scenes from the New American City and the End of Public Space*, New York: Hill & Wang.

De Craeke, L., Di Dio, S. and Vandewynckele, M. (1996) 'Diagnostic social d'un ensemble de Cités Minières, Rapport final, 29 février 1996', unpublished, France: Archives of Communauté du Bruaysis.

Dean, M. (1999) *Governmentality: Power and Rule in Modern Society*, London: Sage.

Declève, B., Macou, A. and Mateu, R. (1999) 'Atelier d'urbanisme participatif de Haubourdin, Mémoire des activités du P'tit Belgique – Rapport d'activités 1998', unpublished, Archives of Ville de Haubourdin.

Declève, B., Macou, A. and Mateu, R. (2000) 'Ville d'Haubourdin, Evaluation participative du Contrat de Ville "Petit Belgique"', unpublished, Archives of Ville de Haubourdin.

Declève, B., Forray-Claps, R. and Michialino, P. (2002) *Coproduire nos espaces publics*, Louvain-la-Neuve: Presses Universitaires de Louvain.

De-Magalhaes, C. and Carmona, M. (2006) 'Innovations in the management of public space: reshaping and refocusing governance', *Planning Theory and Practice*, 7 (3): 289–303.

Denton Hall (1994) Planning agreement relating to the extension of the Marks & Spencer's Store Northumberland Street, Newcastle upon Tyne between City of Newcastle upon Tyne, Marks & Spencer and Scottish and Newcastle Plc. (19 September 1994), prepared by Denton Hall, solicitor for Marks & Spencer. London: Denton Hall.

Department for Communities and Local Government (DCLG) (2002) *Planning for Open Space, Sport and Recreation*, Planning Policy Guidance 17 (PPG17), London: DCLG.

Department for the Environment, Transport and the Regions (DETR) (1999) *Towards an Urban Renaissance: Executive Summary*, London: E. & F. N. Spon.

Department of the Environment, Transport and the Regions (DETR) (2000) *Our Towns and Cities: The future – Delivering an Urban Renaissance*, The Urban White Paper, London: DETR.

Department of the Environment (DoE) (1992) *The Effects of Major Out of Town Retail Development*, London: HMSO.

Desarrollo Urbano de Veracruz (1998) *Plan de Ordenamiento Urbano del Area Metropolitana (Xalapa–Banderilla–Coatepec–Emiliano Zapata–San Andrés Tlalnehuayocan, Veracruz)*, Urbano de Veracruz, Mexico.

Descartes, R. (1968) *Discourse on Method and The Meditations*, London: Penguin Books.

Deusen, V. (2002) 'Public space design as class warfare: urban design, the "right to the city" and the production of Clinton Square, Syracuse, NY', *GeoJournal*, 58 (2–3): 149–58.

Dillion, D. (1994) 'Fortress America', *Planning*, June: 8–12.

Dirsuweit, T. (2002) 'Johannesburg: fearful city?', *Urban Forum*, 13 (3): 3.

Donzelot, J. and Mongin, O. (2004) 'Villes à plusieurs vitesses et économie d'archipel', *Esprit*, 303 (March–April): 7–10.

References

Du Plessis, A. and Louw, A. (2005) 'The Tide Is Turning', *SA Crime Quarterly* (Pretoria), 12 (June).

Dublinate (2000) 'Dawn of new millennium for St. Teresa's Gardens', *Dublinate*, 2 (2): 1.

Eben-Saleh, M. (2002) 'The transformation of residential neighbourhood: the emergence of new urbanism in Saudi Arabian culture', *Building and Environment*, 37: 515–29.

EDAW (1996) *Grainger Town: Regeneration Strategy*, Newcastle: EDAW.

Eisinger, P. (2000) 'The politics of bread and circuses: building the city for the visitor class', *Urban Affairs Review*, 35 (3): 316–33.

Elden, S. (2001) *Mapping the Present: Heidegger, Foucault and the Project of a Spatial History*, London: Continuum.

Ellin, N. (1997) *Postmodern Urbanism*, Princeton, NJ: Princeton University Press.

Engels, F. (1993) *The Condition of the Working Class in England*, ed. David McLellan, Oxford: Oxford University Press.

European Commission (1994) *Europe 2000+: Cooperation for European Territorial Development*, Luxembourg: Office for Official Publications of the European Communities.

European Commission (1999) *Terra Newsletter*, June, Brussels: European Commission, DGXVI.

European Commission (2001) *Draft Joint Report on Social Exclusion*, Brussels: Office for Official Publications of the European Communities.

European Commission (2002) *Joint Report on Social Inclusion*, Luxembourg: Directorate-General for Employment, Industrial Relations and Social Affairs, OOPEC.

Evans, G. (2001) *Cultural Planning: An Urban Renaissance*, London: Routledge.

Featherstone, M. and Lash, S. (eds) (1999) *Spaces of Culture: City – Nation – World*, London: Sage.

Flusty, S. (1995) 'Building paranoia', in N. Ellin (ed.) *Architecture of Fear*, New York: Princeton Architectural Press.

Flyvbjerg, B. (1998) 'Empowering civil society: Habermas, Foucault and the question of conflict', in M. Douglass and J. Friedmann (eds) *Cities for Citizens: Planning and the Rise of Civil Society in a Global Age*, Chichester, UK: John Wiley.

Ford, L. (1999) 'Lynch revisited: new urbanism and theories of good city form', *Cities*, 16 (4): 247–57.

Foucault, M. (2003) *Society Must Be Defended: Lectures at the Collège de France 1975–76*, trans. D. Macey, London: Penguin Books.

Foucault, M. (2007) *Security, Territory, Population: Lectures at the Collège de France 1977–78*, trans. G. Burchill, London: Palgrave Macmillan.

Francis, M. (1987) 'The making of democratic streets', in A. V. Moudon (ed.) *Public Streets for Public Use*, New York: Columbia University Press.

Francis, M. (1989) 'Control as a dimension of public-space quality', in I. Altman and E. Zube (eds) *Public Places and Space*, New York: Plenum Press.

Franck, K. and Stevens, Q. (2007) *Loose Space: Possibility and Diversity in Urban Life*, Oxford: Routledge.

Fraser, N. (1989) *Unruly Practices: Power, Discourse and Gender in Contemporary Social Theory*, Minneapolis: Minnesota University Press.

Fraser, N. (1997) *Justice Interruptus: Critical Reflections on the 'Postsocialist' Condition*, New York: Routledge.

Garba, S. B. (2007) 'Change in the public space of traditional Hausa cities: a study of Zaria', unpublished thesis, Newcastle University.

Gehl, J. (1987) *Life between Buildings: Using Public Space*, New York: Van Nostrand Reinhold.

Gehl, J. (1996) *Life between Buildings: Using Public Space*, Copenhagen: Arkitektens Forlag.

Giddens, A. (1981) *A Contemporary Critique of Historical Materialism*, vol. 1, *Power, Property and the State*, Berkeley: University of California Press.

Glotz, G. (1929) *The Greek City and Its Institutions*, London: Kegan Paul, Trench, Trübner; New York: A. A. Knopf.

Goffman, E. (1959) *The Presentation of Self in Everyday Life*, London: Pelican Books.

Goheen, P. G. (1998) 'Public space and the geography of the modern city', *Progress in Human Geography*, 22 (4): 479–96.

Golkar, K. (2001) 'Moallefehay-e sazand-e keifyyat-e tarrahi shahri' (Components of urban design quality), *Soffeh Architectural Science and Research Journal*, 32: 10–21.

Gomes, F. (2002) 'Urbanización de las favelas y producción de espacio', *Trace. Experiencia Democrática y Ciudadanía*, 42: 28–37.

Goodwin, M. (1993) 'The city as commodity: the contested spaces of urban development', in G. Philo and C. Philo (eds) *Selling Places: The City as Cultural Capital, Past and Present*, Oxford: Pergamon Press.

Gottdiener, M. (1994) *The Social Production of Urban Space*, 2nd edn, Austin: University of Texas Press.

Gove, P. B. (ed.) (1976) *Webster's Third New International Dictionary*, Chicago: Encyclopaedia Britannica.

Goyens, C. and Michialino, P. (1998) 'Atelier de travail urbain Saint Pol sur Mer', in B. Declève, E. Gueuret, B. Montulet and J. Valentin (eds) 'Evaluation participative de l'amélioration des services publics dans le cadre du contrat de ville de l'agglomération de Dunkerque. Echantillon d'actions d'amélioration des services publics', unpublished, Archives of Ville de Dunkerque, France: fiche SP3.

Graham, S. and Marvin, S. (2001) *Splintering Urbanism: Network Infrastructures, Technological Mobilities and the Urban Condition*, London: Routledge.

Graham, S., Brooks, J. and Heery, D. (1996) 'Towns on the television: closed-circuit TV in British towns and cities', *Local Government Studies*, 22 (3): 3–27.

Gregory, D. (1989) 'A real differentiation and post-modern human geography', in D. Gregory and R. Walford (eds) *Horizon in Human Geography*, Totowa, NJ: Barnes & Noble.

Grundy, J., McCombie, G., Ryder, P., Welfare, H. and Pevsner, N. (1992) *Northumberland*, London: Penguin Books.

References

Habermas, J. (1978) *Espace public*, Paris: Payot.

Habermas, J. (1989) *The Structural Transformation of the Public Sphere: An Inquiry into a Category of Bourgeois Society*, Cambridge: Polity Press.

Hajer, M. A. (1993) 'Rotterdam: re-designing the public domain', in F. Bianchini and M. Parkinson (eds) *Cultural Policy and Urban Regeneration: The West European Experience*, Manchester: Manchester University Press.

Hall, M. J. (2000) *The Impact of Environmental Improvements on Town Centre Regeneration: A Case Study of Llanelli, South Wales*, Swansea: University of Wales at Swansea.

Hall, T. and Hubbard, P. (1996) 'The entrepreneurial city: new urban politics, new urban geographies?', *Progress in Human Geography*, 20 (2): 153–74.

Hamber, B. (1999) ' "Have no doubt it is fear in the land": an exploration of continuing cycles of violence in South Africa', *Zeitschrift für politische Psychologie*, 7 (1–2): 113–28.

Hannerz, U. (1980) *Exploring the City*, New York: Columbia University Press.

Harbottle, B. (1990) *Haymarket and Percy Street*, a report by the archaeologist in the County Conservation Team, Newcastle City Council: Planning Department.

Hartwell, C. (1994) Letter on Haymarket development from the Victorian Society to NCC (12 June), NCC files: DET/01/0625/94, Newcastle City Council.

Hass-Klau, C., Crampton, G., Dowland, C. and Nold, I. (1999) *Streets as Living Space: Helping Public Spaces Play Their Proper Role*, London: Landor Publishing.

Hayden, D. (1995) *The Power of Place: Urban Landscapes as Public History*, Cambridge, MA: MIT Press.

Healey, P. (1997) *Collaborative Planning: Shaping Places in Fragmented Societies*, Basingstoke, UK: Macmillan.

Healey, P., De-Magalhaes, C., Madanipour, A. and Pendlebury, J. (2002) *Shaping City Centre Futures: Conservation, Regeneration and Institutional Capacity*, Newcastle: University of Newcastle.

Henderson, T. (1994) 'Store's jazzy plan brings the blues', *The Journal* (Newcastle upon Tyne), 6 June: 3.

Herbert, R. (2003) 'Where fear rules the street', *New York Times*, 9 June. Online, available at: www.nytimes.com (accessed 9 June 2003).

Hester, R. (1984) *Planning Neighbourhood Spaces with People*, New York: Van Nostrand Reinhold.

Hogben, S. J. (1967) *An Introduction to the History of the Islamic States of Northern Nigeria*, Ibadan: Oxford University Press.

Honar va Memari (1977) *Master Plan of Pooladshahr*, Tehran: MHUD.

Hubbard, P. (1995) 'Urban design and local economic development: a case study, Birmingham', *Cities*, 12 (4): 243–51.

Imrie, R. and Raco, M. (eds) (2003) *Urban Renaissance? New Labour, Community and Urban Policy*, London: Policy Press.

INEGI (2005) *Principales resultados por localidad 2005 (ITER), Ciudad de Xalapa-Enríquez*, Mexico City: Instituto Nacional de Estadística, Geografía e Informática.

Jackson, J. B. (1994) *A Sense of Place, A Sense of Time*, New Haven, CT: Yale University Press.

Jackson, T. (1994) Letter on Haymarket development from Tony Jackson to NCC (1 June), NCC files: DET/01/0625/94, Newcastle City Council.

Jacobs, J. (1961) *The Death and Life of Great American Cities*, New York: Vintage Books.

Jacobs, A. and Appleyard, D. (1996) 'Toward an urban design manifesto', in R. T. LeGates and F. Stout (eds) *The City Reader*, London: Routledge.

Jammer, M. (1969) *Concepts of Space: The History of Theories of Space in Physics*, Cambridge, MA: Harvard University Press.

Jivan, G. and Larkham, P. (2003) 'Sense of place, authenticity and character: a commentary', *Journal of Urban Design*, 8 (1): 67–81.

Judd, D. R. (1995) 'The rise of the new walled cities', in H. Liggett and D. C. Perry (eds) *Spatial Practices: Critical Explorations in Social/Spatial Theory*, Thousand Oaks, CA: Sage.

Kapoor, I. (2002) 'The devil's in the theory: a critical assessment of Robert Chambers' work on participatory development', *Third World Quarterly*, 23 (1): 101–17.

Kearns, A. and Parkinson, M. (2001) 'The significance of neighbourhood', *Urban Studies*, 38: 2013–110.

Kearns, G. and Philo, C. (1993) *Selling Places: The City as Cultural Capital, Past and Present*, Oxford: Pergamon Press.

Kallus, R. (2001) 'From abstract to concrete: subjective reading of urban space', *Journal of Urban Design*, 6 (2): 129–50.

Kelly, P. (2003) 'Growing up as risky business? Risks, surveillance and the institutionalized mistrust of youth', *Journal of Youth Studies*, 6 (2): 165–80.

Kenyon, J. R. (ed.) (1990) *Medieval Fortifications*, London: Leicester University Press.

Knox, P. (1995) *Urban Social Geography: An Introduction*, Harlow, UK: Longman.

Knox, P. and Pinch, S. (2000) *Urban Social Geography: An Introduction*, Harlow, UK: Prentice Hall.

Kostof, S. (1992) *The City Assembled: The Elements of Urban Form through History*, London: Thames & Hudson.

Krier, R. (1979) *Urban Space*, London: Academy Editions.

Landman, K. (2003) *A National Survey of Gated Communities in South Africa*, Pretoria, CSIR Publication BOU/I 257.

Landman, K. (2006) 'An exploration of urban transformation in post-apartheid South Africa through gated communities, with a specific focus on its relation to crime and impact on socio-spatial integration', unpublished thesis, University of Newcastle upon Tyne.

Lang, A. (1999) 'Regulation and regeneration: how do development plans affect urban regeneration?', unpublished thesis, University of Newcastle upon Tyne.

Lang, J. (1996) 'Implementing urban design in America: project types and methodological implications', *Journal of Urban Design*, 1: 7–22.

Lees, L. (2003) 'Visions of "urban renaissance": the Urban Task Force Report and

References

the Urban White Paper', in M. Raco and R. Imrie (eds) *Urban Renaissance? New Labour, Community and Urban Policy*, London: Routledge.

Lefebvre, H. (1991) *The Production of Space*, Oxford: Blackwell.

Lefebvre, H. (2004) *Rhythmanalysis: Space, Time and Everyday Life*, London: Continuum.

Lescieux-Macou, A. (2001) 'D'héritiers en batisseurs ... l'atelier d'urbanisme participatif du "P'tit Belgique" ', Mémoire de Maîtrise en Sciences de l'Education, Université de Lille III.

Lichtenberg, E., Constant Tra, C. and Hardie, I (2007) 'Land use regulation and the provision of open space in suburban residential subdivisions', *Journal of Environmental Economics and Management*, 54 (2): 199–213.

Liggett, H. and Perry, D. C. (eds) (1995) *Critical Explorations in Social/Spatial Theory*, Thousand Oaks, CA: Sage.

Light, A. and Smith, J. (eds) (1998) *The Production of Public Space*, Oxford: Rowman & Littlefield.

Loukaitou-Sideris, A. (1988) 'Private production of public open space: the downtown Los Angeles experience', unpublished thesis, University of Southern California, Los Angeles.

Loukaitou-Sideris, A. (1993) 'Privatisation of public open space: the Los Angeles experience', *Town Planning Review*, 64 (2): 139–67.

Loukaitou-Sideris, A. and Banerjee, T. (1998) *Urban Design Downtown*, Berkeley: University of California Press.

Lowes, F. J. (1994) Letter on Haymarket development from Senior Lecturer of the University of Newcastle upon Tyne to Newcastle City Council (13 June), NCC files: DET/01/0625/94, Newcastle City Council.

Lynch, K. (1981) *A Theory of Good City Form*, Cambridge, MA: MIT Press.

Lynch, K. (1992) 'The openness of open space', in T. Banerjee and M. Southworth (eds) *City Sense and City Design*, Cambridge, MA: MIT Press.

Lynch, K. and Carr, S. (1990) 'Open space: freedom and control' (1979), in K. Lynch, T. Banerjee and M. Southworth (eds) *City Sense and City Design: Writings and Projects of Kevin Lynch*, Cambridge, MA: MIT Press.

McClelland, G. (1988) Foreword to F. Robinson (ed.) *Post-industrial Tyneside*, Newcastle: Newcastle Libraries and Arts.

McDonald, G. (1994) Letter on Haymarket development from Eldon Square Capital Shopping Centre plc to Newcastle City Council (11 July), NCC files: DET/01/0625/94, Newcastle City Council.

McInroy, N. (2000) 'Urban regeneration and public space: the story of an urban park', *Space and Polity*, 4 (1): 23–40.

MacLeod, G. (2002) 'From urban entrepreneurialism to a "revanchist city"? On the spatial injustices of Glasgow's renaissance', *Antipode*, 34 (3): 602–24.

Madanipour, A. (1992) *The Principles of Urban Design in British New Towns*, Newcastle upon Tyne: Newcastle University.

Madanipour, A. (1995) 'Dimensions of urban public space: the case of the Metro Centre, Gateshead', *Urban Design Studies*, 1: 45–56.

Madanipour, A. (1996) *Design of Urban Space*, Chichester: John Wiley.

Madanipour, A. (1999) 'Why are the design and development of public spaces significant for cities?', *Environment and Planning B: Planning and Design*, 26: 879–91.

Madanipour, A. (2000) 'Public space in the city', in P. Knox and P. Ozolins (eds) *Design Professionals and the Built Environment*, New York: John Wiley.

Madanipour, A. (2003a) *Public and Private Spaces of the City*, London: Routledge.

Madanipour, A. (2003b) *Cities' Actions against Social Exclusion*, Brussels: Eurocities.

Madanipour, A. (2003c) 'Why are the design and development of public spaces significant for cities?', in A. R. Cuthbert (ed.) *Designing Cities: Critical Readings in Urban Design*, Oxford: Blackwell.

Madanipour, A. (2004) 'Marginal public spaces in European cities', *Journal of Urban Design*, 9 (3): 267–86.

Madanipour, A. (2006) 'Roles and challenges of urban design', *Journal of Urban Design*, 11 (2): 173–93.

Madanipour, A. (2007) *Designing the City of Reason*, London: Routledge.

Madanipour, A., Cars, G. and Allen, J. (eds) (2003) *Social Exclusion in European Cities: Processes, Experiences, Responses*, London: Routledge.

Mahdi, A. (1974) 'The Hausa factor in West African history', unpublished thesis, University of Birmingham.

Makins, M. (ed.) (1998) *Collins Concise Dictionary*, Glasgow: HarperCollins.

Mandeli, K. (2008) 'The realities of integrating physical planning and local management into urban development: a case study of Jeddah, Saudi Arabia', *Habitat International*, 32: 512–33.

Marcus, C. C. and Sarkissian, W. (eds) (1986). *Housing as if People Mattered*, Berkeley and Los Angeles: University of California Press.

Marcuse, P. (2001) 'Enclaves yes, ghettoes no: segregation and the state', paper presented at the International Seminar on Segregation in the City, Lincoln Institute of Land Policy, Cambridge, MA, 25–28 July.

Martindale, D. (1966) 'Prefatory remarks: the theory of the city', in Max Weber, *The City*, New York: The Free Press.

Massey, D. (1985) 'New Directions in Space', in D. Gregory and J. Urry (eds) *Social Relations and Spatial Structures*, London: Macmillan.

Massey, D. (1994) *Space, Place and Gender*, Cambridge: Polity Press.

Massey, D. (1999) 'City life: proximity and difference', in D. Massey, D. Allen and S. Pile (eds) *City Worlds*, London: Routledge, in association with the Open University Press.

Matas, J., Riveros, F. and De La Puente, P. (1988) *El espacio público en el hábitat residencial pobre*, Santiago de Chile: Instituto de Estudios Urbanos, Pontificia Universidad Católica de Chile.

Mauch, J. E. and Birch, J. W. (1998) *Guide to the Successful Thesis and Dissertation: A Handbook for Students and Faculty*, New York: M. Dekker.

Maury, Y. (1995) 'La Négociation des contrats de ville, *Les Annales de la Recherche Urbaine*, 68–69: 43–57.

References

Meegan, R. and Mitchell, A. (2001) 'It's not community round here, it's neighbourhood', *Urban Studies*, 38: 2167–94.

Meyers, W. R. (2003) 'What is public about public space: the case of Visakhapatnam, India', *Cities* 20 (5): 331–9.

Michialino, P. (2006) *Authentic Co-production of Public Space*, Louvain-la-Neuve: Presses Universitaires de Louvain.

Mistry, D. (2004) 'Falling crime, rising fear', *Crime Quarterly*, 8: 17–24.

Mitchell, D. (1995) 'The end of public space: People's Park, definitions of the public and democracy', *Annals of the Association of American Geographers*, 85 (1): 108–33.

Mitchell, D. (1996) 'Introduction: public space and the city', *Urban Geography*, 17 (2): 127–31.

Mittins, R. (1978) 'The history and development of Percy Street – Newcastle upon Tyne', unpublished BA dissertation, Newcastle: University of Newcastle upon Tyne.

Montgomery, S. (1986) 'Planning and urban change in Saudi Arabia', *Journal of Environmental Planning and Management*, 29 (2): 74–9.

Morris, A. E. J. (ed.) (1994) *History of Urban Form: Before the Industrial Revolutions*, Harlow, UK: Addison Wesley Longman.

Mouffe, C. (1999) 'Deliberative democracy or agonistic pluralism?', *Social Research*, 66 (3): 745–58.

Moughtin, J. C. (1985) *Hausa Architecture*, London: Ethnographica.

Moughtin, J. C. (1999) *Urban Design: Street and Square*, 2nd edn, Oxford: Architectural Press.

Moughtin, J. C. (2003) *Urban Design: Street and Square*, 3rd edn, Oxford: Architectural Press.

Moulaert, F., Demuynck, H. and Nussbaumer, J. (2004) 'Urban renaissance: from physical beautification to social empowerment', *City*, 8 (2): 229–35.

Mumford, L. (1961) *The City in History: Its Origins, Its transformation and Its Prospects*, San Diego, CA: Harcourt Brace.

Municipality of Jeddah (2006) *Jeddah Local Plan*, Jeddah: Jeddah Municipality.

Municipality of Jeddah (2004) *Jeddah Structure Plan*, Jeddah: Jeddah Municipality.

Naqsh-e Jahan Pars (1991) *Urban Spaces in Esfahan*, Tehran: MHUD.

Négrier, E. (1999) 'The changing role of French local government', *West European Politics*, 22 (4): 120–40.

Newcastle City Council (1963) *Development Plan Review 1963*, City and County of Newcastle.

Newcastle City Council (1994a) *Report of the Director of Development*, a report submitted to the Development Control Sub-Committee on 1 July, Newcastle: Newcastle City Council.

Newcastle City Council (1994b) *Newcastle upon Tyne Unitary Development Plan, 1994*, Newcastle: Newcastle City Council.

Newcastle City Council (1994c) *Report of the City Estate and Property Surveyor, Director of Development, Director of Engineering, Environment and Protection, Acting Director of Law and Administration and City Treasurer*, submitted to the Regeneration Sub-Committee, Finance Committee, Development Committee and Environment and Highways Committee for decision, Newcastle: Newcastle City Council.

Newcastle City Council (1995) *Report on Haymarket Development*, submitted for information to the Environment and Highways Committee and the Development Committee by the City Estate and Property Surveyor, Director of Development, Director of Engineering, Environment and Protection, Assistant Director of Administration and City Treasurer, Newcastle: Newcastle City Council.

Newcastle City Council (1996a) Memorandum on M&S Haymarket development Outstanding Matters, 27 August, a memorandum prepared by the Chief Planning Officer, NCC files: DET/01/0625/94, Newcastle City Council.

Newcastle City Council (1996b) Letter on Haymarket development from Chief Planning Officer, Newcastle City Council, to Nathaniel Lichfield & Partners, 29 May, NCC files: DET/01/0625/94, Newcastle City Council.

Newcastle City Council (1996c) Memorandum, 15 July, prepared by the Director of Development, NCC files: DET/01/0625/94, Newcastle City Council.

Newcastle City Council (1996d) Letter on Haymarket Development from Chief Planning Officer, NCC, to Nathaniel Lichfield & Partners, 25 June, NCC files: DET/01/0625/94, Newcastle City Council.

Newcastle City Council (2000) *Draft Masterplans for the East End and West End of Newcastle: Consultation and Participation*, Newcastle: Newcastle City Council.

Newcastle City Council (2002) *City Centre Action Plan Review 2001–2002*, Newcastle: Newcastle City Council.

Newcastle City Council (2004) *Green Spaces ... Your spaces: Newcastle's Green Spaces Strategy April 2004*, Newcastle: Newcastle City Council.

Newcastle City Libraries and Arts (NCLA) (1984) *The Sixties: Gone but Not Forgotten*, Newcastle: NCLA.

Newcastle City Libraries and Arts (NCLA) (2000) *Newspaper Cuttings: The City Centre*, Newcastle: Archive of Newcastle upon Tyne City Libraries and Arts.

Newman, O. (1972) *Defensible Space: Crime Prevention through Urban Design*, New York: Macmillan.

NEXUS (n.d.) *Who Are We?* [home page of NEXUS, Tyne and Wear]. Online, available at www.nexus.org.uk/pdf/corporatebrochure.pdf (accessed 28 March 2002).

Niño, C. and Chaparro J. (1997) 'El espacio público en algunos barrios populares de la Bogotá actual', in H. Carvajalino (ed.) *La calle: lo ajeno, lo público y lo imaginado*, Santa Fe de Bogotá, Colombia: Documentos Barrio Taller, Series Ciudad y Hábitat No. 4.

Nolan, Lord (1995) *Standards in Public Life: First Report on the Standards in Public Life*, vol. 1: Report (Cm 2850-l), London: HMSO.

Norberg-Schultz, C. (1980) *Genius Loci: Towards a Phenomenology of Architecture*, London: Academy Editions.

Oc, T. and Tiesdell, S. (1997) 'Opportunity reduction approaches to crime prevention', in T. Oc and S. Tiesdell (eds) *Safer City Centres: Reviving the Public Realm*, London: Paul Chapman.

References

Oc, T. and Tiesdell, S. (1998) 'City centre management and safer city centres: approaches in Coventry and Nottingham', *Cities*, 15 (2): 85–103.

Office of Population Censuses and Surveys (1982) *Census 1981 – County Report: Tyne and Wear*, London: HMSO.

Office of the Deputy Prime Minister (ODPM) (2002) *Living Places: Cleaner, Safer, Greener*, London: ODPM.

Office of the Deputy Prime Minister (ODPM) (2004) *Living Places: Caring for Quality*, London: Office of the Deputy Prime Minister. Online, available at: www.communities.gov.uk/documents/communities/pdf/131006 (accessed 23 January 2008).

Orr, Sir C. (1965) *The Making of Northern Nigeria*, London: Frank Cass.

Pacione, M. (1997) 'Urban restructuring and the reproduction of inequality in Britain's cities: an overview', in M. Pacione (ed.) *Britain's Cities: Geographies of Division in Urban Britain*, London: Routledge.

Page, S. J. and Hardyman, R. (1996) 'Place marketing and town centre management: a new tool for urban revitalization', *Cities*, 13 (3): 153–64.

Pakzad, J. (2000) 'Keifyyat: Motaleb-e Maoavvaq-e Shahrvandan' (Quality: the residents' postponed desire), *Shahrdariha*, 23: 33–9.

Parkinson, M. (1989) 'The Thatcher Government's urban policy, 1979–1989', *Town Planning Review*, 69 (4): 421–40.

Pasaogullari, N. and Doratli, N. (2004) 'Measuring accessibility and utilization of public spaces in Famagusta', *Cities*, 21 (3): 225–32.

Pendlebury, J. (2001) 'Alas Smith and Burns? Conservation in Newcastle upon Tyne city centre 1959–68', *Planning Perspectives*, 16: 115–41.

Pérez Valecillos, T. (2000) 'Espacio público: convivencia y escenario de la sociedad – asentamientos urbanos precarios – caso de estudio: municipio Maracaibo del Estado Zulia, Venezuela', presented at Noveno Congreso Iberoamericano de Urbanismo, Recife.

Perry, N. (1996) Letter on Haymarket development from Nathaniel Litchfield & Partners to Newcastle City Council, 10 June, NCC files: DET/01/0625/94, Newcastle City Council.

PNTDC (1990) *Pooladshahr New Town*, Pooladshahr: PNTDC.

PNTDC (1993) *Pooladshahr New Town*, Pooladshahr: PNTDC.

Poordeihimi, S. (2003) 'Fazahay-e baz dar majmooehay-e maskooni' (Open spaces in residential complexes), *Soffeh Architectural Science and Research Journal*, 36: 25–36.

Pred A. (1984a) 'Places as historically contingent process: structuration and the time geography of becoming places', *Annals of the Association of American Geographers*, 74 (2): 279–97.

Pred, A. (1984b) 'Structuration, biography formation and knowledge', *Environment and Planning D: Society and Space*, 2: 251–75.

Punter, J. V. (1990) 'The privatisation of the public realm', *Planning, Practice and Research*, 5 (3): 9–16.

Punter, J. (1991) 'Participation in the design of urban space', *Landscape Design* (200): 24–7.

Punter, J. (2007) 'Developing design as public policy: best practice principles for design review and development', *Journal of Urban Design*, 12 (2): 167–202.

Rapoport, A. (1977) *Human Aspects of Urban Form: Towards a Man–Environment Approach to Urban Form and Design*, Oxford: Pergamon Press.

Rapoport, A. (1986) 'The use and design of open spaces in urban neighbourhoods', in D. Frick (ed.) *Quality of Urban Life: Social, Psychological, and Physical Conditions*, New York: De Gruyter.

Ravenscroft, N. (2000) 'The vitality and viability of town centres', *Urban Studies*, 37 (13): 2533–49.

Reeve, A. (1996) 'The private realm of the managed town centre', *Urban Design International*, 1 (1): 61–80.

Relph, E. (1976) *Place and Placelessness*, London: Pion.

Renne, P. E. (1997) 'Changing pattern of child spacing and abortion in a northern Nigerian town', Office of Population Research Working Paper 97-1, Princeton University.

Report of Directors (2002) Prepared by the Board of Directors of Strubenkop. Unpublished document.

Riaño, Y. (1990) 'Understanding the cultural dynamics of popular habitats: from spatial activity patterns to local identity in the barrios of Bogotá, Colombia', in M. Bassand and J.-C. Bolay (eds) *International Colloquium: Creative Habitat, Culture and Participation*, Lausanne: Institut de Recherche sur l'Environnement Construit, Commission Nationale Suisse pour l'UNESCO.

Riaño, Y. (1996) 'History of appropriation of barrio outdoor spaces for sports: creating and recreating public space', PhD thesis, *Social Networks in Space: Understanding the Daily Behaviour of Urban Residents in Barrio Mena del Hierro, Quito, Ecuador*, Canada: University of Ottawa.

Riaño, Y. (1998) 'Espacio, redes sociales e interacción cotidiana: hacia una comprensión de la dinámica cultural popular en el barrio Mena del Hierro (Quito)', in J. C. Bolay, Y. B. Pedrazzini and M. Bassand (eds) *Hábitat creativo: elogio de los hacedores de ciudades*, Montevideo: Ediciones Trilce & IREC.

Ricoeur, P. (1985) 'Éthique et politique', *Esprit*, 101 (May): 1–11.

Robinson, F. (1988a) 'Industrial structure', in F. Robinson (ed.) *Post-industrial Tyneside*, Newcastle: Newcastle Libraries and Arts.

Robinson, F. (1988b) 'The labour market', in F. Robinson (ed.) *Post-industrial Tyneside*, Newcastle: Newcastle Libraries and Arts.

Robinson, J. (1996) *The Power of Apartheid: State, Power and Space in South African Cities*, Oxford: Butterworth-Heinemann.

Rodríguez, H. (1993) 'Xalapa: crecimiento urbano, trabajo y economía', *Ciudades. Desarrollo Regional y Expansión Urbana* (Red Nacional de Investigación Urbana, Mexico City), (18): 30–37.

Rogers, P. (2005) 'Youth, urban management and public space: reconciling social exclusion and urban renaissance', unpublished thesis, University of Newcastle upon Tyne.

Rogers, P. (2006) 'Young people's participation in the renaissance of public space: a case study of Newcastle upon Tyne, UK', *Children, Youth and Environments*,

References

16 (2): 105–26. Online, available at: www.Colorado.edu/journals/cye (accessed 12 May 2008).

Rogers, P. and Coaffee, J. (2006) 'Moral panics and urban renaissance: policy, tactics and youth in public space', *City*, 9 (3): 321–40.

Rojas, E. and Guerrero, G. (1997) 'La calle del barrio popular: fragmento de una ciudad fragmentada', in H. Carvajalino (ed.) *La calle: lo ajeno, lo público y lo imaginado*, Santa Fe de Bogotá, Colombia: Documentos Barrio Taller, Series Ciudad y Hábitat no. 4.

Room, G. (ed.) (1995) *Beyond the Threshold: The Measurement and Analysis of Social Exclusion*, Bristol: Policy Press.

Ruddick, S. (1996) 'Constructing difference in public space: race, class, and gender as interlocking systems', *Urban Geography*, 17 (2): 132–51.

Rutter, N. (1994) Letter on Haymarket development from N. Rutter to Newcastle City Council, 14 June, NCC files: DET/01/0625/94, Newcastle City Council.

Rygiel, P. (2000) 'Les Traces de la mobilité géographique', *Actes de l'Histoire de l'Immigration*, revue électronique, vol. 0, 2000. Online, available at: http://barthes.ens.fr/clio/revues/AHI/articles/volumes/mobgeo.html (accessed 18 November 2008).

Rypkema, D. D. (2003) 'The importance of downtown in the 21st century', *Journal of the American Planning Association*, 69 (1): 9–15.

Saalman, H. (1968) *Medieval Cities*, London: Studio Vista.

Sadler, D. (1993) 'Place-marketing, competitive places and the construction of hegemony in Britain in the 1980s', in G. Philo and C. Philo (eds) *Selling Places: The City as Cultural Capital, Past and Present*, Oxford: Pergamon Press.

Saldarriaga, A. (1997) 'Espacio público y calidad de vida', in H. Carvajalino (ed.) *La calle: lo ajeno, lo público y lo imaginado*, Bogotá: Documentos Barrio Taller, Series Ciudad y Hábitat no. 4.

Schmidt, S. (2005) 'Cultural influences and the built environment: an examination of Kumasi, Ghana', *Journal of Urban Design*, 10 (3): 353–70.

Schönteich, M. and Louw, A. (2001) 'Crime in South Africa: a country and cities profile', ISS Paper 49, April, Pretoria: ISS Publication.

Scotland Development Department (1999) *Improving Town Centres*, Edinburgh: Scotland Executive Development Department.

Scruton, R. (1987) 'Public space and the classical vernacular', in N. Glazier and M. Lilla (eds) *Civic Culture and Public Spaces*, New York: The Free Press.

Segovia, O. (1997) 'The woman dweller: public space in Santiago', in J. Beall (ed.) *A City of All: Valuing Difference and Working Diversity*, London: Zed Books.

Segovia, O. (2001) 'Gestión participativa para la recuperación de espacios públicos', *Temas Sociales: Boletín del Programa de Pobreza y Políticas Sociales de Sur*, no. 43.

Segovia, O. and Oviedo, E. (2000) 'Espacios públicos en la ciudad y el barrio', in O. Segovia and G. Dascal (eds) *Espacio público, participación y ciudadanía*, Santiago de Chile: Ediciones Sur.

Sennett, R. (1994) *Flesh and Stone*, London: Faber & Faber.

Serfaty, M. A. (1994) Letter on Haymarket development from M. A. Serfaty to Newcastle City Council, 30 May, NCC files: DET/01/0625/94, Newcastle City Council.

Shaw, S., Bagwell, S. and Karmowska, J. (2004) 'Ethnoscapes as spectacle: reimaging multicultural districts as new destinations for leisure and tourism consumption', *Urban Studies*, 41 (10): 1983–2000.

Shields, R. (1992) *Lifestyle Shopping: The Subject of Consumption*, London: Routledge.

Short, J. (1996) *The Urban Order: An Introduction to Cities, Culture and Power*, Malden, MA: Blackwell.

Silver, A. (1997) 'Two different sorts of commerce: friendship and strangership in civil society', in J. Weintraub and K. Kumar (eds) *Public and Private in Thought and Action: Perspectives on a Grand Dichotomy*, Chicago: University of Chicago Press.

Simmel, G. (1950) 'The metropolis and mental life', in K. Wolff (ed.) *The Sociology of Georg Simmel*, New York: The Free Press.

Simpson, A., Leitch, D. and Wharton, T. (eds) (1997) *Cityscape: Streets for People*, Newcastle: Northern Region of the Royal Institute of British Architects.

Sitte, C. (1986; originally 1889) 'City planning according to artistic principles', in G. Collins and C. Collins (eds) *Camillo Sitte: The Birth of Modern City Planning*, New York: Rizzoli.

Slater, T. (2004) 'North American gentrification? Revanchist and emancipatory perspectives explored', *Environment and Planning A*, 36: 1191–213.

Smith, N. (1996) *The New Urban Frontier: Gentrification and the Revanchist City*, London: Routledge.

Sorkin, M. (ed.) (1992) *Variations on a Theme Park: The New American City and the End of Public Space*, New York: Hill & Wang.

Southall, A. (1998) *The City in Time and Space*, Cambridge: Cambridge University Press.

Squires, P. and Stephen, D. E. (2005) *Rougher Justice: Anti-social Behaviour and Young People*, London: Willan.

Staeheli, L. A. and Thompson, A. (1997) 'Citizenship, community and struggles for public space', *The Professional Geographer*, 49 (1): 28–38.

Staeheli, L. A., Mitchell, D. and Gibson, K. (2002) 'Conflicting rights to the city in New York's community gardens', *GeoJournal*, 58 (2–3): 197–205.

Stone, I. (1995) 'Symbolism and substance in the modernisation of a traditional industrial economy: the case of Wearside', in R. Turner (ed.) *The British Economy in Transition: From the Old to the New?*, London: Routledge.

Swilling, M. (1991) 'Introduction', in M. Swilling, R. Humphries and K. Shubane (eds) *Apartheid City in Transition*, Cape Town: Oxford University Press.

Taichung City Government (2004) *Revision of Taichung City General Plan (TCGP)*, Taichung, Taiwan: Taichung City Government.

Taichung City Police Bureau (2006) *Statistical Yearbook of Police in 2006*, Taichung, Taiwan: Taichung City Government.

Talachyan, M. (2005) *New Towns in Iran*, Tehran: NTDC.

Tavallai, N. (1990) 'Fazahay-e shahri: ravabet-e ejtemaii va farhangi' (Urban space: social and cultural relationships), unpublished Master's degree thesis, Tehran: Tehran University.

References

Taylor, C. (1995) 'Liberal politics and the public sphere', in A. Etzioni (ed.) *New Communitarian Thinking: Persons, Virtues, Institutions and Communities*, Charlottesville: University Press of Virginia.

Thomas, C. J. and Bromley, R. D. F. (2000) 'City-centre revitalisation: problems of fragmentation and fear in the evening and night-time city', *Urban Studies*, 37 (8): 1403–29.

Thompson, P. (2001) *City Centre Provision for Young People in Newcastle*, Newcastle: Brunswick Young Peoples Project.

Thorn High Street Properties Ltd (1994) *Letter on Haymarket Development from Thorn High Street Properties Ltd to the NCC*, (27 May 1994), NCC files: DET/01/0625/94.

Thorpe, D. (1983) 'Changes in the retail sector', in R. Davies and A. Champion (eds) *The Future for the City Centre*, London: Academic Press.

Tibbalds, F. (1992) *Making People-Friendly Towns: Improving the Public Environment in Towns and Cities*, Harlow, UK: Longman.

Tiesdell, S. and Oc, T. (1998). 'Beyond "fortress" and "panoptic" cities: towards a safer urban public realm', *Environment and Planning B: Planning and Design*, 25: 639–55.

Tofiq, F. (1993) 'Gostaresh-e shetaban-e shahr-neshini dar Iran' (Urban growth in Iran), *Abadi* 9: 41–46.

Tönnies, F. (1957) *Community and Society (Gemeinschaft und Gesellschaft)*, trans. C. Loomis (ed.), New York: Harper & Row.

Trancik, R. (1986) *Finding Lost Space: Theories of Urban Design*, New York: Van Nostrand Reinhold.

Triantafillou, P. and Risbjerg Nielsen, M. (2001) 'Policing empowerment: the making of capable subjects', *History of the Human Sciences*, 14 (2): 63–86.

Tuan, Y. F. (1980) *Landscape of Fear*, Oxford: Blackwell.

Urban Green Spaces Taskforce (UGST) (2002) *Green Spaces, Better Places*, London: DTLR.

Urban Task Force (1999) *Towards an Urban Renaissance*, London: E. & F. N. Spon.

Urquhart, A. W. (1977) *Planned Urban Landscapes of Northern Nigeria*, Zaria: Ahmadu Bello University Press.

Usher, D. and Davoudi, S. (1992) 'The rise and fall of the property market in Tyne and Wear', in P. Healey, S. Davoudi, S. Tavsanoglu, M. O'Toole and D. Usher (eds) *Rebuilding the City: Property-Led Urban Regeneration*, London: E. & F. N. Spon.

Valentine, G. (2004) *Public Space and the Culture of Childhood*, Aldershot, UK: Ashgate.

Vall, N. (2001) 'The emergence of the post-industrial economy in Newcastle 1914–2000', in R. Colls and B. Lancaster (eds) *Newcastle upon Tyne: A Modern History*, Chichester, UK: Phillimore.

Van de Ven, C. (1980) *Space in Architecture*, Assen, the Netherlands: Van Gorcum.

Villars, J. (1986) 'Décentralisation. Un point de vue d'opposant', *Esprit*, 110 (January): 81–9.

Viviescas, F. (ed.) (1997) 'Espacio público, imaginación y planeación urbana', in H. Carvajalino (ed.) *La calle: lo ajeno, lo público y lo imaginado*, Santa Fe de Bogotá, Colombia: Documentos Barrio Taller, Series Ciudad y Hábitat no. 4.

Vogel, A. (1981) *Quando a rua vira casa: a apropriação de espaços de uso colectivo em um centro de bairro*, Rio de Janeiro: Instituto Brasileiro del Administração Municipal, Centro de Pesquisas Urbanas.

Voix du Nord, La (1998) 'Editorial: La Ville participe à une action pilote de concertation', 15 October.

Wacks, R. (ed.) (1993) *Privacy*, Aldershot, UK: Ashgate.

Walzer, M. (1986) 'Pleasure and Cost of Urbanity', *Dissent*, Fall: 470–5.

Ward-Perkins, J.B. (1974) *Cities of Ancient Greece and Italy: Planning in Classical Antiquity*, New York: George Braziller.

Weber, M. (1966) *The City*, New York: The Free Press.

Webster, C., Glasze, G. and Frantz, K. (2002) Guest editorial, *Environment and Planning B: Planning and Design*, 29: 315–20.

Whyte, W. (1956) *The Organization Man*, New York: Simon & Schuster.

Williams, J. (2005) 'Designing neighbourhoods for social interaction: the case of cohousing', *Journal of Urban Design*, 10 (2): 195–227.

Winter, P., Milne, D., Brown, J. and Rushworth, A. (1989) *Newcastle upon Tyne*, Newcastle: Northern Heritage Consultancy.

Wirth, L. (1964) 'Urbanism as a way of life', in *Louis Wirth on Cities and Social Life: Selected Papers*, ed. A. Reiss, Chicago: University of Chicago Press.

Wood, I. and Openshaw, E. (1994) 'Drinkers in battle to save their pub', *Evening Chronicle* (Newcastle upon Tyne), 8 June: 6.

Woodward, A. E. and Kohli, M. (eds) (2001) *Inclusions and Exclusions in European Societies*, London: Routledge.

Woolley, H. (2003) *Urban Open Spaces*, London: Routledge.

Worms, J.-P. (1994) 'Reconquérir la citoyenneté pour reconstruire l'État', *Esprit*, 12: 114–37.

Worpole, K. (2000) *Here Comes the Sun: Architecture and Public Space in Twentieth Century Europe*, London: Reaktion.

Xue, C. Q. L., Manuel, K. K. and Chung, R. H. Y. (2001) 'Public space in the old derelict city area: a case study of Mong Kok, Hong Kong', *Urban Design International*, 6 (1): 15–31.

Yin, R. K. (2004) *The Case Study Anthology*, Thousand Oaks, CA: Sage.

Young, J. (1997) Letter on Haymarket development from Newcastle City Council to Nathaniel Lichfield & Partners, 13 January, NCC files: DET/01/0625/94, Newcastle City Council.

Young, P. (1994) 'Revealed: Tyneside's new M&S superstore', *Evening Chronicle* (Newcastle upon Tyne), 4 June: 46.

Young, P. (2002a) 'Carpeting for the wayward skateboarders', *Evening Chronicle*, (Newcastle upon Tyne), 21 September: 10.

Young, P. (2002b) 'Skaters set for own rink', *Evening Chronicle* (Newcastle upon Tyne), 15 October. Online, available at: http://icnewcastle.co.uk/ (accessed 20 April 2005).

References

Young, P. (2003a) 'Expert adds weight to bid', *Evening Chronicle* (Newcastle upon Tyne), 5 December. Online, available at: http://icnewcastle.icnetwork.co.uk/eveningchronicle/eveningchronicle/page.cfm?objectid=13695202&method=full&siteid=50081 (accessed 7 August 2004).

Young, P. (2003b) 'Gangs' brawling blights historic square', *Evening Chronicle* (Newcastle upon Tyne), 20 February: 21.

Young, P. (2004) 'Backing for new style city station', *Evening Chronicle* (Newcastle upon Tyne), 20 July. Online, available at: http://icnewcastle.icnetwork.co.uk/eveningchronicle/eveningchronicle/news/page.cfm?objectid=14444161&method=full&siteid=50081 (accessed 7 August 2004).

Zanjani, H. (1991) *Jam'iat wa Shahrneshini dar Iran* (Population and Urbanization in Iran), Tehran: MHUD.

Index